The Trauma of Moving

Volume 182 Sage Library of Social Research

RECENT VOLUMES IN . . .
SAGE LIBRARY OF SOCIAL RESEARCH

13 Gelles **The Violent Home, Updated Edition**
78 Matthews **The Social World of Old Women**
84 Gelles **Family Violence, 2nd Edition**
94 Rutman **Planning Useful Evaluations**
126 McPhail **Electronic Colonialism, 2nd Edition**
142 Toch/Grant **Reforming Human Services**
150 Frey **Survey Research by Telephone, 2nd Edition**
152 Estes/Newcomer/and Assoc. **Fiscal Austerity and Aging**
153 Leary **Understanding Social Anxiety**
154 Hallman **Neighborhoods**
155 Russell **Sexual Exploitation**
156 Catanese **The Politics of Planning and Development**
157 Harrington/Newcomer/Estes/and Assoc. **Long Term Care of the Elderly**
158 Altheide **Media Power**
159 Douglas **Creative Interviewing**
160 Rubin **Behind the Black Robes**
161 Matthews **Friendships Through the Life Course**
162 Gottdiener **The Decline of Urban Politics**
163 Markides/Mindel **Aging and Ethnicity**
164 Zisk **Money, Media, and the Grass Roots**
165 Arterton **Teledemocracy**
166 Steinmetz **Duty Bound: Elder Abuse and Family Care**
167 Teune **Growth**
168 Blakely **Planning Local Economic Development**
169 Matthews **Strategic Intervention in Organizations**
170 Scanzoni **The Sexual Bond**
171 Prus **Pursuing Customers**
172 Prus **Making Sales**
173 Mayer **Redefining Comparative Politics**
174 Vannoy-Hiller/Philliber **Equal Partners**
175 Brewer/Hunter **Multimethod Research**
176 Chafetz **Gender Equity**
177 Peterson **Political Behavior**
178 So **Social Change and Development**
179 Gomes-Schwartz/Horowitz/Cardarelli **Child Sexual Abuse**
180 Evan **Social Structure and Law**
181 Turner/Turner **The Impossible Science**
182 McCollum **The Trauma of Moving**

The Trauma of Moving

Psychological Issues for Women

Audrey T. McCollum

Foreword by
Elise Boulding

Sage Library of Social Research 182

SAGE PUBLICATIONS
The International Professional Publishers
Newbury Park   London   New Delhi

To Bob, My beloved companion during this journey

For information address:

SAGE Publications, Inc.
2111 West Hillcrest Drive
Newbury Park, California 91320

SAGE Publications Ltd.
28 Banner Street
London EC1Y 8QE
England

SAGE Publications India Pvt. Ltd.
M-32 Market
Greater Kailash I
New Delhi 110 048 India

Printed in the United States of America

Library of Congress Cataloging-in-Publication Data

McCollum, Audrey T.
  The Trauma of Moving: psychological issues for women / Audrey T. McCollum.
      p.   cm. — (Sage library of social research : v. 181)
  Includes bibliographical references.
  ISBN 0-8039-3699-0. — ISBN 0-8039-3700-8 (pbk.)
    1. Women—United States—Psychology—Case studies. 2. Relocation (Housing)—United States—Psychological aspects—Case studies.
I. Title. II. Series.
HQ1206.M366   1990
305.42—dc20
                                                          90-8181
                                                          CIP

FIRST PRINTING, 1990

Sage Production Editor: Diane S. Foster

Contents

Acknowledgements   9

Foreword   11
   By Elise Boulding

Introduction   15
The Inquiry   16
The Issues   21

1. Choosing   27
   Women Who Moved Alone   28
      A Modern Gypsy Seeking Vitality   29
      An Entangled Woman Seeking Differentiation   31
      A Single Mother Seeking Self-Confidence   32
      A Divorcée Seeking Self-Expression   33
   Women Who Chose to Move for Their Husbands' Careers   37
      A Long-Distance Choice   37
      A "Merged" Choice   39
      Images of Power Emerge   40
      Occupation and Choice   41
   Wives Who Had No Choice   44
      Evading Choice   44
      Feeling No Right to Choose   47
   The "Paradoxical Self" Considered   50
      Early Development of the Sense of Self   51
      The Developing Self in the Movers   53
      The Prevalence of the Paradoxical Self   56
      The Ethic of Self-Care   57
   Couples Who Moved to Advance the Woman's Career   58
   Couples Who Moved in Later Life   60
   Résumé   61

2. Losing   63
   Loss of Home   67
      Separating from the Dwelling   67
      Divesting from Precious "Things"   69
      Leaving the Familiar Milieu   71
   Loss of Physical Identity   72
      Hairstyle   73
      "What Are Women Wearing in Minneapolis?"   74
   Loss of Social Identity   75
      A Newlywed   76
      A New Mother   77
      A Retired Woman   79
      Loss of Familiarity   81
   Loss of Friends   82
      Anticipatory Grief   83
      "Moving is Like Dying"   85
      Working It Through   86
      Recoil from Grief   92
   Résumé   94

3. Re-creating a Home   96
   Core Meanings of Home   96
   Limbo of Homelessness   98
   Toward Mastery   99
      Rituals of Possession   99
      Disarray   100
   Self-Expression   103
      "Painting the House Red"   103
      Unexpected Frustrations   105
      Emotional Impediments   107
   Continuity   109
   Repeated Moves   110
   Environs   114
      Goods and Services   114
      Neighborhoods   118
   Reproducing the Past   119
   Résumé   123

4. Friendmaking   124
   The Meaning of Close Friendship   125
      Friendship and Gender   129
      Psychological Roots   131
   Welcome   135
      Welcoming Gestures   135
      Absence of Welcome   137

  Initiative   140
    Initiative, Aggression, and Anxiety   141
    Timeliness of Initiative   145
  Strategies   145
    Collegial Connections   146
    Affinity Groups   147
    Connections Through Children   149
    Special Issues   151
    Traveling in Pairs   152
  Rhythms   154
  Outcomes   159
  Résumé   161

5. Working   163
  Work and the Sense of Self   163
    Dispersion and the Body Self   165
    Dispersion and the Interpersonal Self   166
    Dispersion, Work, and Moving   168
  Occupational Conflicts   171
  Occupational Transitions   177
    Daughterhood into Wifehood   177
    Studenthood into Profession   183
  Occupational Continuity   186
    Striving for Professional Continuity   186
    Striving for Affiliative Continuity   190
  Résumé   195

6. Moving and Marriage   196
  Sources of Tension   196
    Troubled Wives   197
    Unavailable Husbands   201
    Stressed Husbands   210
    Wives of Disappointed Men   211
    Communication Barriers   213
  Resolving the Strains   217
  Résumé   221

7. Concluding   222
  Choice and the Female Psyche   222
    Ambiguous Choices   222
    Helplessness and Power   224
  Re-creating Home: Overview and Outcomes   226
    Meanings of Home   226
    Reconnecting to Home   227
    Other Linkages   228

Friendmaking: Overview and Outcomes   230
    Unexpected Grief   230
    Dilemmas About Initiative   231
    The Work of Friendmaking   232
Work: Overview and Outcomes   234
    Work and Choice   234
    The Sense of Dispersion   235
Other Studies   238
    Mobility and Well-being   239
    Mobility and Choice   249
Pain, Recoil, and Denial   251

8. Intervening   256
Psychological Interventions   256
    Differentiation Between Self and Other   258
    Feminine Paradoxes and Cultural Dualisms   261
    Modifying the Paradoxes   264
    Loss, Grief, and Reconnection   266
    Work and Recognition   270
    Reverberations in the Family   273
Practical Strategies   277
    Researching the Prospective Community   277
    Research for Retirement   280
    Making It Work   284
Reflections   290

References   293

Author Index   299

Subject Index   301

About the Author   310

Acknowledgments

Countless women and several men in Northland have contributed to this work. Many shared deeply personal experiences with frankness and trust, and urged me to persist in telling this untold story of moving—they provided a community of support. Betsy Magill, the Welcome Wagon representative, informed newcomers about my study and forwarded their names to me. Jackie Brill, Molly Brooks, Nardi Reeder Campion, Mary Keller, Thomas McFarland, June Morgan, Karen Nielsen, Anna Salter, Brenda Schwab, and Maggie Steele read earlier drafts or portions of the manuscript, and provided thought-provoking comments. Richard Martz patiently eased my transition from the yellow pad to the word processor, and Kathleen Savage was helpful with a variety of technical skills.

Harry Beskind, Bathsheba Freedman, and Joan Wexler offered a helpful commentary on the completed work from their perspectives of psychiatry/psychoanalysis, developmental psychology, and clinical social work.

Five other women were extraordinary in their sustained interest, encouragement, and validation of the significance of the work. They included Elsa Luker, a frequent mover, and Joan Snell, a long-settled resident. Their patient readings of the evolving manuscript led to many provocative dialogues about the experience of being a woman during the decades of rapid change between the 1950s and the

1980s. Elise Boulding, Karen Endicott, and Marianne Hirsch freely shared their keen insights about women, derived from their scholarly studies in sociology, anthropology, and comparative literature. These women expanded my vision as a psychotherapist, causing me to recognize and rethink my assumptions about women and the cultures that shape our lives. Because of these women, my understanding of the world has been profoundly changed.

My husband, Bob, shared empathically in every aspect of our physical and psychological move to Northland. He gave unflagging encouragement to this research, listened with keen interest to each new finding, and patiently read and reacted to each metamorphosis of the book. Learning of the pain of women who move for their partners caused him pain as well, but also spurred him to examine and express his own private experience. He was a steadfast and beloved partner during every day of this eight year journey.

Foreword

No woman who has followed a partner from one community to another, for whatever reason, can read this book unmoved. The memory flow is soon laden with recollections of unsung adjustments, unnoticed and unlabelled efforts undertaken to make an alien place livable, through many, or few, experiences of moving. Not many families escape this lopsided trauma of women's sacrifice for a partner's career. Yet here is an experience almost totally ignored by scholars, policy makers, and planners; ignored even by the therapeutic community. Audrey McCollum opens our eyes to this blind spot in public discourse, making us realize how extraordinary the act of the apparently commonplace and taken-for-granted act of moving, in fact is.

Plunged herself into a move not at all anticipated to be disruptive in the midst of her own active career as a therapist, McCollum brings her scholarly and therapeutic training to an examination of what she experienced, turning her own pain into a remarkable exploration of how other newcomer women in the community she calls Northland are managing "moving." This is participant observation research at its finest, unstructured interviewing at its best.

The book fires the imagination in many ways. I found myself seeing a whole new dimension of the "Underside of History" (Boulding, 1976) as I read: the stream of women on the move through the ages, laden with children and possessions as they hurry along behind forward-striding males, from the earliest nomadic treks to today's abrupt shifts from countryside to city, from town to town, from urban neighborhood to urban neighborhood.

How often is moving a woman's choice? The extent of lack of choice in the moves to Northland is one of the most striking findings of McCollum's research. Yet these women movers of Northland—presumably like their predecessors through history—do not present themselves as docile or helpless. Rather, the Northland women emphasize how empowering they feel their nurturant role to be, how proud they are that they can make a home for their loved ones under any conditions, anywhere. They fully subscribe to what McCollum calls the "Myth of the Transportable Homemaker."

But there is a price, in loss of identity, depressions, and feelings of worthlessness for women movers. The price is all the harder to pay because it goes unrecognized and unnamed. The unresolved internal polarization between feelings of empowerment and feelings of worthlessness lies at the heart of a woman mover's struggle, and often she does not even know what is wrong.

While husbands fit into a ready-made work structure complete with colleagues (not always successfully, of course), wives have to find their way around a new community unaided and often friendless. Of the 35 partnered women movers (and 7 singles—who made an interesting counterpoint to the study), one third were welcomed into the community in some way, and two thirds were not. Two thirds had no close friends in Northland. One half felt at home after two years, the other half did not. The very thing women need most in order to make friends and make the new place "like home," is energy; but McCollum found the women reporting that they were physically and emotionally drained by the move itself. Yet, most of the women managed. It was hard, but they managed.

There are many wonderful stories about *how* women managed. What makes the book such exciting reading is the realization that there is so much that can be done to make this widely shared experience of moving a more constructive, adventurous and less painful happening for women and their families. For individual women and their partners, just knowing what lies ahead can make a difference. When men enter more fully into moving as a shared experience with their wives, it makes a difference. Why shouldn't they? Yet this is not expected of men. Most of the couples were two-career families; when the women's career needs were met as well as her partner's, the move was less stressful. When they were not, the road was rocky indeed. Yet few couples, even in this day and age, realize in advance the importance of planning for the female partner's career opportunities in the new community. The resulting sacrifice that has no name generates rage for women. McCollum found that some marriages were destroyed as a result.

Successful moving does not only depend on what a couple can do, it depends on what the community can do, and here is where the book poses one of its most significant challenges. How much planning does a town do for its newcomers? A quality of openness to new settlers will show up in all a community's institutions from public and private helping services to church, civic, educational and recreational activities, and this openness interacts with the economic health of a town. What is being talked about here goes far beyond the Welcome Wagon, though the Wagon can be an important first step.

While the book focuses on women as movers, every page witnesses to the importance of the quality of man-woman relations when a move is made—even for the singles. Every insight into what women need is also an insight into what men need, and what children need. (Since children are also unnamed sufferers in moving, I am secretly hoping that McCollum will do a sequel to this book on children as movers.)

McCollum's compassion and insight coupled with her professional and scholarly skills have combined to produce a most unusual piece of research. Good writing makes the book a pleasure to read. THE TRAUMA OF MOVING is written for all of us—women and men, movers and stayers, students and teachers, professionals and planners, and just plain folks.

Elise Boulding

Introduction

An astonishing 43,693,000 Americans moved in a typical recent year.[1] I was caught in that surging tide when my husband was asked to move to the Northland, into a position of challenge and distinction. For him, it primarily meant advancement; for me, unravelling a tapestry of attachments to home, neighborhood, town, friends, and career.

My mate is not a chauvinist. "If you don't want to go, I'll simply say no," he declared, and he meant it. But for reasons it took long to understand, I couldn't ask for that. I acquiesced. He accepted the job.

It was a wrenching move.

The power and the pain caught me by surprise. As a seasoned psychotherapist, sensitive to most realms of human experience, how could I not have known? Over the years, I had repeatedly joined with colleagues to consider the forces that shape personality and behavior. We talked of birth experiences and the qualities of good parenting, we talked of the signposts of healthy development and the tasks of each developmental phase, we talked of learning and schoolmates, we talked of sexuality and marriage and divorce, we talked of illness and death. Strangely, we never talked of moving.

Two psychoanalysts muse,

As old as mankind, human migrations have been examined from many points of view. Numerous studies have considered

15

their historical, cultural, sociological, political, and economic implications. It is remarkable, however, that this theme has received little attention from the psychoanalysts, especially since they themselves have been involved in migration during their analytic careers. (Grinberg & Grinberg, 1984, p. 13)

Weissman and Paykel (1972, p. 24) notice a high correlation between mental depression in women and moving, and point out that the women themselves had not observed that connection. "We suspected that these women did not associate their symptoms with moving, *since it is such an accepted part of American life that it is almost taken for granted*" (emphasis added).

Japanese women movers, seeking medical treatment for depressive symptoms, attribute their malaise to the fact that "the *water* in the new place does not agree with them" (Lock, 1987, p. 143, emphasis added).

Sanford and Donovan (1985) persuasively document the myriad elements in our culture that cause or reinforce low self-esteem in women, but overlook the contribution of moving.

Levinson (1978), studying the issues involved in adult male development, makes no reference to relocation.

The husband of a young colleague, hearing about my book, asks his wife, "What can Audrey be writing about—how you locate a good van line?"

Moving, as powerful and complex psychological work, has been strangely disregarded.

THE INQUIRY

The work of many professionals, whether this is consciously recognized or not, is shaped by life experience. It is an attempt at restitution, resolution, or mastery. When I moved, I needed to make sense of the maelstrom that had seized me. At every opportunity, I asked new acquaintances about their own experiences of relocation. I was soon convinced that moving can open doors to finer living quarters, new relationships, opportunities in the workplace, exciting new realms of experience. It can stimulate growth. But before those potentials are fulfilled, the work of transition can be intense. In families, the work of transition is primarily done by women, on behalf of family members as well as for themselves. Moving is a major realm of women's work in the United States today.

But I needed to understand more. A preliminary scan of published literature yielded the impression that studies were primarily quantitative, primarily focused on single variables or only a few (as quantitative research must be), carried out at a fixed point in time, usually retrospective, focused on outcome rather than process. Moving was viewed from the exterior. There seemed a dearth of material exploring moving from the interior; that is, moving as subjectively experienced by the mover while it was being lived.

I chose to set aside the literature to a later time in order to begin my own inquiry with no preformed belief other than the conviction that moving can be a profound life experience that needs to be more fully understood. My intention was not to make predictions which would be proven or disproven. The study was to be inductive. It was to explore in depth how the experience of moving shapes women's lives, and how the psychology of women shapes their moves.

Why women? Because they were more accessible to me, because they tend more readily than men to open the portals to their subjective experience, because I am one among them and hoped their stories might illuminate my own. And because women's experience has for too long been invisible, the "Underside of History" (Boulding, 1976).

Where was I to find these movers? As my plan was forming, the Welcome Wagon representative came to call.[2] She seemed a natural source of prospects for my inquiry. With keen interest, she readily agreed to give me in sequence the names of each of those newcomers she would visit during the ensuing months.

The ease of finding participants in my study surprised me. I expected to have time to interview 30 women at regular intervals. Among the first 32 whose names I was given, 30 agreed to take part—most with enthusiasm. Only two declined. One explained that "moving is simply something we do," and she didn't want to spend time talking about it. My impression was that she had

achieved a delicately balanced equilibrium that she did not want
to risk disturbing. The other mover admitted she was feeling very
stressed, but did not want to discuss private feelings with a stranger.

Then, with a gathering momentum, word of my study began
to spread through the small city, towns, villages, and granite hills
that comprise the region of Northland. Women told me of other
movers whose stories should be heard. Some called directly and
urgently asked to be interviewed. Soon there were another dozen
participants. Regretfully, because of time constraints, I had to limit
to 42 the core population—those women I would interview
repeatedly over a span of time.

In the months that followed, I was asked by the Women's Network
(an informal association of women of varied ages, backgrounds,
and interests, seeking affiliation, friendships, and support in their
roles as wives, mothers, lovers, widows, divorcées, homemakers,
business women, professional women, artists, and volunteers) to
talk about my study and to lead group discussions. Two planned
sessions grew into seven. Women came to listen and to be heard—
to share the hidden experience of moving.

The core population of 42, and over 100 others in the network
groups, disclosed their thoughts, hopes, fears, joys and tears with
trust and frankness. Many voiced relief and appreciation that they
had been offered a channel through which to express the
unexpressed appreciation that questions were being asked about
a realm of experience that had been too much taken for granted
as inevitable in contemporary life.

In all research, methodological choices must be made. The use
of standardized instruments such as rating scales and questionnaires may yield precise, factual, or manipulable data, yet depth
and richness of insight are likely to be sacrificed. An investigation
of the subjective experience of being a woman undergoing a move
explores self-definition which:

> Is a sensitive construct . . . dependent upon the woman's ability
> to be introspective concerning the way she sees and assesses
> herself within the context of the social roles she holds and
> within her relationships. Thus it is a measure of self-
> knowledge best assessed through extensive interviews rather

than through a structured instrument that might predeter-
mine categories of self-knowledge and however inadvertently,
superimpose a conceptual framework upon the woman's self-
understanding. (Peck, 1986, p. 283)

I chose unstructured, exploratory interviews, initiated with a
simple query such as, "Tell me whatever has been most important
to you about your move." The process was dynamic; my (unspoken)
associations flowed freely between the experience of one mover
and another, between their narratives and my clinical experience,
and between their narratives and contemporary theories of women's
psychological development. These associations will be made explicit.
Themes emerged spontaneously and were explored as fully as
seemed appropriate in research, rather than in a therapeutic
relationship. The most prominent themes were then synthesized
into this book.

My methods were molded by my discoveries as I progressed.
Newcomers were pent up. Most of the initial dialogues were
outpourings lasting as long as two hours. These first sessions told
me that moving could be intense and complex, and that its impact
was likely to fluctuate over time. It was clear that the movers
would need to be interviewed again within a few months. I was
recurrently hearing, "It takes two years before you feel settled,"
so the timespan of my project needed to take that into account.
In all, there was an average of six in-depth, 90 minute interviews
with each mover over the two year period—252 individual
interviews and 7 one-hour group discussions.

Reflecting the mobility in our nation, the core population was
in flux. Eight women moved away before the two years had elapsed,
and 13 moved within Northland once again.[3] These women, who
had grown up in every region of the United States and had come
to Northland from across North America and beyond, were dealing
with moves experienced in the past as well as anticipated moves.
Their stories flowed across time, retrospective and prospective. I
shared deeply with them the experience of 70 moves.

Who were these women? Their ages spanned adulthood from
23 to 79 years. Their parents were tradespeople and farmers, as
well as business people and learned professionals. All except one

of the movers themselves had been educated beyond the secondary school level. By virtue of education and intelligence, they were well equipped to solve life's expectable problems.

Thirty-five women were coupled, married, or with male lovers, and seven were single, including two still unmarried and five separated or divorced (it was by chance, not exclusion, that there were no lesbians). They were Asian and Caucasian. They were Jewish, Catholic, Protestant, agnostic, and atheistic. There were no African Americans in the core population, a reflection of the dearth of African Americans in Northland. Yet, in a symbolic sense, they were included, too. A newcomer is at the margin of the mainstream, and the anxiety and loneliness of her marginality must echo the pain and anxiety of minorities who are chronically outside the mainstream of United States society.

To be sure, the movers were not a pure cross-section of our national population, but they were nonetheless a varied lot, and the variety was increased by the 100 or more who took part in group discussions. And, I would later learn, their stories connected in significant ways with the experiences of other women in other places; for example, Boston slumdwellers (Fried, 1963) and housewives in Australia (Viney & Bazeley, 1977). (A comprehensive discussion of other research is found in Chapter 7.)

Knowing from the outset that the sampling did not meet the criteria of objective, quantitative research, I did not suppose that my findings could be generalized to the United States population at large. But that was not the intent. Rather, my aim was to bring into focus the psychological issues that confront women who move. Whether or not all women face such issues is not germane. If some do, those issues should be the concern of all who care about the psychological well-being of women, and most particularly, those who strive to help and to heal them.

Who was the "I"? I am a clinical social worker trained through long apprenticeship in psychodynamic psychotherapy. My own years of experience and professional growth paralleled enormous growth and change in psychoanalytic thought as it moved beyond the classical drive/defense theory, incorporated ego psychology, object relations theory, and self psychology. Furthermore, under the influence of the Women's Movement, there has been growing awareness within mainstream psychoanalytic thought that many assumptions have been gender blind—either based on a male model of development and generalized to include the female, or expressed without differentiation between the male and female experience. Revisions and refinements are a continuous part of the flow of theory, and as I listen to women's stories, my thinking is informed by these changes.

Psychoanalytic thought addresses the intrapsychic world. A central assumption of clinical social work, and of feminist inquiry as well, is that the individual exists in an interpersonal and societal context. So I turn also to the literature of anthropology, sociology, social psychology, social work, and women's studies to illuminate my work.

THE ISSUES

Most American women will have to face choices about moving, perhaps repeatedly. Many of the passages in a woman's life are apt to be coupled with a geographic move: the passage from home to studenthood, studenthood to workerhood, from single state to coupled state, from daughterhood to motherhood, from motherhood to grandmotherhood, from wifehood to widowhood, and then the passage from accustomed work into retirement.

Some, like our agricultural nomads, the migratory workers, move for survival. For most, moves are in pursuit of betterment. Traditionally, women have followed their men in pursuit of advancement in the marketplace, with its expected rewards of prestige and fortune. Many continue to do that today. But barriers against a woman's own access to varied economic and political spheres are yielding. A woman's anatomy is no longer her destiny— her life need no longer be organized around the inevitable functions of her uterus. Her life can be sculpted in more shapes than ever before, and in more places than ever before.

Choice is ephemeral. Unless it is exercised with insight and concern for self as well as others, it readily eludes us. For women, my study will show, there are obstacles against making wise and responsible choices about moving (Chapter 1). Aspects of feminine psychology—a tendency to merge with loved ones, contradictory states of both helplessness and power in their sense of self—may cause women's choices to be more illusory than real. And there is a dearth of understanding of the challenges they are likely to face during a move. To choose without knowledge—of self as well as circumstance—is not to choose. It is simply to acquiesce. And that may result in bitter disappointment.

Moving causes extensive loss (Chapter 2): loss of home in which a woman's sense of competence and continuity may be embedded; loss of identity expressed in physical appearance and in the myriad roles involved in work and play; loss of the feelings of effectiveness and the recognition linked to work; and loss of close friends who nurture a woman, confirm her sense of self, and reinforce her self-esteem. Lost aspects of self as well as lost others must be mourned, yet the mover's grief is unanticipated and arouses self-doubts, guilt, and shame.

Home has many meanings (Chapter 3). Enfolding, safe, strong, and warm, it is a parental representation. Before it can be recreated, there is a limbo of homelessness that kindles deep anxiety. Home is a realm of mastery. The strangeness, confusion, and disorganization of transition threaten the sense of competence that is a cornerstone of self-esteem. Home is an extension of self, expressing taste, experience, and values; affirming continuity; representing identity to others. Powerful emotions and practical impediments interfere with the recreation of home, and the reintegration of self connected with it. Sensory linkages foster it. The state of feeling at home includes but extends beyond the dwelling to physical milieu, neighborhood, and town.

Major moves heighten longings for intimate friendship, deeply rooted in women's psychology (Chapter 4). While movers mourn their lost intimates, most lack the comfort of being welcomed by new acquaintances. The dilemma of when and how to take initiative arouses anxiety about expressing aggression, as well as fear of rejection. Making friends is a realm of energetic work involving advance and retreat, hope and disappointment, attachment and loss. The newcomer's self-esteem is painfully at risk while new bonds slowly deepen.

An inner sense of dispersion makes women especially vulnerable to the disruptions of moving, and is heightened by moving (Chapter 5). Movers struggle anew with inner conflicts—the pull towards affiliation against the tug towards the marketplace, ideals of accomplishment against ideals of nurturance. Their work priorities must be realigned, their work identity redefined. If a woman moves to support the aims of husband or lover, the development or continuity of her own work in the business or professional marketplace is interrupted. The networks that sustain a woman's work of affiliation (mothering and marriage), as well as the strategic integration of resources that allows a woman to combine the work of affiliation and professional work, are dissolved by a move. New systems of support must be designed. The development of a realm of work commanding recognition outside the home is central in feeling connected to a new community.

Conjugal relationships can be severely strained by major moves (Chapter 6). The pain of loss, as well as the man's transitional unavailability, can arouse anger in the woman, and she may struggle with resentment and envy of his fulfillment through work. Male movers are anxious and lonely also. Moving heightens the need of both partners for "maternal" nurturance and "paternal" recognition of accomplishment, and familiar sources have been left behind. Communication barriers increase estrangement, whereas acknowledgement of needs and limitations can result in deepening interdependence and growth.

When the van arrives, the woman's task of rearranging the furniture can pale before the challenge of reshaping her life!

It is time to pull away the veils of denial, to reveal the story of costs as well as gains. Without understanding the complexities of moving, a woman feels guilt, shame, and anxiety about those inner turmoils that are inevitable but seem inexplicable. Her self-esteem can be deeply threatened. Without understanding the commonality of her emotions, she feels isolated in a bleak passage with no exit. Sadness, loneliness, and fear can be compounded by scornful self-blame and hostile blame of loved ones.

There are wider reverberations as well. In an impersonal and impatient society ravaged by hunger, illness, homelessness, loneliness, and violence, women must conserve in their lives the essential continuities: the elements that affirm their existence; confirm their significance; release their creativity; and nourish the concern that flows out towards their loved ones, their environment, and their world. Heedless, frustrating, and repetitive moves deplete their capacity for concern.

Furthermore, in an era when male and female roles are in flux, powerful energies are needed to realign relationships and restructure those social institutions that lock women and men into gender-related but need-thwarting roles. If women's creative energies are squandered in heedless, frustrating, or repetitive moves, they will be unavailable for societal change. In that way, American mobility can hold women in the cage of political powerlessness.

Most of the movers' stories were pressing to be told. I was entrusted with very private and deeply moving communications about moving. I have protected their trust by disguising their identities so that only they will recognize themselves. Yet, to preserve the immediacy of their experience, and in the hope that clinicians and scholars will recommend this book to clients and students, I have used the movers' own narratives, told in the language we all share. Where the language of theory is needed, I have tried to make concepts accessible to clinicians of various theoretical persuasions, as well as the educated general reader.

The movers' stories, and the insights they contribute, can cause us all to question our assumptions about moving and sharpen our attention to the needs of the mover. Recognizing the issues around which preventive or therapeutic intervention can be useful, and the ways in which intervention can be offered (Chapter 8), health and mental health professionals—clinical social workers, clinical psychologists, family physicians, pastoral counselors, psychiatric nurses, psychiatrists—will be able to reach out with greater understanding and effectiveness towards patients and clients who are considering a move, in the throes of a move, or reconstructing their lives after a move. These clinicians, as well as scholars concerned with the psychology and sociology of women's development, can serve as conduits through which greater understanding of the mobile woman can flow into society at large.

NOTES

1. According to the Bureau of the Census (Current Population Reports, 1989), 42,551,000 individuals one year and older moved within the United States, and 1,142,000 moved into the United States during the census year 1986-87.

2. The Welcome Wagon is a national organization administered through regional supervisors. Its program is carried out at the local level by representatives, or "hostesses." The aims are both commercial and civic. As many newcomers as can be identified are called upon. They are informed about the institutions and facilities of the community, and about the goods and services provided by local merchants. In some locales, Welcome Wagon also becomes the nucleus of social interactions among newcomers. This has not been the custom in Northland.

3. Within five years, I found in an informal survey, 23 of 42 women had moved away from Northland, once again engaged in the complex work of transition.

O N E

Choosing

Moving begins with choice, but for whom? In the past, the tradition of virilocality was strong in our culture and most others as well. Where man went, woman went too, and that was a mandate widely embodied in law. Until recently, it was an assumption rarely questioned. The ideal wife of the 1950s was self-effacing and husband-serving—she was nourished by his approval, sheltered by his earnings, enhanced by his accomplishments, identified by his name, and this "goodwife" moved with her man. But now, after two decades of dialogue energized by the Women's Movement, after two decades of rethinking the roles, rights, and relationships of men and women, the assumption of virilocality is being challenged.

The study of moving offered a rich opportunity to explore the myriad nuances of choice among some contemporary women. Complex and interrelated questions could be discerned within the movers' stories.

Why did these women move? Why were they moving to Northland? Were their goals concerned with love relationships, career development, or other realms of self-development? Was the balance between their aims similar or different among single and coupled women? Did they realistically consider whether their aims could be fulfilled in Northland?

Did movers experience a sense of choice about moving? Did they exercise that choice or abdicate it to others? Did they make choices responsive to their own wishes and needs or only to the needs and wishes of others? Did coupled women share the decision to move with their partners? Did they seek involvement as women making decisions to safeguard or enhance their own well-being, or as wives helping a husband make the decision that would serve his goals?

The study of choice was serving as a prism, reflecting many facets of a woman's being. Much was revealed about each woman's sense of self—that is, the composite of sensations, images, memories, fantasies, emotions, and ideas that comprises the mental representation of *me*.[1] Much was revealed about each woman's relationship to herself as well as to others, the psychological boundaries between herself and others, and the value assigned herself and others.

It became apparent that the sense of self of many, perhaps most, of these movers was imbued with paradoxical qualities such as helplessness and power, unworthiness and heroism. Among the coupled women especially, contradictions within their sense of self seemed to have interfered with their capacity to make choices about moving that would safeguard their well-being. It became important to understand why these women might have developed such a "paradoxical self."

All of these questions and insights were discerned as the movers' stories unfolded. They will, therefore, be revealed and explored in the context of typical tales.

WOMEN WHO MOVED ALONE

Contemporary single women seem to move to pursue educational or career goals. Yet it is not easy to know how often or how fully those moves are also concerned with affiliation, connected to a pull toward or away from relationships—with parents, siblings, heterosexual or homosexual lovers. The relational agenda may not be readily apparent.

Among the single women in my core population of 42 movers, the relational motive was as important as the occupational one. The major impetus for moving had arisen out of a relationship with a man. Each woman felt she had lived in the shadow of a man, or felt at risk of being entangled in the claims of a man. Some had undergone or were intending divorce, and several were testing out problematical relationships by living independently. They had all challenged themselves to explore, expand, and reaffirm their sense of self now that they were on their own. In this sense, the relational motive was paralleled by a "narcissistic" motive.[2]

A Modern Gypsy Seeking Vitality

"I feel as though I'm on a river, rushing through the rapids. But when I come to calmer water, I won't simply float. Rather, I'll sink—sink into lethargy and hopelessness." This was Susan's tale.

Winsomely flamboyant, expressive, and highly intelligent, Susan thought of herself as spontaneous, playful, and creative. But she lived with a fear of boredom, the boredom that would mean sinking into lethargy and hopelessness, into emptiness, nothingness. So she fled that inner danger. It didn't suffice to flee it in imagination, books, plays, or fantasies. She had to flee it in reality.

"I'm always searching for new experiences. I can't just read *National Geographic*. I have to actually be in those places." Susan moved and moved. She moved from place to place and from man to man, temporarily experiencing life through each man, mantling herself with his identity. As she shared his specialness, she felt special herself.

Lately she felt again the encroachment of dreaded boredom in her career and, particularly, in a love relationship that had lost its zest. She felt no longer special but taken for granted. So, once more in flight, once more seeking, she came to visit relatives in Northland, and here she experienced a tantalizing sense of connection.

"I was in an antique shop one day and I saw a very old cabinet." She was intrigued and examined the workmanship closely. "On the back of it a name was carved. It was the name of my great-grandfather!

"There's something very special about New England. You're in touch with the past and you're in touch with nature," she mused, glancing out at the ancient interfolding hills as we talked in the autumn. She felt an affinity, a subtle melding with the landscape that allowed her to participate in Northland's specialness. "You have to know how to look at November," she explained, "you have to be able to see all the varying shades of gray, you have to be able to see the mauves. I can do that. And I can smell the rain coming. That's another continuity for me; when I lived in Oregon I could smell the rain coming. And I smelled moist leaves here one day and that took me back to my childhood home, the home I lived in when I was nine."

So this psychological nomad—seeking other places, other people to ignite her fragile feeling of aliveness and specialness, trying out new identities like costumes in her changing roles and relationships, unsure of her true self—felt lured by the glimmer of continuity with her personal and familial past and her affinity with the surroundings. She seemed to belong. So on her visit she accepted a job, found an appealing house, and swooped into Northland a month later.

Young adults of the 1970s were labeled by Tom Wolfe and others "the Me Generation," and the name has persisted. From a moral perspective, that label is pejorative, connoting selfishness in contrast to altruism. But from a mental health perspective, it highlights the prevalence of the private struggles being enacted within our culture, struggles of many individuals, like Susan, to develop and maintain over time a clear, cohesive sense of self, imbued with vitality and dignity. These are struggles occupying a major focus of attention in contemporary psychoanalytic thought. They can be considered narcissistic struggles in that they concern the cohesion, continuity, and valuation of the self.

Susan fled from a dreaded state of inner emptiness, searching for a self that would feel authentic, and for the emotional nutriments she had lacked in childhood when her mother was immersed in the needs of her chronically ill father, and both parents were erratic in responding to the developing child. There are many modern nomads who are propelled by needs that are similar if somewhat less intense. But they are more usually men, I believe, because men have a greater propensity and more readily available resources to try to relieve an internal void through external change (several such men were the husbands of movers in my population, and as a clinician I have seen many).

An Entangled Woman Seeking Differentiation

Louise appeared to move for professional advancement. But her parallel aim was to differentiate herself from a man, to clarify her own needs, wishes, and rights both within and outside of the love relationship—and to test the resilience of the relationship.

She had met her lover, Migel, while in nursing school, and after graduation she moved without hesitation to Baltimore where he was in professional training. Life there was endured, not enjoyed. Living from financial necessity in a deprived neighborhood, Louise recoiled from street behavior both seen and heard—unsupervised children, children being the targets of yelled obscenities and physical abuse, and women endangered in the dark. Neighbors in her building drew back from her overtures. "They seemed to want their own spheres of privacy." So after her workday, when her lover studied, Louise huddled alone in her apartment. She watched TV or slept, falling prey to meaningless boredom. Rather like Susan, though much less intensely, she relied upon stimulation outside herself to replenish her vitality.

When her lover graduated, there was a shared interlude of travel and of struggle as Louise and Migel confronted their religious, ethnic, and value differences. Louise had to break loose, feeling entangled in the chauvinism of her lover's family, fearing that she would either be caught in a state of chronic rebellion or capitulate to their expectations and lose her individuality.

Though marriage was central in her life's goals, so was a professional career. She recalled cautionary tales from her divorced mother and unhappy friends about women who abandon careers to follow their men and then resent them for it. Personal recognition felt essential to her.

Northland was familiar from her childhood, and she knew there was excellence in her field of nursing. She accepted a staff job, imagining promotion to a supervisory post. She hoped, even expected, that her lover—missing her intensely—would follow later to build his own professional career in Northland.

A Single Mother Seeking Self-Confidence

Women whose lives have been deeply intertwined with a man's often become aware that the boundaries between self and other seem blurred. There is an illusion of merging with the partner into oneness, into a protective cocoon. Hatching out of that cocoon, a woman can feel as fragile as a moth.

Nellie, mother of two young children, was frightened about her move, although she also felt a sense of escape, a thrust toward disentangling from her marriage to a self-centered, demanding, and often absent man. She had felt lonely and unvalued. The Latina wives she was living among were sympathetic, but resigned to their own subservient roles. "That's the way it is for women," they sighed.

Her unhappiness was intensified by the environs—no trees, few parks, heavy traffic polluting the air, street dangers, and slums fringing the urban core.

Life came to feel unbearable. But Nellie had been reared to be a wife. "I grew up expecting to be supported. My father was a domineering man, a controlling man. I've always seemed to need a strong man." She had been drawn to a man in her father's image, a man whose attitudes intensified the childlike feelings alive in the woman. She felt indecisive, unsure of her judgment, with little sense of confidence or competence. Because she did feel so pliable, so easily influenced, she had to mobilize herself somehow to leave. To some degree she shared with Susan a dread of losing her self, sinking into lethargy and hopelessness.

She fled that danger, finding a kernel of strength in herself and perhaps, as well, being energized by the women who surrounded her. They had spoken in contradictions, she told me, both accepting their outward subservience yet celebrating their private power. The hearth was in their control, and they mocked what they saw as their mates' "struttings and posturings."

Recognizing her need for an ally, Nellie came to be near a sister in Northland. Then began the struggle each single mover faced in her passage into independence—the struggle against isolation and loneliness; the struggle to withstand the recoil of those who still feel threatened by unattached women and exclude them from social doings; the struggle against the danger of being preyed upon; the struggle to grow, to develop a career in the marketplace and live independently; to experience herself as an individual connected with yet differentiated from others. These are the struggles that many single women and most single mothers face in our society. They are struggles that can be dramatically intensified by moving.

"I'm very frightened," Nellie confided, "very frightened about whether I'll make it on my own."

A *Divorcée* Seeking Self-Expression

Madeleine, divorced for several years and holding a responsible job had "made it." Yet she felt a tidal wave of pain at the prospect of moving to a modest apartment and selling the large house where she had reared her family. In fact, the divorce had been set in motion by her husband's insistence that they move away from that home every winter to further his career, and her protest against that seasonal unraveling of her life. Soon after the marriage deteriorated, the house did also. Madeleine felt unable to cope alone with an unpredictable well and a malfunctioning drainage system, unable to shovel off the mounds of snow so the emburdened roof wouldn't buckle.

But there was another reason for moving out—not the contracture of physical helplessness but the expansion of psychological growth. Madeleine needed money that could release her from her humdrum job and allow her to concentrate on her poetry; the poetry that could express and affirm her nascent self-as-woman, distinct from self-as-mother and self-as-wife. Distinct but still so fragile, even in her sixtieth year.

"I see myself as the instrument through which energy flows to create my work," she told me solemnly. "I can't yet feel I own the poetry because then I would feel responsible for it, there would be the risk of exposing myself. So I try to detach myself from it." Yet her comments about the powerful poems she showed me told us both that the creative process was allowing her to untangle and release some strands of her inner being. Although exposing her uncertain self-as-woman felt hazardous, she was delighted with the premonitions of acclaim when her first poem was published.

"I used to be a daddy's girl and I've been like that all my life," she reflected, almost echoing Nellie. She recognized her long-standing need to attach clingingly to a man and then vicariously experience his strength. She had clung to her husband and to lovers after him. She strove now to experience her distinctness; she groped for personal sturdiness. But she also recognized her need to be understood and encouraged, and had chosen to move within Northland so that her network of confidantes would be undisturbed.

* * *

The seven single movers, aged 27 to 72, strove to use moving as a catapult into growth and change. Trying to pull away from troubled attachments to men, these movers needed to rework their separation in their minds, understanding the causes of the relational failure, assigning the responsibility, accepting whatever guilt felt inevitable, trying to find the release of self-forgiveness. That reworking required gazing at their lives as though in a mirror, trying to look with a level gaze and scanning for a surer sense of self. Several sought psychotherapy to accomplish that.

But in spite of their complex feelings about lovers or husbands, they were clear that they now made their own choices, and were responsible for their own destinies. They strove to understand their priorities, and to design new lives that would fulfill their needs. They identified the elements of Northland life that would foster such fulfillment: a satisfying job and—at least as important—a close relative or friend to offer encouragement and comfort. Even the revitalizing seasons, with their opposites of exposure and shelter, endurance and relief, harshness and gentleness, were factored in.

These movers felt entitled to seek that fulfillment. They felt entitled to take good care of themselves. They did, at least, until the tug of a love relationship again clouded their choices.

Louise capitulated to her lover's chauvinism. Experiencing frustration in his first, somewhat tentative, attempt to find a professional opportunity in Northland, Migel reclaimed Louise through sexual blackmail—having an affair to express his protest at her absence. Angry and humiliated, feeling forced to choose between the possibility of professional advancement and this man, Louise rationalized that her profession was less important to her than she had supposed. She returned to Migel and their engagement soon was announced. Whatever earlier relationship this uneasy choice may have reproduced, it was clearly influenced also by her move to Northland. A newcomer without time and opportunity to develop new close friendships, still intensely lonely, her professional future quite uncertain, Louise needed Migel to feel deeply connected to someone. This ambivalent relationship seemed better than none.

Another single mover's effort told a more hopeful tale. Reni's first marriage had been eroded by her hidden anger. It was, in fact, the move she had made with her new husband that she had resented—a move causing her to leave a job she loved, a move that opened the first rift between them. "I never had a voice in the decision." But this young woman had never claimed a voice. It never occurred to her to question her husband's right to decide. She only became aware of her fury at him as she struggled to understand why her marriage was failing.

Reni left Philadelphia to distance herself from her husband as the divorce proceeded. "He wasn't about to move again," she realized, and she wanted neither to encounter him nor to have memories of him kindled by friends and by the environs.

Feeling lost and deeply anxious—"I had no address, no phone number, I wasn't even sure what my name was after the divorce"— she sought refuge in Iowa, where she had grown up. Sustained by a summer job in her professional field, there she met a man who would become her lover.

For Reni, alone among the single movers, Northland was unknown. Her sense of self now anchored in her professional identity, she came to accept an appealing job at week-ending distance from the city where her lover lived. As their relationship intensified, she began for the first time to grapple with those questions she had failed to face with her former husband: Must it be assumed the woman's identity is transportable? Must her career be interrupted rather than her partner's? Should her fulfillment be attained primarily through him rather than being parallel and intertwined with his? Is she truly entitled to take care of herself? Reni's lover joined her in the effort to find answers that would fulfill them both.

* * *

The questions that engaged this couple were avoided by most of the coupled movers in the core population. Whereas single movers had made choices intended to fulfill their own needs and aims, to affirm and expand their experience of self, the choices of coupled women seemed clouded with ambiguity, laden with hidden conflict. I heard about ambiguous choices, conflicted choices, even illusory choices from most of the women who moved to Northland to advance their husband's careers.

Within the core population, there were 30 such women. For half of their husbands, a move was expected. These men were beginning or ending postgraduate education, or their jobs were in jeopardy. They had no alternative to moving except to abandon their careers, although all but two had considerable choice about where to go.

The other half did not have to move. They chose to move because they were dissatisfied with their jobs or striving for advancement. Apparently by chance, since corporations do exist in Northland, none of these men were enmeshed in a system requiring frequent "transfers" as the price of promotion. But some among them had moved and moved, perhaps—like Susan—driven by their own inner restlessness, their own dread of boredom and emptiness, questing for ever greater recognition and reward. And their wives supported their quest.

Seven of these women felt certain that they had made active choices, fully sharing the decision to move with their husbands. Ten believed they had been somewhat involved in the decision-making. Thirteen of these capable, intelligent, educated women felt that they simply had no choice. Yet none had seriously considered not moving with their men. How could this be understood? It seemed important to begin by looking more closely at what women really meant by sharing the choice.

WOMEN WHO CHOSE TO MOVE
FOR THEIR HUSBANDS' CAREERS

Plans and dreams are often intermingled, but at important junctures they must be distinguished from each other. I expected that those women who were confident they had shared the decision to move would have brought into focus their personal preferences and needs as well as their husbands'. They would have explored how fully the new milieu could fulfill those needs; investigating career opportunities, housing, recreational, cultural and educational facilities; population characteristics, climate, cost of living—whatever elements that could most affect their lives.

In fact, this was far from the case, as Mildred's story showed.

A Long-Distance Choice

"We made our decision to move here together," she volunteered—a young woman who had never seen Northland when that decision was made. Her husband, David, had come to investigate a prospective job, but he came alone. The trip seemed too costly for her to come too.

She had impressions of New England, appealing impressions from David's relations. She was ready to leave a western city with a monotonous climate, smog, a transient population, ethnic tensions, and poor schools. She wanted to live in a "small, friendly community where people would care about each other." She imagined that Northland would include such places, and actively encouraged her husband to accept the job there rather than another job they were considering in a New England metropolis.

Mildred had married young and began training as a physician's associate several years afterward. Mothering two children was satisfying, but not quite enough. She reached for personal growth and recognition. She felt competent and respected in her field, and had friendly colleagues and opportunities to work toward advanced professional credentials. Mildred well recognized the importance of her professional life—the sense of contributing, the appreciation of patients and colleagues—in maintaining her self-esteem. She expected to continue that career after moving and also supposed that the workplace would be a major source of new friends.

Yet this self-aware young woman decided to move without actively investigating the potential for openings in her field. She made assumptions that proved unfounded. She gathered inadequate information by phone, later recognizing that the one administrator she talked with had been "falsely optimistic" if not frankly misleading. With wry insight she acknowledged, "Maybe I would have learned more if I could have afforded to come for a visit, but maybe I simply didn't ask enough questions on the phone. Maybe I was using denial, and I really didn't *want* to find out that the only available jobs were during the night hours."

Indeed it did seem that by failing to gather enough information, Mildred had avoided knowing about the bleak realities she was to confront after the move: denigration of her professional degree; scarce job openings and those at hours incompatible with family life; and low salary scale.

And although she knew which school district she wanted to live in for her children's benefit, Mildred did little investigation of the cost of living in that community relative to the incomes she and her husband could expect. Once in Northland, forced to work outside her field in an unskilled job that felt demeaning, working at irregular hours that interfered with making friends, and financially unable to enjoy or provide for her children the many available recreational activities, Mildred felt increasingly alienated from the community she had expected to be friendly and caring.

"We made our decision to move here together," Mildred had declared. Yet it seemed her sense of choice was illusory, based more on fantasy about Northland than on fact. Had it been crucial that Mildred made her ill-fated choice from a 3000 mile distance? Most other wives did have chances to visit and investigate Northland. Surely that would have made a difference. Yet it did not make the kind of difference I would have supposed, differentiating plans from dreams. Sally's tale made that clear.

A "Merged" Choice

"Choosing the school was a clear *we* proposition," Sally told me with conviction. She and her husband together investigated 13 postgraduate programs, focusing on the quality of each program, its cost, and location before choosing the one that Alan would attend. Together they decided on Northland.

They decided on Northland in spite of the fact that, as Sally told me vehemently, "I hate the cold. It frightens me. I feel nauseous when it's very cold. I feel unsafe. I don't want to go out. I chill easily. I need the temperature indoors to be 75 degrees." From prior exposure to northern climates, she had known those things. She had simply disregarded the fact that cold would pervade her life here for four years or more.

Having lost her mother in early childhood, Sally's vision of her future was centered on family life, on creating for her children-to-be a nurturing milieu such as she had not had (perhaps also to give herself a second chance, a chance to experience vicariously through her children the mothering that she had longed for). But Sally understood that she would need to provide income until her husband finished his training. And she enjoyed her work in graphic arts.

Yet she failed as much as Mildred to investigate opportunities herself, to factor into the decision her own prospects in Northland. "I just assumed there would be jobs in my field. [In Cleveland] the newspapers were full of openings." Nor did Sally investigate salary levels and the cost of living. "I was stunned when I realized how low the salary scale in my field was here and how hard it was to find a job."

Sally was convinced the decision to come to Northland was firmly mutual, shared with her husband. Indeed it was. Yet, except for her need to be with him, the choice had altogether related to Alan's needs, not to Sally's. In this 23-year-old woman of the 1980s, "goodwife" of the 1950s seemed quite alive. She involved herself in the decision as Alan's wife, helping him arrive at his decision, but not making an informed decision of her own. Her aims had been merged with Alan's needs.

Images of Power Emerge

Did any of these women who believed they had fully shared the decision to move allow themselves to know what they were choosing?

Ellen seemed to know a lot. The firm in Northland was the fifth she had visited with her husband. During a three-day stay they investigated his prospective job, cultural facilities, the school system, access to large cities, and child-care facilities. But as I listened closely to Ellen's spontaneous account, I noticed that she, too, was emphasizing the values of Northland for her husband and young children. Ellen's needs seemed as totally melded with those of her family as Sally's.

Only by inquiring directly did I learn what she had explored in Northland for Ellen as a woman, apart from wife and mother. Then she confided that she was an experienced children's librarian, and admitted the disappointment she had felt on learning of the limited opportunities for work or advanced training in her own field. Unlike others, she had allowed herself to know that her professional growth would probably be stalled before the final decision to move was made. Ellen did not avoid this reality as others did, but she minimized its significance. "I had been considering a possible career change anyway, so I wasn't *intensely* disappointed." The discouragement she felt was set aside, priority being given to the welfare of husband and children. So in actively choosing to move, Ellen consciously chose to disregard a major aspect of her selfhood. She would not risk her family's well-being, only her own.

To be sure, through nurturing she felt nourished. This form of vicarious self-care is common among women. But another influence was operating as well. Ellen saw herself as the matrix of her family, responsible for supporting them through the transition, responsible for making things go well in their lives. Her self-esteem seemed significantly embedded in her competence and her power to do this.

Ellen described a sense of empowerment that was revealed by many movers. It was a nurturant power that included but extended beyond sustaining life and promoting growth in physical realms. It was psychological power as well, power to influence relationships, power to shape human lives.

But that sense of power was paralleled by feelings of vulnerability. "I like to have things under my control. When I don't feel competent, I'm uneasy and anxious," Ellen confided. "The move has been a heavy weight." (How could it be otherwise, I wondered silently. How could she make things go well for her loved ones even though diverse influences beside her own would impinge on them?)

Occupation and Choice

It is often supposed that women whose lives are embedded in the work of affiliation (wifehood and motherhood)[3] would yield decisions about moving to their husbands because the men are the wage earners. It would follow that a coupled woman's sense of choice about moving would be strongly enhanced by her own involvement in professional work, and her own financial contribution to the family. Yet among the Northland women who moved to advance their husbands' careers, this did not seem to be the case. To be sure, six of the seven who had "fully" shared the decision with their partners had themselves been engaged in business or professional careers. But this very fact showed how misleading numerical correlations can be. It was not their professional careers that spurred them to take an active role in the decision. In fact, like Mildred, Sally, and Ellen, they even failed to ensure that professional opportunities would be available for themselves.

Altogether, more than half of the 30 wives who moved to advance their husbands' careers were involved in their own businesses or professions when the decision to relocate was reached. Yet there was only one who actively and realistically planned for the continuity of her own professional life before deciding to move. That was Barbara's tale.

"I felt ready to move on," she told me. "It seemed as though I'd said everything there was to say in New Orleans. I wanted to come here. Martin and I both wanted to get back to the seasons. For me, autumn means exhilaration, getting back to work after the laziness of summer. There, the fall was hot, everyone went to the beach. It made me feel irritable and impatient." She felt a need for that exhilarating energy since the creative people she had been living among were "very laid back—producing wasn't that important to them."

Barbara was a photographer. She had worked at many jobs, but never tried to sell her creative work. She hadn't felt ready until just before they decided to leave New Orleans. Then there had been a surge—it had felt like time to begin moving her work out to other people, to exhibit or publish. Her husband's family was in Northland, and they could arrange the variety of introductions into the artistic community that she would need to become known.

Even under the umbrella of their sponsorship, making contacts meant taking a risk and that felt very hard. What if people didn't like her photographs? She'd have to convince herself that she's still a good person, and that her work is really good. She feels as though there is an inner voice in her mind—it seems to be a male voice—that tells her that perhaps her work is no good. The voice is very critical, very judgmental. When she becomes aware of it, "then I don't feel like God's finest creation. I feel like a hellish worm." Barbara speaks with wry humor. She is not deluded, but well aware she describes an "introject" of considerable power.[4]

Barbara's self-esteem was clearly in delicate balance, and there was another shadow across her hopes. She had read a book of essays, three authored by Northland women (Ruddick & Daniels, 1977). "They found it disastrous here. They found that it was a male-dominated community and they felt unrecognized. That made me really uneasy. But I felt there must have been changes since they wrote. In fact, during my visit I went into a grocery store, and I saw a young father marketing with his baby. That was encouraging!"

So Barbara, keenly aware of her readiness for artistic recognition, aware that her self-esteem could plummet sharply, set aside her misgivings and risked moving to a community that might repudiate her work. She, too, seemed to place herself in jeopardy.

Yet there were differences. Barbara was unusually insightful about herself. Pain and turmoil earlier in her life had led her into a journey of self-discovery in group psychotherapy before she came to Northland. She recognized her vulnerability and, whereas other women disregarded obstacles or overlooked risks, Barbara explored the risks and accepted them with open eyes. She recognized her need for professional fulfillment and believed in her right to enjoy it. She was clear that Northland offered a potential network to support her in her aims.

It seemed to be Barbara's unusual self-awareness, not her career, that set her apart. Having a professional career seemed to have made these women no more attentive to their personal needs and aims (distinct from those of their partners and children) than being embedded in domestic life. With an almost uncanny skill, movers disregarded some element in Northland life that was likely to be central to their well-being. Whereas professional women like Mildred and Sally overlooked the paucity of jobs (among other things), full-time homemakers such as Polly took care of themselves just as inconsistently.

Polly and her husband had visited five centers offering training in his field, and then Polly had chosen Northland University for him and he had concurred.

"Northland seemed magical. The foliage was brilliant in October, it was close to Maine and lobster, we had heard about the Connecticut River and the prospect of canoeing, we ski and we like the mountains, the training program seemed excellent, the air was cold and I imagined being in front of a fire. And the colonial architecture was so appealing."

But in her torrent of enthusiasm, Polly allowed images to serve as realities. She imagined that they would buy one of the appealing colonial houses but failed to inquire about real estate prices. Knowing her life would be centered at home, she had neglected to investigate the sorts of homes that would be available. Her fantasy was to be shattered, her disappointment intense.

* * *

All of the coupled movers who "fully" shared with their husbands
the decision to move in order to advance the husbands' careers
were under 40 years of age. They were not reared as traditional
wives of the 1950s. So it was unexpected to find that most had
disregarded themselves, or deceived themselves, or unwittingly
sabotaged their goals. Like the single women, they felt entitled
to make active choices in their lives, yet there was an incongruity
between their illusion of choice about moving and the realities.
Consciously or unconsciously, they overlooked some problematical
aspect of life in Northland that would be central to their well-
being—the harsh winter, lack of professional opportunities, the
adverse salary/cost of living ratio, the limited availability of
attractive, affordable housing—aspects that these resourceful
women could actually have found out about and factored into their
decisions. Could it have been that they unconsciously felt
undeserving of fulfillment? Or was it that they privately imagined
themselves capable of overcoming any obstacle? How were they
different—if they were—from movers who felt they had no choice
at all?

WIVES WHO HAD NO CHOICE

Evading Choice

Not choosing can be a deliberate choice. It can transfer unwanted
responsibility to another person's shoulders. Tina made that clear.

"Since it was Jim's career that was involved in this move, I let
him decide. It would be his responsibility if things didn't work
out. Then I could blame him—and I would, too!" She was
humorously candid. But she also conveyed that her marriage was
vibrant with aggression as well as warmth and love. Through
stormy arguments, Tina and Jim had negotiated change from
traditional roles to an egalitarian partnership. He was involved in
domesticity; she had achieved success in business. "I want to be

treated as a colleague, not an appendage." But it was as an appendage, not a colleague, that Tina chose to move.

The responsibility of choice was unwanted because Tina was absorbed in realigning her own work priorities. She had been closing down a too-successful business—an exhilarating success that became so demanding Tina had too little time for her preschool children. And the needs of the children felt compelling. "I adored my daughter. But after my son was born, I had such special feelings about him I wanted to take more time to be a mother."

And the responsibility was unwanted because the move evoked frightening images: "I was afraid New Englanders would be snobby, cliquey, and preppy." People would feel disdainful of the university where she and her husband earned their degrees. There would be great emphasis on proper clothes and social activities. She would be expected to go to faculty teas where "you'd be supposed to crook your pinky when you picked up the cup" (she giggled at this Victorian absurdity), where wives would gossip and she would feel like an outsider and be afraid to leave the room lest they talk about her. She had experienced just such a tea during an earlier visit to the East. And she dreaded the cold, imagining snow drifting up over the windows, the roads blocked, running out of food and fuel, being physically endangered. "I guess I purposely exaggerated my fears, trying to convince myself they were unfounded," she admitted.

Her choice not to choose seemed an avoidance of troublesome feelings and fearful thoughts. She was able, in fact, to isolate her emotions from her thoughts, and to feel detached. "I just didn't feel anything much about the move." Being frightened was intolerable for this active, competent woman; it was alien to her sense of self. "Things will work out right for me, they always have in my family." But, in fact, this move was not to work out right for Tina, or for Jim.

Choosing not to choose can be purposeful for other reasons. It can allow a woman to evade disturbing conflicts, and avoid resolving them. "Moving can give you a way out of a difficult situation," reflected Terry, who also deliberately yielded the decision to her husband. Terry's difficult situation involved severe tension between her urge to please and her urge to perform, between affiliation and professional accomplishment—the tensions that plague so many women.

She had studied engineering "because I was good at it. I never really loved it." After a setback beyond her control, she decided not to complete an advanced degree. She accepted a technical job and won her boss's respect by working stoically through a time of bereavement. Terry charged herself with high expectations— ideals that mirrored her father's perfectionistic standards. When she wanted to shorten her workday to have more time with her husband, she would have found it hard to tell her boss, to risk losing his esteem.

"I have that awful need that women have—to please people— even if it means giving up something myself. Like when I was a child, I would serve cocoa to my friends, and even if there wasn't going to be enough for me I would serve them and it would make me feel good to meet their needs that way" (here was another voice speaking of self-fulfillment through nurturance, power through provision). Moving away would allow Terry to avoid telling her boss she hadn't enough cocoa for him, metaphorically speaking.

There was another conflict as well, the tug of profession against the pull of marriage. Terry recognized that she and her husband wouldn't have much time for each other if they were both full-time professionals. "Who would do the maintenance—the cooking, shopping, cleaning?" She had friends who lived that way. Their marriages suffered or ended in divorce. If she had really loved her work it might have been different, but she put their relationship first. For a time, she would avoid the conflict. "I was prepared to follow him wherever he decided to go."

Terry was reluctant to leave Seattle. She, too, feared the severe winters in Northland. She knew she might have trouble finding an interesting job in a smaller community. She knew she and her husband, Brad, were shy and unsure about making new friends. But she chose to disregard her fears. She would simply allow the move to happen.

Tina and Terry both felt competent as professional women and felt a sense of partnership with their husbands. They thought they were clear about modifying their professional aims in favor of close family life. So they seemed to accept the move from a perspective of strength. Yet just like those women who believed they did exercise choice, they discounted aspects of Northland life that could impinge strongly on their well-being. Unlike some of the others, whose disregard for self seemed unconscious, their disregard was intentional. They avoided factoring in aspects of life in Northland that were associated with images of helplessness and vulnerability— images of being overcome by the harsh winter, of feeling disdained or lonely, and of being jobless. Their strength was grounded in avoidance and denial, and it was brittle.

Feeling No Right To Choose

Tina and Terry were among the few women who purposefully decided not to choose. For most who had no sense of choice, the issue entered another sphere. They felt they had no right to choose. All but one of them had moved repeatedly—as often as 15 times in 20 years. They had allowed themselves to be pulled along in the jetstreams of their husbands' careers.

There were striking similarities among these women. Their families had been geographically stable, so moving had not been a prominent childhood experience or an expectable life-style. All were two-parent families with role division along traditional lines: The income-producing father was nominal "head of the family," and the mother stayed at home.

All the movers had experienced at least one parent as perfectionistic, imposing very high standards concerning behavior, academic and extra-curricular achievement, and social success. The girls were brought up "to please," they were first to please their families and then, ultimately, a husband. They were supposed to please by trying their utmost to comply with the expectations of others—not fulfilling their own unique potentialities, but trying to become whatever others needed them to be.

With only an interlude for advanced education and perhaps a brief experience in the workplace, these women passed from daughterhood to wifehood. They married early, with little opportunity to consolidate a sense of themselves as both connected to and yet distinct from others, secure in their own competence.

Their moves after marriage fostered dependence and feelings of helplessness, since attempts to develop a profession that might have continuity, or even just marketable skills, were repeatedly interrupted. When these women, each of whom ultimately succumbed to depression, even imagined refusing to uproot once again, they would confront their felt incapacity to live independently—an incapacity both economic and psychological.

"I always accepted Henry's choices," said Kate. "I seriously questioned his decision only once, but that was on the grounds of his position in the business. I never felt it was legitimate to question for myself. I always felt that my role was transportable. I never even considered not going with him or separating. I would have felt too anxious about making it on my own, and life without him would have been unthinkable. And it never occurred to me to ask him to choose between his job and me."

Andrea's words almost echoed Kate's. "It never crossed my mind that I had a choice about it. He always made the decisions—he said, 'everyone moves this much,' and I believed him. I never had thoughts of not going with him, or leaving him. I do love him and I've felt very dependent on him."

"I was intensely angry at Bill when he was considering this job in Northland," Debra confided, "but I didn't feel I had any choice. His happiness is important to me, and he supports the family, so it was up to him." Debra's anger was aroused when she realized that moving would rupture a tapestry of sustaining personal connections, but she was unable to use the energy of that anger to assert her own needs. Unprotestingly, she accepted Bill's right to make the decision. And although he could have continued supporting the family in the respected position he already held, it didn't occur to her—or the others—to encourage her husband to develop and grow right where he was.

Feeling helplessly dependent and accepting the rightness of self-sacrifice, women such as these seemed at first to fit the stereotype of goodwife, a stereotype that was both expressed and reinforced by the classical psychoanalytical view of the truly feminine woman as passive and masochistic (Deutsch, 1944). These movers seemed unsure of their worth; their self-esteem seemed low. They felt no entitlement to decide where they wanted to live their married lives.

"I always felt that my role was transportable," Kate had said, and this was implied by the others. Such women subscribed to what I began to view as a myth, the "myth of the transportable homemaker." This is a myth that disregards the intricate web of supportive connections that enables a woman to find satisfaction in the work of full-time wifehood, motherhood, and homemaking— a web of connections that enables her to tolerate the fragmentation, discontinuity, repetition, frustration, and isolation that seem inevitable in even the most fulfilling domestic life. It is a myth, widely accepted in our culture, that declares, "I can do that anywhere."

Yet, there was clearly a contradiction at work, since the feelings of helplessness, dependence, and unworthiness that were revealed are inconsistent with the idea, "I can do it anywhere."

"I've always expected accomplishment of myself—as a good student, a good athlete," Kate confided. "I expected myself to be a good wife and that meant supporting my husband in his career aims. I felt it was up to me to make it all work for the family." Here again was that heroic expectation—I had heard those same words from others.

"I expect myself to be a supermom," explained Andrea, expressing guilt about her moments of irritability at the children and her wish for respite—a baby-sitter or day care. "I feel very disappointed in myself when I'm not the kind of mother I think I should be." The kind of mother she thought she should be was omnipresent, omniscient, ever patient, comforting, and helpful—even through multiple moves.

"Many women's identities have to do with qualities of being, not doing," observed Debra. And thus she made it evident that in myriad, complex ways, she was what Andrea strove to be— sympathetic; encouraging; a skillful strategist who supported her husband and children emotionally and in their occupational, educational, and social undertakings. Being the matrix of the family was her central role, her career, and she privately recognized its value.

"My husband thought our 11 moves were fun," Anna said wryly. "But he never knew anything about them. He would go off and I would put the glasses on the shelves, get the boxes unpacked, get my children settled in school, help them find new friends, and

when he came home there I would be, ready to take care of him."
Anna conveyed that she was both victim and heroine. Her husband
never knew what the moves entailed because, in fact, she chose
not to tell him. She should, she could, do it all alone. But why
did she need to shield him? And why was Debra so reluctant to
confront her husband with the realization that her psychological
provision might have value comparable to his financial provision?
Protective attitudes toward their men were implied by many of
these women, and directly expressed by a few.

"I see my husband as more fragile, myself as more resilient,"
one mover reflected. "I have to be the one to make the changes
because I'm more adaptable. I have confidence in my capacity to
cope. I feel kind of maternal toward him."

Such communications were not of helplessness and dependence,
but of power. "It was up to me to make it work for the family."
That is a deceptively simple statement, but an astonishing one in
its implications. These women revealed images of themselves as
having boundless capacity to tolerate disruption and loss, to be
strong, adaptable, resilient, resourceful, and to absorb and heal their
families' stresses and respond wisely to their needs. These were
images of a nurturant power.

It was evident that the "no-choice" movers experienced
themselves in terms of opposites. Their sense of self included
contradictory qualities of helplessness and of power, of unworthiness and of heroism. They devalued themselves and yet
overestimated themselves. Their self-esteem was not consistently
low; rather, it was labile, shifting between depths and heights.
Embodying such contradictions, their sense of self could be viewed
as paradoxical, and I have designated it as "the paradoxical self."

THE "PARADOXICAL SELF" CONSIDERED

How could the informal narratives of these movers' lives begin
to explain the contradictions in their senses of self? To understand
deeply the influences that have shaped an individual personality,
one needs to explore the subconscious realms of the mind. My
inquiry did not allow for such depth. The movers were not my

therapy clients. But an understanding of how the sense of self develops does illuminate their tales, and for that understanding I turn to contemporary (post-Freudian) psychoanalytic thought.

Early Development of the Sense of Self

In the view of Mahler, Pine, and Bergman (1975), building on the work of Hartmann (1958), Jacobson (1964), and Spitz (1965), birth sets in motion a developmental surge from an undifferentiated state toward psychic separateness, or individuality. First is biological birth. Psychological birth is more gradual. The amniotic membrane has ruptured, but the vulnerable baby is still shielded by a membrane of care. In the earliest months, girls and boys alike experience a relationship with their mothers (or primary caregivers) so close that for the infant and, at moments, for the mother as well, the boundaries between self and other seem to be blurred. It is as though the two are merged into one in a symbiotic state. Slowly, responding to a multitude of sensations, communications, and growing capabilities, the infant (girl or boy) separates out of that melded unity and begins to experience him- or herself as a separate individual. The infant develops mental representations of self as well as of mother (and other caregivers), and gradually becomes able to sustain those representations even in the mother's absence.

While the distinction between self and non-self is still wavering— during the first 18 months to two years of life—the infant seems to imagine that his or her wants have great power. For example, a state of inner craving such as hunger seems magically to produce a nourishing breast or bottle. Such gratification, as well as developing skills—the capacities to throw or run for instance—contribute to a heady experience of exhilaration and empowerment. But at the same time, the toddler frequently feels his or her weakness. A tiny girl who first confronts waves at the seashore—waves that wash inexorably over her feet in spite of her commands that they stop, in spite of her protest, fear, or fury, vividly experiences a collision between her imagined power and her actual helplessness.

When the caregiver responds empathically to the toddler's needs, comforting and encouraging, respecting her actual capabilities but not expecting too much, the child's feelings of competence are increased. Such well-attuned parental responses, in the view of Winnicott (1965), facilitate the development of an authentic self. And, in Kohut's perspective (1971), as the toddler's heady feelings of power are accepted and enjoyed, as her accomplishments are "mirrored" by the appreciative caregiver, there can be gradual modification of the grandiosity. A more realistic sense of self is shaped. The young child can enjoy the surf, approaching and retreating in accommodation to its rhythms. She is learning her capabilities and her limits. She is also learning to distinguish between the safe togetherness of braving the surf in her mother's arms (which Kohut would likely see as necessary merging with the power of the idealized parent), and the scary separateness of exposing her small body to its power all alone. She is learning about difference—her tiny thighs can't withstand the tumbling waters as her mother's sturdy ones can.

So the surge toward becoming an individual means to experience separateness from others, as well as difference from others. At the same time, the emerging self is shaped by experiencing relatedness to others. Stern rejects Mahler's belief that the infant "hatches" out of a symbiotic union. In Stern's view, during the developmental period that would correspond with her symbiotic phase, "infants consolidate the sense of a core self as a separate, cohesive, bounded, physical unit, with a sense of their own agency, affectivity, and continuity in time" (1985, p. 10). He argues that development does not proceed primarily in the direction of autonomy, but just as much in the direction of subjectively experienced interpersonal connection. Stern's model is consistent with the "self-in-relation theory" of Miller (1976, 1984) and her colleagues Jordan (1984), Kaplan (1984), and Surrey (1985, 1987), who believe that relatedness is central in female development from infancy throughout life (whereas boys are socialized away from that interpersonal nexus).

It is difficult to think our way into the mind of a preverbal infant. Theoretical disagreements notwithstanding, there is no doubt that babies and caregivers are reciprocally involved from birth and experience separateness, relatedness, difference, and sameness as well. From early in the female infant's life, mental images are being formed of the characteristics of her caregivers and of her interactions with caregivers, and these in turn shape the evolving mental images of self. Baby becomes like the caregiver through conscious imitation as well as unconscious identification—it is as though parent images and self images become superimposed, like a double exposure in which one image blends into the other.

The Developing Self in the Movers

How can all this be useful in understanding why some movers had no sense of choice, why they seemed to experience themselves as both powerful and helpless, valuable and unworthy and with needs not clearly differentiated from those of their loved ones? It is not possible to know how empathic, how attuned to their needs, the first caregivers of these women may or may not have been. So it is unclear whether their earliest, fragile feelings of competence were nourished even as the tiny girls were sympathetically encouraged to accept their limitations. But it is clear that their first caregivers were their mothers. So their first, central experience of power was with a woman—the awesome, absolute power a mother exercises in her capacities to nourish or to deprive, to soothe or to frustrate, to encourage or to control.

And for these women, maternal power was prominent through their childhood, although experienced in paradoxical ways. Their fathers had been labeled as the traditional head of household— the one who provided financially, the one whose word was said to carry the greatest weight. Yet all but one of the women (whose mother was recurrently ill) remembered that their mothers had seemed to be the more powerful parents. Father was said to have the power; mother actually exercised it. These mothers were seen as stoically enduring their husbands' absences and disturbances, or as making the decisions crucial to family life, or as dominating their mates, or as single-handedly maintaining the continuity and stability of the home. From early in their lives, the movers must have been identifying with those powerful mothers, gradually incorporating into their mental representations of self the attributes of those mothers who could "make it all work."

Then another major influence entered the developmental arena. Each of these movers recalled the very high expectations set forth by one or both parents, usually the father. Such expectations would be likely to have two meanings. First, as the child was experienced by her parent as an extension of the parent's being, a gratifier of the parent's needs and dreams, and insofar as the child accepted that burden within herself, the development of her own authentic and stable sense of self would have been impeded. Her own unique characteristics, potentialities and limitations—distinct from those of her parents—would not have been adequately recognized and appreciated by them or by her. In the language of self psychology, she would have served as a parental "self object," serving functions for the parent that she or he could not provide for her- or himself.

Second, parental approval, even love, depended on fulfilling those expectations, so the little girl would have incorporated those high standards into the realm of her developing mind that includes both conscience and ideals. In addition to the elements of self derived from identification with the invincible mother, there were now also elements derived from internalized parental exhortations, (usually paternal and well illustrated in Barbara, who spoke of "that inner voice—a male voice" that was critical and judgmental and that often caused her to feel "like a hellish worm"). Together, these maternal and paternal elements would have coalesced into an extraordinary ideal of personal perfection. (To be sure, every individual forms images of her ideal self, which she strives to fulfill through her lifetime. But there is great difference in the attributes of such ideal selves and, especially important, great difference in the degree to which they are realistic and attainable.)

It is likely that there were contradictory influences as well. In the families of each of these women, from the first moments when the baby's femaleness impinged on her parents' consciousness, there would have been subtle communications as to what *femaleness* means and how much it is valued; communications through the way the infant was held, played with, looked at, and spoken to. In traditional families in which father is nominally the "head," that image is often supported by a denigration of the female, sometimes subtle, sometimes blatant—a denigration in which both mother and father may participate. So it was very likely conveyed to the little girl that femaleness has to do with passivity and dependence, weakness and vulnerability—perhaps even worthlessness. And those communications would also have been absorbed by the infant's mind.

There was at least one more influence contributing to the hopes and expectations that these movers had for themselves. It was exemplified in Debra's growth into womanhood. Her mother, often ill and dysfunctional, had not seemed overtly powerful (although illness can exert a covert power of its own). Debra saw herself as proudly moving into her mother's shoes, fulfilling the role— in exemplary fashion—that her mother had abdicated, and emotionally supporting her father. And it seemed that the special relationship she developed with her father was re-created with her husband. Others among these women spoke of their special affection for their fathers (even their perfectionistic fathers). It is likely that they, as well as Debra, enacted with their husbands the sustaining, nurturing roles they might have wished to play, or did play, with their fathers.

It is certain that the way these movers experienced themselves— their contradictory states of helplessness and power, their contrasting feelings of inferiority and superiority, their difficulty distinguishing their needs from those of loved ones—were shaped by many dimensions of their early experience. And clearly, to fulfill the expectations represented by their ideal selves, they overstretched their adaptive capacities. They became depressed. When a woman's ideal self and what she recognizes as her actual self are no longer in harmony, then the internalized voices that comprise her conscience speak in sharp rebuke, and healthy love is withdrawn from the self. A fall in self-esteem inevitably follows.

It is ironic that each of these movers had concealed her pain from her husband. As Anna portrayed it, "My husband thought the moves were fun. He was amazed when I finally told him what they had done to me." But by the time she did tell him, she was ragefully depressed and her marriage was in jeopardy. Except for two women whose husbands were so self-absorbed as to have little capacity to understand or empathize with their wives' distress, the "no-choice" movers recognized that their husbands would probably have been concerned and responsive had they realized the emotional toll the uprootings were taking on their wives. It was goodwife, with the high expectations she had internalized, who had not allowed him to know—or had not even admitted to herself that she had these limitations.

The Prevalence of the Paradoxical Self

The characteristics of the "no-choice" married movers seemed particularly striking. Yet those women were not so different from the wives who felt a clear sense of choice that, on scrutiny, seemed to be an illusion—for example, Mildred, who had failed to find out that her professional life would reach a dead end, Sally, who ignored the cold climate she dreaded and chose Northland to fulfill Alan's aims, and Polly, who fantasized a cozy, creative domestic life in a colonial house that she could not possibly afford. Consciously, such women felt they had the right to choose, and their conviction communicated dignity and self-respect. Yet their disregard for their own well-being was as blatant as among the "no-choice" movers. It seemed that unconsciously they, too, felt undeserving and yet powerful enough to overcome any setback.

Once I had recognized this contradictory motive, and the contradictory self-representation it seemed to reflect, it was apparent that many women were revealing it—whether or not they had actively chosen to move. There seemed to be a coupling of opposites in delicate balance. There was Terry, for example, who had to be seen as superworker or else risk humiliation, and moved to evade that dilemma. There was Tina, who had avoided the images of Northland that made her feel vulnerable and frightened, and had been swept into the move asserting that things always worked out for her. There was Ellen, whose self-esteem was grounded in her power to make the move work out well for her family, and who felt incompetent and anxious if she was unable to accomplish that.

Contradictions in their senses of self were revealed by many movers, and limited their capacity to make effective choices. Motivated (consciously or not) by a sense of helplessness and unworthiness, such movers disregarded aspects of their being that would need fulfillment. Motivated by heady feelings of heroism and power, they discounted their apprehensions and imagined themselves capable of dealing with whatever frustrations and challenges they might encounter. Both states contributed to unrealistic evaluations of what they faced, and sometimes led to overwhelming disappointment. Without doubt, some disappointments could have been avoided if these women had been able to attend realistically to their needs, and to provide themselves with more effective care.

The Ethic of Self-Care

The perspective of a mental health clinician, through which motivations, attitudes, emotions, and behaviors are judged as adaptive or maladaptive, normal or pathological, includes sociocultural and moral assumptions, and these are often unacknowledged. So, in considering the movers, this question should be asked: What of altruism? Were not the women who moved to further their husbands' careers manifesting those very qualities idealized (especially in women) by mid-twentieth-century United States society: good sportsmanship, loyalty, generosity, self-effacement, devotion to other? Is questioning their motives to espouse a late-twentieth-century exaggerated devotion to self?

The reasoned voice of Gilligan (1982), examining moral judgment among women grappling with major life choices, speaks to this question. The movers, like women Gilligan studied, were indeed guided by an ethic of care for others. Many of the movers were altogether focused on care for spouse, care for children. But their ethic did not fully incorporate self-care. They had not fully acknowledged the interdependence of self with other. They had not attained what Gilligan described as her vision of maturity in feminine morality, embodying an integration of rights for self and responsibilities to other—a morality that guides a woman to act responsively toward herself as well as toward another, a morality that I would accept as an indicator of psychological (and societal) well-being. Such a "mature" ideal self and conscience (the realms of the mind in which moral values are embedded) seemed to guide only a few of the women in the core population. Chris' story was the clearest example.

COUPLES WHO MOVED TO ADVANCE
THE WOMAN'S CAREER

Chris was among two couples who moved to Northland to advance the woman's professional career. Both at the cutting edge of societal change, the women modeled distinct and different styles of choice. Diana's move mirrored the move of a traditional man with his spouse. Giving highest priority to her professional growth, she accepted a job in Northland, and was followed by her lover. Diana cherished the relationship, which was later sealed in marriage, but she was unwilling to compromise her nascent professional career for its sake. In this way, she took the stance so long assumed by men, and so long endured by their wives. Far from unconcerned, she nonetheless accepted that her lover might be frustrated in his search for professional opportunities, and that together they might face periods of separation while he worked elsewhere. An unusually self-sufficient woman, she felt clear about the boundaries of her care—her lover's success was his responsibility and not hers.

Chris came to Northland for postgraduate training accompanied by her scientist husband who had no job waiting for him and no assurance that he would find one. To that extent, her venture and Diana's were in tandem. But then they diverged. Whereas Diana emulated a male tradition, Chris reached for a fresh design.

Like the "no-choice" women movers, Chris had grown up in a traditional family. Her father was the wage earner, and her mother's homemaking continued into the evening after father came home to relax (a man, he works from sun to sun, but woman's work is never done, she ruefully chanted). Chris sensed her mother's resentment of that disparity, but she also believed that her parents valued each other highly as individuals, respected the role each played in the family, and shared in making most decisions. There seemed to be a parity of power if not in workday.

She experienced them as strict disciplinarians in her earlier years, but felt well trusted by high-school age. Unlike the parents of many other movers, her parents wrote no script for her life but let her make her own choices. They imposed no goals on her, but encouraged her to pursue her own. Chris' parents seemed able to perceive and respect her as a young person who was unique in her own way, distinct from themselves rather than an extension of themselves. And their capacity helped Chris to crystalize her sense of self.

"I knew a wide variety of people and I knew clearly how I was different from them and how I was the same. I knew who I was, and I had a strong sense of my own value." Indeed, with quiet dignity Chris communicated a conflict-free and modulated self-esteem that was apparent in few movers. It seemed embedded in a family acceptance that was not dependent on accomplishments, but was simply a response to her being.

Chris was 18 and Paul, 19, when they met. They talked endlessly about their ideas and their life dreams, and knew each other deeply when they married after graduation from college. "We grew and changed together," said Chris, recognizing that the ideal set forth by her church had been that of subservient wife, wife serving her husband's needs. Gradually that ideal became transformed within her. "It happened in an evolutionary way." And a pragmatic way. Chris was often late coming home from her first job. "If Paul wanted dinner before eight he had to learn to cook. And he did." She experienced marriage without subservience. "I saw it as two people serving each other," and in this respect Chris' view was strikingly different from those women who gave primacy to their husband's needs.

She worked to support Paul through his scientific training, and then she felt the need of graduate school to open new career pathways for herself. "Paul contributed to my decision from his understanding of me, helping me face important issues, but the decision was mine. I had to decide if it was worthwhile to make the investment, to take on a huge student loan when I knew it might be for a short-term return. I want to be a mother, maybe in about five years, and then I'll probably only work part time because I'd want to be home with the children—but I decided I really was worth the investment. It would help me grow as a person."

Once Chris had resolved that question, she and Paul decided together which program to choose. "I took a risk coming here because we had no assurance he'd find a job in his field. He was prepared to bag groceries and I was prepared to have him do it."

Three months later she told me, "It's been a great relief that Paul's found satisfying work. That takes the burden of guilt off my shoulders." "The burden of guilt? You told me you were prepared to have him bag groceries," I reminded her. "Yes, for a while. But I would have felt very badly if he hadn't found meaningful work because I care about his happiness. There probably would have been some tensions we'd have had to deal with, but I think we could have worked that out. We care very deeply about each other's well-being and growth."

The sense of mutuality was echoed again. More clearly than any other mover, Chris seemed to express an ethic of care grounded in interdependence. And the interdependence seemed to allow this couple to experience a true sharing of choice.

To be sure, it might be thought that Paul was enacting a self-sacrifice comparable to those enacted by many wives. Without interviewing Paul, I could not judge to what extent he had actually risked his own well-being. Whatever the risk, however, it was to be temporary. As Chris' two-year program was nearing completion, Paul did again make claims for the primacy of his career. The next move was primarily to serve his aims.

COUPLES WHO MOVED IN LATER LIFE

What of couples whose moves were free of the imperatives of career? There were three who moved in their later years: one in anticipation of retirement; one in conjunction with retirement; and one after retirement. All three were quite familiar with Northland. Whereas the move of one wife was among the smoothest in the core population, two of these women were to suffer intensely painful feelings of loss. They too had had difficulty clarifying their own needs sufficiently to anticipate whether their new milieu would be fulfilling or not.

RÉSUMÉ

Moving begins with choice. The exploration of a woman's choice reveals much about her relationship to herself as well as to others, the psychological boundaries between herself and others, the value assigned herself and others.

Among the 42 women in the core population, the single women moved to fulfill aims that were primarily concerned with the equilibrium and development of their sense of self. And they felt entitled to do so.

Among the coupled women, however, only a minority had allowed themselves to recognize and act as responsively toward their own needs as toward the needs of their loved ones in deciding to make this major move. This was true irrespective of their age, irrespective of their occupation, irrespective of their familiarity with Northland, and irrespective of their subjective sense of choice.

Many movers had difficulty distinguishing their needs from those of their loved ones. And these women revealed what I have termed "the paradoxical self." That is, they experienced themselves in terms of paradoxical qualities—helplessness and unworthiness on the one hand, power and heroism on the other. These internal contradictions, which apparently arose from early psychological development, interfered significantly with their capacity to make need-fulfilling choices about a transition that would have complex reverberations in every realm of their lives.

NOTES

1. I have found it useful to follow Maltsberger and Buie's differentiation (1980, p. 63) between image and representation of self. Thus,

> A self or object *image* is the view of oneself or another at a particular time in a specific situation, remembered, perceived, or imagined. *Representations* (of self or objects) are more enduring schemata than images, constructed by the ego out of the multitude of realistic and distorted images which the individual has had at different times.

For ease of expression, the terms *self-representation* and *sense of self* are used interchangeably throughout this book.

2. My thinking about the ways in which these movers experienced themselves has been much influenced by the work of psychoanalyst Heinz Kohut (1971, 1977, 1980), noted for his contributions to an understanding of the development, characteristics, and conflicts concerning "self." Whereas classical Freudian theory posited a normal developmental progression from narcissism toward object love, Kohut argued that there is a separate line of narcissistic development, parallel to object relations, throughout life. He affirmed the existence of healthy as well as pathological narcissism.

In classical psychoanalytic thought, narcissism was understood as "libidinal cathexis of the self"—that is, pleasure-seeking energy flowing toward the self. In the popular view, this has been understood as self-love, and the term narcissism has had pejorative connotations. I find more useful the idea that "Mental activity is narcissistic to the degree that its function is to maintain the structural cohesiveness, temporal stability, and positive affective colouring of the self-representation" (Stolorow, 1975, p. 179). Therefore, throughout this book, the term *narcissism* will refer to the continuity and integration of the sense of self, as well as to self-esteem.

3. I have chosen not to follow the prevalent dichotomy between the concept of *work* and the concept of *mothering*. Such a dichotomy denies the difficulty and complexity of mothering, and denigrates its significance in society. In my view, work is the investment of time and energy toward fulfilling a serious goal; a career is a realm of work to which there is a high level of commitment and usually some progression over time. It could be argued that women making a primary commitment to family life are engaged in a domestic career. However, to avoid inevitable objections (Laws, 1976), I use the term *work of affiliation* (rather than domestic career) to denote wifehood, motherhood, and daughterhood to aging or disabled parents, as well as the development and nurturance of friendships. I use the phrase *work in the marketplace* to denote the exchange of goods or services for goods (usually but not always money) or services. I use the term *profession* to denote not only the learned professions such as medicine, law, or education, but also any field of financially compensated work involving special training.

4. Barbara's "inner voice," as well as similar presences described by other women, can be understood as an example of states

> in which a hostile presence is experienced as part of the self, albeit as an unpleasant, burdensome part. In these states, the patient suffers from a chronically nagging and disapproving conscience . . . In these cases the critical presence is integrated, however loosely, into the self-representation (Maltsberger & Buie, 1980, p. 65).

Such inner presences are often termed *introjects*. Mental representations of qualities of another person have been integrated into the mental representations of the self, and are experienced as part of the self.

T W O

Losing

Most movers suppose they are making a gain, passing through an entrance into a new state of being. Whether they pass reluctantly and fearfully, or hopefully and joyfully, they imagine a state of betterment. Indeed, in this nation moving has been a metaphor for betterment since the earliest pilgrim landings, since the great westward migrations, since the surges toward imagined treasure lodes. The land of opportunity has been a restless, mobile land.

Yet every entrance is also an exit. Every gain is also a loss. Since the dream of betterment through moving is a cherished dream, we rarely shine as bright a beam on the exits and losses as on the entrances and gains. But without that illumination, many women are left alone in the shadows—alone, bewildered, and ashamed.

"A move can be really high stress even when you want to do it," declared a newcomer in a Women's Network discussion. *"You don't anticipate that,* so your reactions are confusing and frightening. You expected to feel good about it. You think you should feel good about it, but you don't. *So you think there must be something wrong with you."*

There were murmurs of agreement around the room. This mover was making two crucially important observations.

Many newcomers had been enthusiastic about their moves. They expected them to be happy experiences. They were bewildered and dismayed when they realized that their pleasure was intermingled with, or overshadowed by, sadness they hadn't foreseen. They had moved before, yet it seemed that the painful emotions associated with earlier moves had been forgotten—a repression perhaps reinforced by the pervasive denial within our culture of the stress of moving. The unexpected upwelling of pain was a source of anxiety and shame, complicating the psychological work to be done.

Contrary to what might be expected, the distress had little relationship to choice. Whether the move was wanted or not, whether the newcomer had actively chosen to come or not, almost all of the movers struggled with intense feelings of loss. There were losses of objects, animate and inanimate. There were losses of elements of the sense of self, here defined as the gestalt of mental representations of one's physical qualities, personality characteristics, capabilities, limitations, values, emotions, and fantasies—all that one is. There were losses of identity, here defined as the outward expression of self through which one is recognized and responded to, the interface between self and other.

Movers felt shrouded by the sadness those losses aroused. This was true of women who moved with loved ones as well as those who moved alone. In reading their stories, the clinician will wonder whether these women were aggrieved or depressed, whether their responses were normal or pathological. Those terms are sometimes used with ambiguity, so a clarification of their meanings may help to provide a context within which the movers' experiences can be understood.

Grief, in the view of Jacobson (1971), is a prolonged and profound state of sadness; *sadness* is an emotional response to suffering caused by experiences (or fantasies) of loss or deprivation. Sadness concerns loss of pleasure. There is preoccupation with happy experiences of the past combined with painful desires to regain them. There are feelings of helplessness and hopelessness, but the stability of self-esteem is maintained. The sad person feels deprived but not bad and worthless or empty. Involved are predominantly "libidinal cathexes"—attachments fueled by pleasure-seeking energy—but not aggressive conflicts. And here Jacobson seems to follow closely the distinction made by Freud (1917) in his classical differentiation of mourning and melancholia.

In contrast to grief, Jacobson suggests, depression inevitably involves aggressive conflict, either conflict in relation to external reality or conflict within the psyche. There is a heightened aggressive cathexis of objects and/or self—that is, an increased flow of aggressive energy toward the other or toward the self. Depression may result from an attempt to resolve ambivalence against the other by turning the intolerable aggression against the self, or it may be the result of primary narcissistic conflict—a discrepancy between the actual and ideal self-representations. At the core of depression is an experience of failure. And here Jacobson's view concurs wtih Zetzel's concept of depression, a "basic ego state characterized by loss of self-esteem" (1970, p. 88). Depression may include feelings of inertia, indecisiveness, worthlessness, futility, helplessness, hopelessness, sadness, guilt, and shame. In deep depression, along with inhibition of thought and action, there is withdrawal of affect as well.

In contrast to Freud (1917) and Jacobson (1971), Abraham (1924) and others such as Fenichel (1945), Kubler-Ross (1969), McCollum (1981), and Siggins (1966) have recognized the almost inevitable association of anger with grief—anger at the object or circumstance causing deprivation or loss. Perhaps the distinction between grief and depression should be thought of as relative rather than absolute. Siggins (1966) suggests that the intensity of ambivalence toward the object—the balance between love and hate—is particularly significant. Also significant, since Jacobson (1971) writes not simply of aggression but of conflict concerning aggression, is whether the hostility can be tolerated and gradually mastered without a deep plunge in self-esteem. If it is accepted as relative, Jacobson's differentiation is useful: Grief is a state of sadness provoked by loss; depression is a state of diminished self-esteem provoked by failure.

Among clinicians, depression tends to be thought of as pathological. Yet both Jacobson (1971) and Zetzel (1970) point out that it may also be an appropriate or "normal" response to life's inevitable disappointments or failures. The experience of movers is permeated with loss, disappointment, and failure, as the stories of the Northland women will show.

* * *

Donna, introspective and articulate, told of the variety of losses women can face in their moves. She had moved to France several years before, newly married to a scholar who had been awarded a prestigious fellowship. That move, soon after college, was imbued with excitement. It gave Donna a welcome opportunity to pull away from her birth family, to gain some wanted independence from her too-helpful parents as she began rearing her own children. It was the emancipating move that many young people seek to affirm their surge into adulthood—an emancipating move in which separation anxiety is usually assuaged by the comforting awareness that home still exists. And Donna's move allowed her to get a fresh perspective on U.S. culture at a time when she was feeling alienated from its materialism and racism.

After five years, the fellowship ended and there were no more funds. The only opening in Donald's specialized field of research in linguistics was in Northland. For the couple, there seemed little choice. It would have been wrenching for Donald to give up that realm of work. Donna, whose primary work had been mothering, was scarcely equipped to support the family financially. On the positive side, coming back to the United States would allow a renewed closeness to Donna's family that felt welcome now that she was more secure in her adulthood, as well as career advancement for Donald.

But even as she thought about those prospects, Donna realized the sense of affinity to France that she had developed. Her sun-drenched house was open to the surround, with a grove of eucalyptus that yielded its pungent scent to the midday heat. She felt a love of the land, a connectedness to it.

The rhythm of life was pleasantly languid, and Donna noticed less pressure on women to "go into the outside world" than she imagined in the United States. Her role as a young mother seemed valued; it was shared with a close-knit circle of friends, and supported by expertly staffed well-baby clinics. In her daily rounds of neighborhood shops with their succulent fresh produce, the unfailing "Bonjour, Madame Prescott" conveyed welcome recognition.

Donna's capabilities were recognized in other contexts as well. She was committed to the Leboyer method of natural childbirth—gentle childbirth—and was a leader in a voluntary educational organization encouraging its practice. And there was another network of friends among the scholars, a circle in which Donna felt her social, emotional, and intellectual life to be nourished.

Her daily life, like the daily life of many homemakers, was unremarkable—so unremarkable that the intricacy of its fabric could easily be unnoticed. Yet to leave France meant to detach from a spectrum of roles, meanings, and affiliations. It meant to lose home, neighborhood, friends, some realms of work—myriad strands of connection and identity which all the movers had to unravel. Or tear loose.

LOSS OF HOME

Separating From the Dwelling

To leave home is to leave a dwelling. My population included those who changed dwellings because they needed to move, like Ruth, and those who moved because they needed to change dwellings, like Jennifer. Both women moved within Northland. Although other meanings of home would emerge as the study progressed (Chapter 3), these women made it clear that because so many elements of the self can permeate a dwelling—taste and values, personal and family history—the pain of leaving can be intense.

Ruth and her family, wanting to be actors in the "counterculture" movement of the 1970s, had lived in seclusion in the remote hills of Northland where young people were turning away from a chaotic world, trying to recapture their self-sufficiency, creativity, and a sense of their power to shape their own destinies if not the nation's. They were setting about it with saw and hammer and nail. "We built our own house," Ruth explained. "Every detail was just as we wanted it. That was the hardest thing to leave. It was an expression of ourselves and we loved it."

Ruth was among the few coupled women who made a genuine, active choice. Her motives for moving (from the countryside to a Northland town) and her husband's were intertwined. They needed more accessibility to his clients, new career opportunities for her after a home-based business had failed, better schools for the children. Those needs were reshaping their values, bringing about some compromise with what they had earlier repudiated. They wanted to change their lifestyle, become part of the mainstream. They wanted to "part the curtains and look in, at least to taste it!" (the tumbling metaphors communicated both the urgency of Ruth's wish and her anxiety about it).

But their rural home had established the boundaries they needed between themselves and others, boundaries that were now unexpectedly being stripped away. "We had a lot of privacy," Ruth explained. "We tend to let our feelings show—we're not always quiet in our family. Here in town we feel very exposed." This volatile family was exposed to the eyes and ears of close neighbors.

In important ways, dwellings shape relationships. They foster closeness or they allow needed distance between family and the outside world. A family can be themselves in privacy, shielded from others, as Ruth's had been, or they can be themselves by opening their home and absorbing others.

"We left our house 10 days ago," mourned Jennifer, who reluctantly moved in her eighth decade. She moved from a cherished home that she and her husband felt physically unable to maintain into smaller quarters. "We loved our home. It was built for us, the first one with a cathedral ceiling in the area," she told me, her pride in its specialness bringing a momentary glow to her saddened face. "It was big, and we often had our out-of-town friends come and stay. We entertained a lot. I love to entertain." Entertaining nourished friendships. But Jennifer reached further. Educated, eager to be effective in a broader world, but the wife of a banker in an era when it was frowned upon for a privileged woman to command a salary, she opened her home to students from abroad.

Those women, whether now coupled or single, who were most aggrieved to lose their dwellings were primarily women whose lives had been embedded in domesticity. They experienced their homes as a magnetic center that drew their friends to them. They experienced themselves as the hearth to which came friends and family for comfort and renewal. They radiated energy, skillfully enhancing their family's interactions with the outside world. Their children's accomplishments were fostered, school friends cordially welcomed. And through the hospitality they offered, these women nourished relationships that could offer support and recognition of their husbands in their careers. In their dwellings, these women felt effective; they were empowered. And then it was lost—the dwelling and, at least for a time, that power.

Dwellings define boundaries within the family as well, offering secret nooks and crannies, shelters from the frictions and irritations of daily life. For Jennifer, smaller quarters meant a grievous loss of privacy between her husband and herself, exaggerated now that both were home in their retirement. It meant unwelcome annoyance because he seemed "underfoot." And this, of course, is an issue for all families whose living space must contract because of the householders' physical limitations, financial setbacks, or because the cost of housing in a new community is unexpectedly high.

Divesting From Precious "Things"

A woman's sense of self can be expressed in the physical structure of her dwelling, and in the accoutrements of that dwelling as well. Giving up possessions can be a relief—a divestment from burdensome clutter—or an experience of grievous loss. It may be both.

"My mother was a collector," recalled Terry, who had passively accepted the move her husband wanted, realizing it allowed her to evade conflicts about her career. "And I guess I inherited that trait. I really enjoy having things around. But I know that keeping things is an avoidance too, an avoidance of having to make decisions about them and having to reexperience the feelings and memories associated with them. You have to do that before you can clear things out."

As she packed for her move, Terry could only tolerate that re-experiencing in small doses. So she brought with her many possessions connected with her parents, both recently dead. At times, as she continued to sort through those things, it became unbearable. "I try to detach myself, to avoid thinking of the meanings or the emotional connections."

In keeping with the high expectations she imposed on herself, she had felt it was her responsibility alone to start the sorting and do the packing before she came to Northland, and then once again when she moved from a rented apartment in Northland to a house the couple bought. "My husband was even more disturbed by the packing up than I. He couldn't sort through the things associated with his family. He'd become immobilized. I'd find him reading an old letter and crying." Her words were akin to those of another woman, a wife who felt no choice about moving: "I see my husband as more fragile, myself as more resilient. I feel protective, even a little maternal toward him."

Such a view of feminine strength was prevalent among the movers; it was an aspect of their self-representations that had emerged as they discussed choosing to move. Thus among the movers who were coupled, it was usually the woman who did the sorting and packing. Whether or not many husbands other than Terry's would have been "immobilized" by the intense emotions stirred up, it was the women who were expected, and expected themselves, to endure those feelings.

"I hadn't realized how much 'things' meant to me until I had to start making choices," said Jennifer. "We couldn't bring everything. Some things, the oriental rug, the dining room table, were part of the family, had been part of it for so very long." Her eyes misted. "We had a huge world map up on the wall and each time a family member would take a trip we'd stick a pin in it to commemorate the journey. We don't have space for that here."

Movers who come from a distance, as Terry and others did, or who have limited money to have their possessions transported, as the majority had, or who move into more restricted space as

Jennifer and others did, all have to divest themselves of possessions. Giving furniture or books to relatives or friends, as a few movers did, somewhat assuages the sense of loss. Through the gift a feeling of connection to the receiver is sustained. One can imagine the special chair and the special friend in a satisfying relationship. The connection with the chair is maintained through the friend, the connection with the friend through the chair. If the gift is to a relative, the line of continuity through family feels strengthened.

But the divestment can be exquisitely painful. Leaving behind a broken rocking chair in which the first-born was soothed to sleep, a piano around which there was caroling at Christmas, a rusty tricycle, a mural that recorded a family's peregrinations— leaving behind whatever embodies special memories and experiences—can feel like an amputation. It is the loss of a segment of family continuity, of personal history, the loss of a fragment of self.

To be sure, the experiences and relationships embodied in those artifacts may have been securely internalized. But at the moment of choice, their tangible representations become freshly imbued with emotion. With the losing of the inanimate object, the passing of the experience or relationship is likely to be newly mourned.

Leaving the Familiar Milieu

The mover's sense of connection can extend beyond her possessions, out of her dwelling, into the physical surround. Nostalgia for place can be intense.

"'My special love was for the view," grieved Madeleine, the divorcée who, like Jennifer, moved out of a family homestead that was now too burdensome to maintain; she sold her memory-filled home with its sagging roof to support her work as a poet. "There was an intimate view of meadow on one side and a distant view of mountains on the other. I felt as though the trees and grass and hills were part of me, an extension of myself. I felt at one with it. I was so afraid of losing that." Those views had stirred reveries, those images found voice in Madeleine's poetry. But more, the permanence of those trees and hills was calming. The connection she felt to that stability helped to soothe her fears about her own mortality as she entered her seventh decade.

For many movers, the surroundings had been a realm of mastery. "I walked through the forests, I climbed the mountains. I possessed them. They belonged to me," recalled a young newcomer in a moment of passionate longing for the western countryside she lived in before.

"I miss the ease of life," said Terry, reminiscing about the balmy environs she had left. "The weather didn't impede anything—my I-want-to-go-home feeling here is kindled by cold weather. I have a dread of winter from the horror stories I've heard. They say it makes the hairs in your nostrils freeze, and you catch your breath as though you had jumped into icy water. People all turn inward and it's hard to get around."

"I feel anxious about the winter," echoed a Texan. "I haven't ever driven through snow before. It takes so much energy, clearing the driveway, starting the car. And people seem to disappear. I took the baby out for a walk and there was hardly anyone on the street. I've heard they don't come out again until spring." It was both helplessness and isolation that these women feared.

To be sure, some movers had felt alienated from the environs they had left, especially large cities. They were glad to move away from street crimes, racial tensions, schools in turmoil. But even if the milieu left behind was far from ideal, it was familiar. Boundaries between known and unknown, between safety and danger, were understood. Problems were identified, but resources and solutions were recognized as well. Since we try to control our world through cognition, the unknown may feel unsafe.

LOSS OF PHYSICAL IDENTITY

Identity, the outward expression of self, the interface between self and other, is grounded in the body. At first contact with another, the physical self is responded to, perhaps with a gesture and usually with words: "You look wonderful today." "You're looking tired." "You've lost weight." "What a tan you've got!" Whether welcome or not, such comments affirm the continuity of existence. Not to be recognized—and the newcomer is not at first recognized—is a loss of physical identity that can feel uncanny.

"It was as though nobody saw me." "I was invisible." "I felt like a ghost." These uneasy comments were made by a number of movers, and their similes vividly conveyed the anxiety they felt. To be unseen can kindle the deepest human dread, that of disintegration of the self, nonexistence.

Hairstyle

Such dread can become focused on hairstyle. "The way my hair looks is absolutely central to my appearance," explained a newcomer who worried about risking an unknown hairdresser in Northland. One among those many women who had trouble making claims for her needs, she felt guilty about spending money on herself. But still, on any pretext that could involve the family too, she went back to the state she had left for her haircuts. "If it's cut wrong, it takes so long to grow out, so long to make repairs." Women with the time and financial means traveled surprising distances back to their trusted hairdressers. Frivolous as that could seem, it was a serious attempt to ward off the threat of lost identity.

Hair has complex meanings. Haircutting has been used to symbolize separation from a previous world or stage of life in traditional cultures around the world (Van Gennep, 1960). A baby's head is shaved to signify his entrance into life; a girl's head is shaved as she enters the state of marriage; a widow's hair is cut to sever her bond to her husband; hair may be cut after death to symbolize separation from worldly life.

In our own society, the first haircut traditionally marks the transition from babyhood to boyhood—and that loss of babyhood has been quietly mourned by many a mother who has preserved a severed curl as a memento. Haircutting has been expected of young women turning away from society to enter religious orders. A linkage between haircutting and separation seems to run deep in human experience.

Hair may be chosen for rituals of transition because it is an easily recognized characteristic, having its unique color, length, and arrangement—in our own society, the flowing locks of the 1960s "Flower Children" or the "Afros" of the 1970s were distinct. Hairstyle expresses individual identity as well as affiliation with a group—it symbolizes a balance between separation and connection, whereas the haircut is connected with separation and loss. Small wonder that the styling should only be entrusted to a familiar person, and that the risk of an altered appearance produced by an inept or unfamiliar hairdresser should be dreaded. Hairstyle is a prominent way the mover can preserve and express her physical continuity.

"What Are Women Wearing in Minneapolis?"

Clothing, as much as hairstyle, is a selective declaration of physical identity. Elements of self are concealed, elements are transformed, and elements are revealed through the clothing one chooses to wear. It is an expression of the ongoing, yet ever-changing experience of self in a social context. There is a balance between conformity with and variation from the accepted styles of a community. After a move, the interplay of self-concealment, self-transformation, and self-disclosure must be reworked, and a new fit between individual preference and group norm must also be achieved.

"Every time we began settling in a new place," reminisced a frequent mover, "I would find a way to ask one of the women I met, 'May I see your closet? What are women wearing in Minneapolis?'" Perhaps particularly because she had moved so often, felt marginal so often, there was an urgency in her wish to conform, an urgency in her need to look like an insider and feel like one as well.

"This town seems very homogeneous, very class conscious," observed Terry in a discouraged mood. "There seem to be 'right' neighborhoods, 'right' schools to have gone to. And there's clearly a 'right' way to dress." Terry had encountered elitism in Northland, as one does in most, if not all, communities. Feeling a painful absence of a "right" fit between herself and her new town, she had the illusion of a homogeneity that excluded her. It seemed most visibly expressed in fashion. Twenty months after her move she confided, "Some of my clothes still feel uncomfortable to wear." Those were the clothes that expressed her exuberance, clothes that felt too flamboyant in her new milieu.

Northland homogeneity was, in fact, an illusion. There are many variations of style adopted by the many subcultures within the region—farmers and peace activists, academics and tradespeople, corporate executives and artists. But Terry's sense of the incongruity of her clothing expressed a more general lack of congruence between herself and her new community. She had not yet found her niche, her own subculture. It seemed with Terry, and with others who expressed similar feelings, that the sense of incongruity was fed from both sides—from the newcomer's uneasy awareness of being marginal, and from signals that a settled community absorbs newcomers most readily when they learn how to conform. That was sometimes made explicit.

Ten months after she moved, another newcomer recounted with mingled humor, embarrassment, and outrage that a neighbor had cautioned her that her style of dress was inappropriate for her small town. "I dress up for church, and sometimes I wear dresses during the week. I enjoy the way it makes me feel. Just because you're home with your children, do you have to wear painter's pants? I think you should be free to dress as you wish, but her comments made me feel very uncomfortable." In contrast to Terry, who concealed aspects of her personality by avoiding her exuberant clothes, this mover had used her style to reveal her true self, and that self was rebuffed.

LOSS OF SOCIAL IDENTITY

Parallel to their concern about losing aspects of physical identity, women were anxious about the loss of social identity that moving involved—social identity embodying the roles a woman plays in society. Those roles can be recognized by the woman as expressions of her capabilities, and can lead to recognition by others. It is both the internal and the external recognition that confirms her selfhood and her specialness, and gives positive meaning to her life.

Moving is often caused by, coincides with, or results in a transition from one life phase or predominant role to another. In such a dual passage, the continuity of a woman's sense of self as well as her recognition by others is interrupted. Here is another narcissistic disruption that must be struggled through without the support of close friends or trusted colleagues. It must be passed through while a husband or lover is absorbed in his own passage. Even when the entrance into a new primary role—a profession, wifehood, motherhood—is joyful, what has been left behind can be as intensely felt as what has been gained.

A Newlywed

"People here don't recognize me as an individual!" an offended and angry young newlywed told me. Her move coincided with her transition into wifehood and disrupted a nascent career in business. That had not been difficult to set aside, because her commitment to it was tentative. But she felt diminished by the loss of her identity outside of marriage. "I feel a sense of outrage that both his family and mine now see me as just the minister's wife who is expected to trail around behind him, and that they ask how *he* is getting along here but not how I'm getting along. And that's true of a lot of people I've met here—they don't recognize me as an individual," she told me indignantly. This young woman of the 1980s was being regarded as a traditional "goodwife," a consequence of marriage that she was far from ready to accept.

Wherever she lived, there would have been a struggle to transform her identity in the minds of her husband's traditional family and her own, claiming her distinctness from her mate as well as her connection to him. But the move stripped her, in a sense. No longer a student, no longer a business woman, she had no credential, no occupational label, other than "wife" to present to the new community. There are traditional women in Northland, there are radical feminists, there are all variants between. It was not that Northlanders could only perceive this newlywed as an appendage of her husband, but rather that she felt she had lost any other identity to present to them. Reorganizing her own sense of self without support (her husband was absorbed in his pastoral concerns), she may have communicated her uncertainty. Others respond to the way we perceive and label ourselves.

A New Mother

The loss of her professional identity, and its label, was central in Jan's transition. She was settled in her marriage before her move. She had spurred her husband to consider changing jobs because his corporate responsibilities interfered too much with their personal lives. Was Ted married to Jan or to his firm? She took initiative in helping him locate alternatives, and urged him to consider a position in Northland, familiar to her from years before.

Jan was an editor, challenged and fulfilled. But with a new baby on the way, she wanted to set aside her professional career and immerse herself in mothering. So during her exploratory visit to Northland with Ted, she made no effort to investigate opportunities for her own professional future, assuming they would be available when she wanted them. Like other movers, she relied on assumptions. Nor did she learn of the low salary scale in her field (or even the high cost of real estate, in spite of her intention to center her life at home). These oversights would have seemed astonishing in a woman with Jan's acumen, had they not been such a common occurrence among the movers. Jan actively chose Northland, but much more for her husband than herself.

After she was here, the loss of her professional identity made Jan deeply uneasy, unexpectedly anxious. And the anxiety persisted for many months.

"I feel as though I'm floating," she told me. "It's as though nobody really knows who I am."

"Would it have been different if you'd stayed in Houston?" I asked. "You might have decided to give up your editorial work there too, so you could be involved in full-time mothering for a while." Yes, it would have been different, Jan explained. Even if she had stopped her newspaper work, others would still have known her as an editor. Through the continuity of their recognition, her image of herself as a professional person would have had ongoing confirmation.

Within four months of her move, Jan's wish for her professional career became intense. Like the newlywed, she had experienced a wounding lack of recognition from people newly met. Domestic work felt unfulfilling.

"My husband and I used to share the boring chores—that made them easier—and I paid someone to clean. I've been freaking out here. I want to get settled, but there's so much housework to do. I've discovered I hate it. It's repetitious and monotonous and there's no recognition. Oh yes, my husband compliments me on a good dinner, but that's not enough. I enjoy mothering and I feel I'm good at it [her alert, responsive, sociable infant seemed to attest to that]. But I need affirmation from other people." Her baby could respond only in terms of his own need-fulfillment; he could not confirm Jan's specialness as a person distinct from himself.

Clear that she wanted time at home with the infant, Jan needed many more months to locate possible part-time jobs in this unfamiliar territory. The few in her own field were abysmally paid and almost invariably full-time as well. Not until 16 months after moving did she find an interesting, permanent part-time job. It was not directly in her field, but related closely enough.

Six months later, she confided that the emotional pull toward professional life felt less urgent now. Recognition in the public world had assuaged the intensity of her need. In the consciousness of Houston she had been a professional woman. Now, in the consciousness of Northland, she existed as a professional woman once more. But the interlude of lost professional identity had lasted close to two years.

To the clinician, it could seem that Jan's narcissistic crisis was unduly intense and prolonged. Yet we do not, in fact, know what is normative during major transitions. Following Stolorow's proposition that "Mental activity is narcissistic to the degree that its function is to maintain the structural cohesiveness, temporal stability, and positive affective colouring of the self-representation" (1975, p. 179), it was evident that most of the movers experienced significant narcissistic disequilibrium. Anxiety such as Jan's signaled an impending loss of "positive affective colouring of the self-representation"—loss of self-esteem.

A Retired Woman

Affirmation from outside is crucial for many women (and men as well). Closely intertwined is the glow that arises from inner affirmation—the well-being experienced from fulfilling one's own ideals. A move can dim that glow. Among those who moved later in life, after their children were grown (or nearly so), only Rose simultaneously retired from a profession—a long career as a history professor.

"I think of myself as a happy person, a fortunate person," she had told me in the first flush of jubilation about her move. Rose's ideal self was clearly a contented self. She seemed to be a stoical woman who had little tolerance for troubled feelings; she warded off those emotions that felt "negative," a word she often used. Perhaps because of that sturdy psychological insulation, her sense of lost identity was less immediately felt than other women's. She spoke of the first premonitions of unease seven months after her move. When her husband accompanied her to the supermarket, an unaccustomed practice, she wanted to protest. It made her feel like shrinking away from him, she explained—not wanting to be seen shopping together. "Why is that?" I wondered, thinking of younger women who long for such sharing. "Because it brings to mind an image of *uselessness*," she told me anxiously. She was picturing two elderly people with nothing to do but go to the store.

Two months later, Rose seemed to be floundering. "Maybe we made a mistake trying to make two major changes at once," she suggested. The dual passage of retirement and moving was much more stressful than she had expected.

Rose had felt fully entitled to share the decision to move with her husband. Familiar from summer vacations, Northland was appealing. But, as the move was being planned, Rose seemed not to have formed clear ideas about how her life could be meaningful there. Her decision to move seemed to be based on vague expectations.

Now she was missing her academic life keenly. Housekeeping didn't give her a feeling of competence: "It's too easy," she declared. She felt uncertain about how to find new ways to feel effective. It was difficult to think of herself in roles that wouldn't command the level of respect, and self-respect, that she had enjoyed in her professional career, so she was cautious about casual volunteerism. And she wanted flexibility. Her children were grown but Rose wanted to be free to visit them and receive their visits; she wanted to be supportive to a husband who was groping to redesign his own life.

Sixteen months after the move, she admitted to feeling depressed. "I don't feel as though I'm contributing anything to anybody," she said with a tinge of despair—despair connected with her situational plight and also, it seemed, despair that she was engulfed by emotions that felt alien. The loss of the glow of competence and the satisfaction of helping others through her professional work, as well as the loss of shared concern and affirmation from her colleagues, resulted in a loss of meaning in Rose's life. There was a painful discrepancy between the mental representations of her ideal self—happy, capable, contributing to others—and what she was experiencing as her actual self. Such is the discrepancy that results in a fall in self-esteem and is central in the state of depression.

Rose felt unaffirmed from within. Jan, the editor, and the young newlywed felt unaffirmed from outside. The difference was primarily one of emphasis. Younger movers acknowledged more frankly than older ones their need for external recognition. Among the older, it was only hinted or implied. Yet approval from within the self and approval from outside are interwoven.

Those women who had set aside their business or professional work when they moved were in marriages they wanted, new or longstanding. But marriage alone was not sufficiently sustaining. In leaving communities that validated their professional identities they had lost a significant source of narcissistic equilibrium. They had lost what Kohut (1980) terms the mirroring back of worth that everyone needs to confirm her or his sense of self, and to replenish healthy self-love throughout the life cycle. It was a loss that left them anxious and intermittently depressed.

For other women the move, and prior moves as well, had interfered with the possibility of ever developing careers in the marketplace, or had thwarted the consolidation and advancement of such careers. As one frequent mover said ironically, "Moving so much gave me a way out. I didn't have to decide what I wanted to be when I grew up!" By agreeing to the moves, she and others like her had evaded the developmental task of clarifying their identities as women, connected with but distinct from their mates. And this avoidance was a source of the continuing helplessness and dependence so many of the frequent movers had revealed. In a vicious cycle, the helpless/devalued aspects of their self-representations were repeatedly reinforced.

But it was not only professional careers that were disrupted and professional identities that felt lost. Jennifer's life, for example, had been committed to the work of affiliation. But her move in her eighth decade was experienced as a frightening loss of adult competence. Like many older adults who move out of homes in which family life has been nourished, homes that the fledglings have left, homes that now seem too large to heat and maintain and to afford, Jennifer had moved into a smaller dwelling. As this lively, creative, intelligent woman had confronted her incapacity to take care of a home she loved deeply, a home in which her social identity was embedded, the sense of loss was exquisite. She was sad, anxious, outraged. "It feels like diminishing, it's an experience of diminishing—and I feel furious about it." Her feisty spirit echoed Dylan Thomas' outcry to ". . . rage, rage against the dying of the light" (1957). Indeed, whether consciously felt or not, raging and grieving are intertwined.

Loss of Familiarity

Some movers experience little change in their core social identity. Women primarily committed to the work of affiliation sustain their roles as wife or mother; women who move to accept a professional opportunity continue to be recognized as physicians, bankers, or administrative assistants. But these women's lives have been embedded in a familiar structure, shaped by commitments to household tasks and the rhythms of their children's school days, their husbands' or lovers' homecomings, aerobics workouts, art classes, volunteer work, Friday night potluck suppers with other couples—a web of interconnections that a move will rupture, a web of interconnections in which a woman enacts a multitude of roles that together shape her identity. That is unraveled.

"I feel very unsettled. I need things to be predictable, to have a routine. I feel very distressed if I don't know what's coming next." The anxiety this homemaker expressed seven months after her move was experienced by many others. Time and energy was needed to regain the familiar rhythm of daily life and to reconstruct the total fabric of identity.

LOSS OF FRIENDS

"Every morning as I drove across the river on my way to work I would think, 'there isn't a single person in this town who really cares whether I'm here or not'," recalled a settled Northlander, reliving her move of eight years before in a Network discussion. Her bleak thought expressed one of the deepest dreads that people can experience: being unrecognized, unresponded to, uncared about—not existing in the consciousness of others. Being utterly alone. The Northlander's desolate cry brought into focus that an object loss can also be a narcissistic loss—a loss of those responses that help maintain the stability and continuity of the sense of self. Her outcry was echoed by many others whose moves had ruptured close relationships.

A few women had moved a short distance within Northland and preserved their friendships with nearly the same intimacy as before. A few had left behind their close friends during earlier moves, and had never been able to replace them. A few frequent movers had given up trying to form attachments after their friendships were repeatedly interrupted.

"After we made several moves, it didn't seem worth the bother to try and meet people, because then I'd have to anticipate the hurt of leaving them again," explained one of them, a "no-choice" mover who had relocated 11 times in her 15-year marriage. She had become more and more solitary and withdrawn.

Except for these few, movers felt the pain of separation from loved ones as central in the pain of moving. It was felt whether or not the move was wanted. It was felt by single women and coupled women, women who moved for husbands or lovers, women whose husbands or lovers moved for them. Several younger women felt saddened by the separation from family members. For most, who had pulled away earlier from their birth families, it was the loss of intimate friends that kindled deep grief.

Anticipatory Grief

It was kindled, but in some women it had a long fuse. Tina, for example, who had abdicated the choice about moving and yielded to her husband's wish, went through the motions of preparing to leave in a state of detachment. Feelings were isolated from thoughts and actions.

"I was like a zombie. I really felt nothing much about moving at all. I was absorbed in closing down my business and in the children. Then the day before the van came with the packers, my husband told me to choose the clothes I'd need for our cross-country drive. I went to the closet and stared at the clothes and I was immobilized. I couldn't even think. Then I suddenly started to cry and I cried for two and a half hours and I yelled and I screamed. I told him to go alone, I and the children would stay behind. I didn't want to leave, no, I didn't want to leave." Her grief burst explosively through the defensive wall.

Others cushioned themselves against their grief even longer than she. The intense activity of sorting and packing and dismantling their homes; negotiating with van lines and realtors; closing down memberships, bank accounts, charge accounts, milk deliveries and trash pickups; changing postal addresses and magazine subscriptions; attending farewell parties—this accelerating surge of activity could stimulate an emotional "high" and mask the awareness of impending loss. And that momentum and elation could last after the move in the flurry of interactions with realtors, shopkeepers, bankers, librarians, carpenters, plumbers, and more, all deflecting attention from the experience of loss.

The appreciation of the reality of the separation was sometimes obscured by earlier circumstances. "At first it didn't seem any different from other times when I had gone away for a term," noticed a recently graduated student.

"We all separated from each other during summer vacation anyway," Rose, the retired history professor, pointed out. Her summertime move to Northland scarcely felt different at first from other seasonal peregrinations.

These various defenses against the pain of loss—isolation of affect, avoidance, denial—served to delay its onslaught. Perhaps they were useful in allowing the mover to remain highly active and organized, especially as it is usually the woman in a family who is the primary strategist in a move. Yet women who invoked such defenses became especially vulnerable to an explosive breakthrough such as Tina's, and especially vulnerable to anxiety and shame because the upwelling pain was then so unexpected.

Many women felt aggrieved about impending losses as soon as the move was planned. Some, like Donna, tried to assuage sorrow with reason.

"I tried to stay aware that things there would change, that some of our friends would be leaving too. I tried not to idealize our life," she told me, recalling the six months of intense sadness before she left France for Northland. Her grasp of those realities coexisted with her sadness, but did little to relieve it.

The sorrow of the movers was compounded by the sadness and the outrage of their friends. "Our friends wined us and dined us and said, 'how can you do this to us?' We knew our lives would grow away from each other—they felt that I was deserting them," Rose recalled pensively. She was, in fact, deserting them.

All who move away desert those who are left behind. Those who stay have to wrestle with sadness and anger and envy and fear for themselves, mingled with gladness and hope for the mover's good fortune. Those who leave must wrestle with regret and guilt about the pain they are inflicting on colleagues, customers, clients, and patients, as well as family and friends.[1]

When human bonds are torn apart, there is a longing for comfort. Indeed, a particularly observant newcomer noticed that before she moved she had begun grieving intensely for those special people who seemed to be nurturing—not only affectionate friends but also a sympathetic supervisor, concerned colleagues, a kind doctor, and her hairdresser. So I learned yet another meaning of the loss of the hairdresser. It is not just the result—haircut or hairstyle—that is important to women, but also the special care a hairdresser provides.

There are few ways in which an adult American woman allows herself to have her body tended by others. Hair care is among them. Long after the child can bathe herself and toilet herself and mostly dress herself, she needs her mother's help with shampooing and combing out the snarls and brushing the locks into a becoming style. The hair of a small girl is the focus of loving and admiring ministrations. The hair of a woman is a focus around which she can continue to experience gentle nurturance, motherly bodycare. The hairdresser can be a symbolic mother who can support the mover through her passage.

"Moving Is Like Dying"

Jan, the editor, had begun grieving as soon as she decided to move. "I was surprised and upset at the intensity of my sadness—it's like death in its intensity," she told me in dismay. That parallel was frequently drawn.

"My greatest fear is being nobody, having no one close to me—maybe it will be unbearable and I will just die." This true despair was voiced by a young Northlander dreading her forthcoming move. She experienced not only the object loss ("having no one") but also the narcissistic loss ("being nobody") inherent in separating from close friends. Those friends, who were objects of her affection, also validated her worth and confirmed her existence. Being nobody meant psychological annihilation. Many movers feel they are "nobody" before they form new connections in a new community.

"Moving is like dying," Jennifer told me sadly. "It's a kind of death. It's coming to an end." Moving within Northland, she had experienced only minor geographic separation from her intimates. Yet elements of her connection to those friends felt lost. In losing her home, she feared that her capacity to be a fully competent woman who effectively fostered relationships was ending.

"Moving is like dying," Madeleine, the divorcée, exclaimed in our first conversation. "I felt at one with my home. I was afraid of losing it, of feeling alone. It's like dying, because dying means aloneness." The separations and losses of moving had stirred fears of her own aging and death, as they did with other older movers, and revived memories of past deaths in her family. Indeed, it is common that loss in the present reawakens memories of losses in the past; grief from the past merges into present grief and deepens it.

Whether a move was wanted or not, whether the losses associated with moving were object losses or losses of self, they were felt with such intensity as to be associated with death in the thoughts of many movers. Indeed, with the elemental wisdom embodied in the rituals of preliterate people, *rites de passage* from one state of being to another or from one territory to another often incorporate an enactment of death and rebirth (Van Gennep, 1960). Symbolically, moving is first a kind of dying.

Working It Through

Sustained grief would be unendurable. For most women, there were rhythms of grief, ebbs, and floods. There were upwellings, often unexpected.

Sometimes the trigger was recognizable. A young mover received a magazine from Atlanta seven months after leaving, with photographs of her old neighborhood undergoing renovation. Her nostalgia was sharp, and she felt a twinge of outrage. "It's all going on without me. How dare they?" she exclaimed, only half in jest. There was a surge of sadness, there was painful recognition that in the consciousness of Atlanta she had ceased to exist, and there was longing for reunion.

Grief also welled up without apparent cause, perhaps first signaled in a dream.

"I dreamed that my husband and I were on a ship, about to embark on a journey. We went into the dining salon. A circular table was arranged with immaculate linens and flowers. Around it guests were seated, and we somehow knew that they were waiting for us, waiting to surprise us. Then I noticed that they were our oldest friends, our dearest friends from Chicago. I felt a surge of joy, and I started toward them to hug each one. I hugged Janny . . ."

"Then my husband woke me up. I saw I was in Northland, and I started to cry. Later on that morning, glancing at my appointment book, I noticed that this was the very week we embarked on our move to Northland one year ago. It seemed uncanny."

Uncanny as the temporal coincidence seemed to this mover, she described a phenomenon familiar to clinicians. The unconscious sector of her mind had responded to the anniversary of her move. The sadness and the longing welled up again. The complex task of grieving was unfinished.

Grieving for those who live has been less well examined than grieving for the dead. In bereavement, as Fenichel has written (1945, pp. 303-394),

> The tie to the lost object is represented by hundreds of separate memories; for each of these memories the dissolution of the tie is carried through separately and this takes time. . . .
>
> Every mourner tries to simplify his task by building up a kind of substitute object within himself after the real object has departed. For this he uses the same mechanism all disappointed persons . . . employ—namely, regression from love to incorporation. . . .
>
> Mourning consists of two acts, the first being the establishment of an introjection, the second the loosening of the binding to the introjected object.

Even while the intense emotional attachments to the deceased are being gradually given up through these two processes, transformations may take place within the mourner's personality. That is, characteristics of the lost person are permanently internalized, and are manifested in the mourner as new ideals, traits, or interests (Loewald, 1962; Siggins, 1966).

Theoreticians have believed that it is easier to loosen ties to an introjected object rather than an external one. Yet the mover must let go of ties to objects that are no longer present but continue to exist in reality. In that the lost objects are only partially lost, the relinquishment may be less painful but more complex. Movers made it clear that letting go is rarely abrupt and rarely smooth. There is reaching forward and pulling back, a *danse macabre* of grief.

Most women invested large amounts of time, energy, and money in communicating with friends in other places, trying to soften the impact of loss. Some arranged for visits back and forth. "We've had so many houseguests that I feel as though I'm running an inn," chuckled Rose. "But I must say, I love it. In a way it feels as though the separation hasn't happened—and I write long, personal letters. You can really think about all you want to say, so it lasts longer than a phone call."

Bittersweet. Those communications could mask the sense of loss. But they could also make it more acute. Letters from distant friends could confirm that the separation had really happened. They could stir intense sadness and longing for reunion. Long-distance phone calls would arouse the gladness of reconnection. But when the receiver went down, the sadness would simultaneously descend.

Jan, who had grieved for her lost identity as an editor, mourned her lost friends as well. Being married and having a cherished infant did not forestall the melancholy—nor did it for other coupled women. Four months after she came, Jan told me, "One day last week I looked out the window. Everything looked so barren and gray, a few flakes of snow drifted down. I felt so sad and so bleak. People here have been friendly from the start, but I have moments when I feel unbearably sad. I miss my dear friends so intensely." Clearly, the welcome and friendliness that had flowed toward Jan from Northland residents had not begun to fill the void. Pleasure-seeking energy was still directed toward distant friends; having not yet loosened those ties, she was unready to form new ones.

"My sadness gets reopened every time I hear from my friends," she said. And Jan's pain was compounded by a growing sense of estrangement. She went back to Texas for a visit six months after her move and was dismayed. She was unable to feel responsive toward her closest friend, Nilda, a confidante with whom she had shared the joys, hopes, fears, and disappointments of everyday life. "I couldn't seem to feel anything much at all. It hit me that the relationship couldn't ever be the same as it was before, because of the distance." With that realization, there was an emotional withdrawal, and Nilda noticed how closed off from her Jan was.

Then there was a reversal. Months later, Nilda came to Northland to visit, and Jan sensed her friend retreating from her. The visit was confronting Nilda with the stark reality of the separation, and she was intensely disturbed. In turn, each woman was trying to fend off pain by withdrawing affection and denying her own need. (It did not seem appropriate to point this out, but I suspected that the estrangement had also been fed by unacknowledged anger. Not only would the "desertion" of Jan's leaving have kindled anger in Nilda, but the subsequent emotional withdrawal of each woman was a mini-abandonment that may have aroused anger in the other.)

It was not until 20 months after Jan's move that the estrangement began to heal. By now, Jan had reclaimed her professional identity in Northland, and her self-esteem was more secure. The intensity of her need for Nilda's concern was somewhat reduced and made the separation more bearable. And Jan's connection to Nilda had been maintained through her memories and through the silent dialogues that we carry on with those who are physically absent but psychologically present. Yet the external relationship was still important. On another visit to Texas, Jan made a point of spending private time with Nilda, time for confiding, and she noticed a feeling of reconnection. Jan came away from this visit realizing that the relationship could continue, "just like people's relationships with their families continue," less intense but meaningful.

Others who were able, emotionally and financially, to persist in preserving their attachments as Jan had persisted, noticed similar transformations. No longer sharing the psychological substance of daily life, the mover recognized a loss of intimacy. This sometimes prompted a recoil, an emotional distancing from the "lost" confidante. This may have been the counterpart of the "regression from love to incorporation" in mourning; that is, there was a loosening of the tie to the external object, and a redirection of emotional energy toward the internalized object. As the tie to the object felt internally preserved, a cautious outflow of affection may have felt safer, followed by the warming realization that the relationship, although less intense, would stay alive both internally and externally in spite of separation. Yet this healing happened slowly.

Whether grief was first experienced in anticipation of the move, whether it was fended off until later, however it ebbed and flowed, it was inescapable for most movers. As, indeed, it should have been. Good cheer in the face of loss may be applauded—it usually is, being labeled courage—but it does not necessarily foster emotional health. Although the validity of their belief has been questioned (Wortman & Silver, 1989), many clinicians have observed that an absence of grief, the incapacity to mourn a significant loss, can diminish both physical and mental well-being. When the powerful emotions of mourning—sorrow, anger, and its frequent companion, guilt—are buried in the mind, they find expression in disguised forms. Illnesses can develop as the body's immune system is weakened, or unexplained depressions can manifest later (sometimes as puzzling variants of the anniversary reaction). Or the absorption of psychological energy in keeping the painful emotions out of awareness can produce a state of inappropriate emotional detachment (Deutsch, 1965; Siggins, 1966). And, just as significant, since mourning can be understood as a process that allows for adaptation to loss or change, the avoidance or absence of mourning can interfere with the acceptance of loss and change (Pollock, 1977).

Almost a third of the core population, and many who joined in group discussions, had felt so overwhelmed by anxiety or depression linked to their losses that they sought psychotherapy. There was no evidence that these women were more disturbed than the others. They were, however, more motivated to understand the reasons for their unhappiness and less fearful that seeking help betrayed a shameful weakness. Several pointed out that it was only in therapy that they became fully aware of the powerful emotional impact of their moves—they had been attributing their troubled feelings to other causes.

The majority did not avail themselves of professional help, yet only a few women passed through their transition without experiencing moments of deep distress. Those in distress struggled to contain it.

"It's very disturbing to feel a wave of bleakness and not to be able to explain it," a newcomer confided four months after her move. "It makes me feel out of control." Here was another woman whose unanticipated sad and anxious moments felt shameful, alien to her ideal self; here again was the dissonance that pulled women to the brink of depression. "I have to involve myself in work around the house or else I could just float away on it." The tasks anchored her attention, kept her from floating away on that oceanic sadness, and then the accomplishment gave her a small experience of mastery, a small dose of self-love that assuaged the bleakness.

"I go horizontal," said another. "I go horizontal with a book. I withdraw and read and think." Others invoked similar self-soothing strategies, retreating into their inner worlds to connect with images and memories and daydreams that evoked a feeling of comfort.

Some tried to shrink their distress by contrasting it to greater pains.

"I said to myself, come on, get your head together," a recent mover declared at a dinner party. "I said, 'a lot of your friends have lost their husbands. Be glad because you still have yours.'"

Donna recalled that her depression seemed most intense about six months after her move to Northland. "Then one day I happened to glance at something that had Anne Frank Street written on it. And I began thinking about Anne Frank [a young Jewish girl hunted down and killed by the Nazis in Holland (Frank, 1983)] and how she would wish just to be alive. That helped to put my own sadness in perspective." In such efforts to gain perspective, the mover imagines a greater pain—loss of life—and by contrast feels relief that her own pain is less. But such relief is usually temporary. Donna is not Anne Frank, she is Donna, and only her own experience has true reality.

The strategy may, in fact, rebound by arousing guilt. The mover reads in the newspapers about the death from leukemia of a four-year-old, about devastating famine in Africa, about the menace of nuclear annihilation. By contrast, her own preoccupation seems trite and she feels unjustifiably self-centered. Then the grief she has felt in response to loss arouses guilt and shame. So the grief is compounded by a fall in self-esteem, the substance of depression.

"Isn't it a question of whether you see the glass as half full or half empty?" inquired a Northlander at one of the Women's Network meetings in which movers disclosed their inner struggles. Not really, I thought, because the reality includes both the fullness and the emptiness, and both must be experienced: the emptiness of loss and the fullness of memory and of new attachments—the entrance and the exit.

Recoil from Grief

That questioner had been a settled resident. Movers were confronted with the stark fact that the settled community was reluctant to know about the sadness they were feeling.

"Everybody seems to be all smiles and happiness at being here. The mood I'm in, people wouldn't want me around. I'm a real downer."

"We have to wear our having-a-good-time masks when we go to gatherings."

"People insist that you like it here. They ask, 'don't you just *love* Northland?'"

Indeed, that question was asked many times, and with urgency. "Not yet," one mover thought silently. "My nose is pressed against the window of Northland life, but I'm still outside it. I'm lonely and missing my old friends intensely. But this person needs me to love Northland."

A long-settled Northlander told me wryly, "When I first came from the West, people asked how I liked Northland, and I told them the truth. It took years to heal the breach!" Movers unwilling to take that risk had to wear a smiling face, suppress authentic reactions, be on guard, and show less than usual spontaneity. They could not be their true selves, and that intensified the lonely feeling of being a stranger.

Why should settled people insist that newcomers love their town, their village, their farmlands? Because the interconnection between self and other is intricate. On the one hand, the self has developed in part through conscious imitation and unconscious identification. Images of the responses and attributes of important others have been incorporated among the developing mental images of self. In this sense, other is embedded in self (Buie & Adler, 1982; Jacobson, 1964; Mahler et al, 1975; Winnicott, 1965).

The opposite is true as well. Self remains to some extent embedded in other throughout one's lifetime (Kohut, 1980). Other includes people primarily, but also includes the milieu that is significant to the self and is partly experienced as an extension of self. Other, composed of various objects of attachment, responds to the self in ways that validate one's identity, reinforce self-esteem, confirm the very sense of being. If a newcomer seems to repudiate the milieu by failing to love it, those residents whose selves are embedded in it may feel diminished and recoil. "Don't you just love Northland?" is a way of asking, "Don't you just love the elements of life that are significant to me?"

If the newcomer's sadness or anxiety or loneliness arouses guilt in the resident because—enmeshed in the needs and commitments of her own life—she has failed to reach out, the resident may turn away. Or if the newcomer discloses pain that the resident feels helpless to assuage, the resident's feelings of competence and self-regard are threatened, and she may recoil from that discomfort as well.

And the resident, unless this is her birthplace, has struggled through her own transitional pain. Since she chose not to move away, she has experienced a reconnection and reached a state of equilibrium, even if fragile. The distress of the newcomer can disturb that equilibrium. It can cause painful resonances, reawakening forgotten grief. And if that grief felt alien to the resident's image of her ideal self, she would of course shrink from experiencing it again.

That threat can be experienced by recent movers as well. Rose, the history professor, made that clear. "Would a different group of movers have been more adequate?" she wondered, as we talked about the study more than three years after her own move. When

I reminded her of the anxiety, sadness, and depression she had vividly described earlier, she explained, "Yes, I do remember saying those things. But being depressed or anxious seems like being out of control and so I don't want to think about that now. I don't want to know about it." In striving to extinguish the memory of her own earlier "inadequacy," she limited her capacity to feel empathy for other movers, or even for herself.

The resident's recoil can erupt in harsh judgments. "People who have so much trouble with moving must have real flaws in their characters!" declared a long-settled Northlander who heard me describe my project. Maybe so, I thought silently. But are there any perfect personalities? Isn't being flawed basic to the human condition? And isn't it an expression of flawed compassion to heap shame on newcomers already in pain?

RÉSUMÉ

In moving, these women experienced myriad losses. There were losses of elements of self that had been expressed and given recognition through physical appearance, in the home, through diverse social roles, and in work. There were losses of highly valued relationships, or significant transformations of relationships that continued. Losses included both objects of love and sources of love, all playing a significant role in maintaining the cohesiveness and continuity of the mover's sense of self, and her self-esteem.

Sooner or later, whether they had wanted to move or not, whether they moved alone or with partners, almost all of these women experienced grief—sometimes so intense as to be compared with bereavement. Unprepared for their pain, they felt anxious and ashamed.

Movers experienced an absence of empathic response in the new community, which inevitably intensified their loneliness and sadness and reinforced self-doubts and shame. In contributing further threats to the mover's self-esteem, it increased the likelihood of depression.

Yet there was no moratorium for the mover. Ironically, while her energy was absorbed in feeling, understanding, containing, expressing, and dispelling the powerful emotions associated with loss, she needed simultaneously to confront the challenges of reconnection.

NOTES

1. Those in the healing professions may be concerned that they are doing harm. For the clinician, especially one engaged in long-term psychodynamic psychotherapy in which the relationship between client and therapist is at the core of the therapeutic work, the experience of leaving can be exceptionally intense. The working through of termination means enduring the rage, reproaches, fears, sadness, and despair of clients. There may be a daily barrage of such powerful emotions for weeks or even months before the clinician's move. She must monitor the powerful responses that are stimulated within herself, steadfastly focusing on the client's needs even while her own ambivalence about leaving is incessantly kept alive.

THREE

Re-creating a Home

CORE MEANINGS OF HOME

"As I move toward it, the house seems to reach out and enfold me. Home means feeling safe," a mover explained. In each interview, when the topic of home was broached, I explored its meanings.

Another gestured with encircling arms. "Home is where you can be yourself, completely natural—where it feels safe and where it *is* safe to have feelings and to let them show."

"I come back at the end of the day and as I approach the front door I feel the warm anticipation of going into my cozy apartment. I slip into a wrapper or caftan and plan my evening in front of the fire."

"I love the wide, strong floorboards in the house, and the woodstove. It's elemental to cut the wood and bring it into the stove. I like to feel its texture. The stove is warm and strong, it defines home within the range of its warmth. The hearth is home."

Enfolding, safe, cozy, strong, warm—these meanings seemed evocative of the "holding environment" conceptualized by Winnicott (1965) to represent the benign maternal presence that fosters integration in the infant. An older mover made the connection directly: "The house I left was my womb. I sheltered in it," she mourned. This precise linkage was expressed by other women as well.

"I feel like a room with permeable walls, like a house that people easily move through." "I feel like a motherly being, a house that people freely enter. I feel warm, like a room." These were the voices of two college students in a Women's Studies class, two young women groping for words to express their sense of femaleness.

House (or room) and woman (or womb) are linked in dream, myth, and symbol worldwide. In preliterate Melanesian cultures, cult houses in which exclusively male transactions and sacred rituals are enacted are nonetheless understood to be female structures imbued with female essence (Errington & Gewertz, 1987; Meeker, Barlow, & Lipset, 1986). In advanced Western cultures, a school, college, or university and its physical structures is known to its students as *alma mater*—nourishing mother.

Consciously recognized or not, *home* can be a metaphor for mother, not only the real mother but also the mental representation of mother that slowly forms in the mind of the child, coexisting with the actual mother and then gradually substituting for her presence. Home can represent the internalized mother that adults carry within their minds throughout their lives.

Knowing that the home-mother is there makes absence feel safe. "It's a place of belonging, of knowing your way around. It's a familiar place you can go away from, confident that it will be there, unchanged, when you return," a mover explained. It is that confidence that helps young people make their emancipating moves away from the homes of their birth families. Although those homes (and families) need at times to be repudiated in the struggle toward autonomy that is expected in our culture, they still do exist. The image of their unchanging existence can be a touchstone of safety.

Leaving and losing are not the same. To lose one's home can mean to lose the sense of shelter, safety, and warmth that it embodies. It can mean to reexperience, at least unconsciously, the pain and danger of separating from the actual mother of long ago. It can mean to feel like the toddler who dashes exuberantly out of sight and then becomes aware that she is separate, alone, helpless, small, and scared.

Several months after her move, Priscilla awoke from a dream, drenched in cold sweat. "I was on a ship again, and my husband was at the helm. He declined to follow the course I asked him to set. We berthed at an oriental city. Then I was walking urgently through narrow, tortuous passages trying to find my way back to the ship that would take me home. But my way was impeded, blocked by street vendors and rickshaws and crowds of slowly shuffling people, and the alleys kept diverging. I felt directionless, always moving, but not knowing where I went. I was bewildered, then frantic. I awoke to a bleak dawn. Where was my home?"

LIMBO OF HOMELESSNESS

Priscilla felt adrift in a limbo of homelessness, and such an anxious state was described by many movers. The feeling of connection to home had been severed. Priscilla recognized that from a dream, but for others it was a trip away from Northland that brought the disconnection into sharp focus.

"After our vacation," recalled Donna (who grieved for her sun-drenched life in France), "we drove up to the house and neither my husband nor I knew where we were. Of course we really did know, but there was no sense of recognition, no feeling of coming home. It was very sad to realize that after nine months here."

Jan, the editor, felt a "weird" absence of belonging anywhere when she journeyed back to Texas three months after her move to Northland. "I felt I didn't belong there any more, but we feel we don't belong here yet either." And she still felt disconnected when she and her husband returned from a trip a year later. "The autumn foliage was glorious then. But it didn't seem true that we live here; it didn't seem real," she told me uneasily.

Movers such as these were describing a disturbing dissonance between thought and feeling. Cognitively, they well knew where they were. But they missed the emotional ties (the cathexis) that imbue an experience or a place with a full sense of reality. They did not belong.

For some movers the interlude of psychological homelessness was brief, but for many it was prolonged. The work of transforming a dwelling into an enfolding, safe, cozy, strong, warm shelter was time-consuming and energy-absorbing. It was a complex process that involved gaining a sense of mastery in the new environs; it involved imprinting qualities of self in the dwelling; it involved reestablishing a feeling of continuity; it involved expressing one's identity to others. It involved allowing emotional connections to develop, so that good feelings from the past could flow into the present and infuse the new surround.

These were challenges for single and coupled women alike. The men who moved with coupled women, with few exceptions, immersed themselves in studies or professional careers. It was the women who were expected, and expected themselves, to carry out this complex psychological and practical work, recreating home for their families as well as for themselves.

TOWARD MASTERY

Rituals of Possession

"Home means feeling safe," movers had told me. This was, in fact, a central attribute. Safety arises from being strongly sheltered, warmly sheltered—passive states. It arises as well from active states, from achieving a sense of mastery. For many women, the first step in the direction of mastery, "possessing" the dwelling, was a ritual of cleaning that had the quality of an exorcism.

"The first thing I had to do was clean the kitchen," recalled Barbara, the photographer. "It was already clean, but I had to do it again to make it mine. I can have crumbs on the counter and if they're my crumbs that's fine, but if it's someone else's crumbs, that's filth. I had to scrub out all the cabinets to know what was there, to make sure there weren't any lurking crusts of toast." There was a lilt of self-mockery in her voice, but the message was serious. "And then there was new shelf paper and then doing the bathrooms. My husband cleaned them but I had to do it again. And then, at last, I could arrange all our own things."

Barbara focused on traces of the most elemental human processes, eating and excreting, functions that form the earliest linkages between infant and mother. A free spirit in her own creative work, she was not unduly meticulous. Rather, those crumbs and crusts and drips seemed to be the vestiges of other presences and other attachments that had to be banished before Barbara could begin to feel truly connected to the house.

Donna claimed her house in a similar way. After her sad return from a trip, when she felt no recognition of home, she spent two days vigorously cleaning and tidying. "That seemed to make the house belong to me again," she told me, a little puzzled. That seemed to be another exorcism, impelled by unconscious needs.

Through the women's rituals of emptying, washing, mopping, and tidying, the vestiges of other presences were swept and wiped away. And then the new occupants could begin to claim ownership. They could begin to explore, test out, find their way around.

"They didn't know how to turn on a light switch, use the hot and cold water taps, flush the toilet" (Lapin, 1987). This observation about Cambodian refugees in New England was published after my project was finished. But it connected directly with the expressed needs of the Northland movers, all familiar with Western technology, and it spotlighted the helplessness that movers in a strange milieu anywhere may have to overcome.

"I like to find out exactly how things work in a new house— I mean how many steps to the light switch, how hard you have to push the handle to make the toilet *really* flush." Few movers were as whimsically graphic as this one was, her words almost exactly echoing the bewilderment of the Cambodians, but it was clear that each newcomer needed to go through her own rituals of familiarization. Each one had particular things she needed to find out and control in order to begin to feel safe in her new domain.

Disarray

A few women were able to achieve a sense of mastery swiftly, although with intensive effort. They spoke of their feelings of urgency. Speed was an effort to bypass or abbreviate the physical turmoil and its psychological concomitants—anxiety, confusion, disorganization—because those states were intolerably threatening to their view of themselves as effective people.

But disorganization, confusion, and anxiety were unavoidable for most movers (single or coupled), either because of external circumstances, their own internal responses, or—most often—both. In fact, malfunctions that might be dealt with effectively, philosophically, or humorously in settled life were likely to disrupt seriously the mover's sense of competence.

For a year, Reni, who moved alone, away from a failed marriage and into a new job among strangers, shared her house with mice and bats. They frightened and disgusted her. Whereas other movers carried out rituals of exorcism, clearing away the detritus of other presences, Reni's attempts were thwarted. Each day there was new excrement in the drawers; cooking a simple meal meant rewashing the soiled utensils. She resented the intrusion, the claims on her energy and time. She resented the reality that the rodents were out of her control. And, burdening her more, she felt ashamed of her fear, disgust, and resentment. "My colleagues make light of it—they think I should be able to deal with mice. And I'm stubbornly refusing to move again. It just takes too much energy to pack things up, find out about new places."

Reni was depleted. Her sense of competence was diminished by the invasive rodents, her self-respect was diminished by her fear and disgust. And thus the grief aroused by the losses linked to moving—loss of her marriage, friends, colleagues, work, identity—was compounded by the fall in her self-esteem. There were layers of loss and pain dragging Reni into a depressive spiral, a spiral that she described hesitantly, as though it revealed a flaw in her character. This talented professional woman, friendly and outreaching, ready to risk a new love relationship when another had grievously failed, had not even had the comfort of understanding that her reactions were consonant with the stresses she was enduring.

When either nature or technology run amok, even the settled householder is unnerved. For the mover, invasive rodents, shrilling alarms, or bursting pipes are both metaphor and reality. Myriad troubled feelings about the move can be attached to the frozen pipe or the swooping bat. Yet they are also disturbing impingements upon the mover's fragile equilibrium.

The physical disarray involved in Reni's move was extreme. Yet even expectable disorder aroused unexpected distress among movers. For Dorothy, a self-reliant 73-year-old woman whose move out of an unhappy marriage was emancipating and joyful, the transition at first had the quality of a frightening dream. "It was traumatic! The worst thing was the disorganization. For years, whenever I've had a nightmare it's been in the same form: Something is about to happen and I'm not ready. The disorganization of moving gave me just that nightmarish feeling, the feeling of not being ready."

"It's very confusing not knowing where things are. Old people get confused," said Jennifer, who moved from her cherished family home to smaller quarters. "And it makes me feel anxious. I feel anxious about everything." Jennifer's treasured antique rug became a metaphor for her unsettlement. She couldn't induce it to lie flat. Whichever way the furniture was arranged, the rug slithered into new wrinkles. Jennifer didn't feel smoothly or safely grounded in her new dwelling. Indeed, since humanity evolved from the tree-swinging primates, the sense of being safely grounded has been a foundation of security, both physical and emotional. Its opposite, the image of falling forever, is one of the primal fears, originating in early infancy (Winnicott, 1965).

"Old people get confused," Jennifer repeated. "Tell your readers not to wait until they're old to make their moves." Indeed, she targeted a risk for the older mover whose retrieval of recently acquired information may be less reliable than more distant memory, and who may rely on elements in a familiar environment to stimulate recall.

Dorothy and Jennifer were the two oldest, but young movers felt confused as well. "It's very disorganizing because you can't find things," said one of the youngest. "You want to write, and the pencil has a broken point, and you can't find the pencil sharpener, and you don't want to buy a new one because you know it's there somewhere." Months later, she moved again, this time from her rented house into a purchased one. "I *still* can't find the pencil sharpener," she chuckled, but with an edge of exasperation. "There was one attached to the wall here but the truckers broke it off!"

Not being able to smooth the rug or not finding the pencil sharpener, the can opener, the turkey platter at Thanksgiving— these are small challenges to competence. Small challenges with large psychological consequences—loss of feeling safely grounded, of feeling oriented in space, oriented in relation to the surround, the walls, the stairs, the furniture, or even, "How many steps to the light switch?"

Among those women who need order, predictability, and a sense of control in their lives—and most do to some degree—these disruptions arouse anxiety. Dorothy was able to tolerate that anxiety, working through it in her dreams and accepting it as a psychological cost of moving. Other movers such as Reni could not. Judged as unacceptable by an unforgiving conscience allied with unsupportive colleagues, her sense of incompetence led to a fall in self-esteem and a temporary state of depression.

Depression and anxiety were powerful impediments against recreating home, and could readily set in motion a vicious cycle. Those states impeded recapturing the feelings of effectiveness that women had enjoyed in their previous homes, and, in turn, the loss of effectiveness fueled anxiety and depression.

SELF-EXPRESSION

"Painting the House Red"

Our cave-dwelling ancestors garnished their walls with paintings that represented their experience of the world, imagined and real. Tribespeople on remote Pacific islands plait pandanus leaves into intricate and symbolic designs to form the walls of their simple, thatch-roofed dwellings. The linkage between the psychological world of men and women and the shelters they arrange seems close. The urge toward self-expression has power. Among Northland movers, this was confirmed.

"Feeling at home means the house has become an extension of yourself," movers explained. "It's an expression of yourself."

"You get your place so it smells and sounds just the way you want it," a young newcomer told me in a glow of anticipation.

"We've painted the house *our* color, red!" rejoiced Ellen. Through the red paint she took possession of the house, her being seemed to flow into the house, and its red glow warmed her emotionally and reflected back her own exhilaration. Exhilaration was prevalent among the movers who could release these expressive drives.

"I love decorating houses almost better than anything!" exulted Dorothy after she had passed through her nightmare of disorganization. She played with colors, and she opened the ceiling with a skylight so that the internal blues and golds echoed the sky and the sun.

"I began to feel at home as soon as my furniture arrived," said another, who then undertook a joyful and extensive remodeling of her rambling house. She created niches to display an important collection of folk art, each piece embodying the memory of some venture of discovery shared with family members, the collection also expressing her own artistic flair.

A dwelling begins to become a home when it is imprinted with its occupant's personality—when the colors of the walls, the patterns of the fabrics, the arrangement of the furniture, the placement of artifacts, and the hanging of paintings express her ideas, emotions, daydreams, and memories. Through such decoration, the urge toward expression is fulfilled, special qualities of self are reflected back in validation, and the self is revealed to others. Her home declares a woman's identity, as a newcomer's arresting tale confirmed.

"I don't feel we are intensely materialistic, but we do like having our things around. They express our taste, our experience, our values," this thoughtful woman explained as she reminisced about the move preceding the one to Northland. "I found dealing with the moving people very difficult. They treat women like bits of fluff; they're very condescending. We had acquired a number of antiques and my concerns about how they were packed weren't taken seriously." The stage seemed to be set for disaster. "Then, en route, the van caught fire and all our furniture was destroyed— only some books and knickknacks were saved. So I entered that new community with no furniture. It was like those dreams in which you go out and find yourself naked! Our furniture would have communicated some things about me to our new acquaintances. It was as though part of my identity was missing."

Unexpected Frustrations

Usually less dramatic than a burning van, practical problems nonetheless thwarted the urge toward self-expression in most movers. Many lived in rented dwellings, either temporarily or for the entire two-year period. Some lived among the furniture and artifacts of strangers, jarring to their own tastes. Unlike those movers who were able to "exorcise" the vestiges of other presences, these women felt engulfed by them.

"I've absolutely hated living in someone else's clutter," an edgy mover exclaimed, feeling as though her personal boundaries had been invaded. And the alien spirit of another woman's rented house seemed to be symbolized when the owner's plants became jaundiced in spite of the newcomer's careful tending, and, one after another, drooped to their death. It felt as though they rejected her tenancy.

The equation of home and identity was so close that it deterred some movers from exposing their temporary habitats to others, especially the untested others of a new community.

"The place simply wasn't an expression of me, and I didn't want people to see it," confided a 34-year-old who made no attempt to invite new acquaintances in during the ten months she lived in a rented apartment. This was a warm, outgoing woman who was very experienced in moving, and had become aware that appearances count. She feared that, from the evidence of her distasteful surroundings, visitors might form false impressions of the woman who lived within. Her confidence about how she would be received was temporarily fragile. Akin to those women who needed hairstyles and clothing that felt authentic, that would declare their true selves to a new community (and, hopefully, be accepted), she needed a dwelling that felt authentic.

Other movers, in unfurnished rented quarters, were constrained by their leases against extensive decorating.

"I had so much wanted a two-story colonial that I could decorate to express my own taste and my own ideas," Polly, who also was interested in folk art, told me. This was Polly who had chosen Northland as the locus for her husband's training and her own domestic life, enthralled by images that might have been drawn from pages of *Vermont Life*. Her fantasy had been shattered by the sober realities she confronted. She voiced her intense disappointment in her affordable prefabricated house, "this shack," as she termed it, that she and her husband had rented from a distance, sight unseen.

Polly was among the many who accepted temporary housing that they found inadequate. There were myriad words of protest and resentment that might be echoed in many parts of the United States today.

"I'm really worried about the cost of fuel; this place is so poorly insulated."

"We've been cold all winter. We couldn't afford enough fuel to set the thermostat above 60 degrees."

The high cost of fuel and of housing in certain areas of Northland was a shocking revelation to most movers. Since this information is readily available, it was surprising that so many had failed to inform themselves before deciding to come.

"We had a copy of the newspaper sent to us," Polly explained, "and we studied the real estate ads. There were attractive houses that seemed affordable. We didn't realize they were miles out in the boonies." This intelligent young woman had not thought to procure a map or write a letter of inquiry to realtors advertising their properties. And even during her investigative visit, Polly had not discovered that the attractive houses close to her husband's workplace were not affordable.

For many movers, hopes and fantasies were supplanted by dreary realities—realities not confronted in advance, realities that might have given a different shape to expectations, and perhaps to decisions as well.

"This doesn't feel like it's our house yet." This was the discouraged voice of a newcomer a year after her move. She now lived in a house she owned, a compromise house that was the most she could afford. "It's cramped, it's cluttered and confused. I dislike the wallpaper. There's not enough light."

She was among the movers who lacked the financial resources to buy fresh carpeting, enlarge a window to welcome more sunshine, or even replace furnishings they had left behind. Most of the newcomers had had to absorb the cost of moving, some from great distances (a few had expenses paid by their new employers). And some of those who had owned their previous houses had difficulty selling them promptly. Only when those homes were finally sold were funds available to begin transforming a new dwelling into a home. It seemed that the expenses of relocation, and the implications of those costs, had not been fully taken into account when decisions to move were made.

Emotional Impediments

"Why didn't the movers think it was challenging, why didn't they think 'nesting' was fun?" asked Rose, who looked over a draft of this chapter four years after her move and was unsettled by it. That was one of the many junctures at which I thought critically about the findings, searching for unrecognized bias. This questioner was one of the few fortunates who could choose just exactly the new house she wanted. And she was among those with little tolerance for troubled feelings in herself or others. Her ideal self was a happy self, and she tried to obliterate the memory of the interludes of anxiety and depression that had shrouded her earlier in her own transition.

"Why didn't the movers think it was challenging, why didn't they think 'nesting' was fun?" The answers came from the movers themselves. From the outset, a few did think it was challenging, a few did think it was fun. But many more told me that not only practical problems impeded self-expression in their new dwellings, but their emotional states did as well—just as their emotional states had slowed the recovery of their senses of mastery and competence. Women who felt depleted or depressed after their move could scarcely muster the energy or interest to make their new dwellings attractive. And some stressed movers became too anxious to decorate their new habitats with pleasure.

A young newcomer, whose move (in tandem with a new marriage and entry into professional life) seemed "like a frightening transition into adulthood," found that becoming a householder felt "almost overwhelming." Having bought a house almost a year after her initial move into rented quarters, she felt immobilized at the prospect of furnishing it. "I haven't been able to deal with all those choices.

When you make a decision you have to give something up," she explained, accurately pinpointing what is often overlooked, the fact that any choice involves both gain and loss. Even the choice of a chair involves the loss of the chair not chosen, or the loss of the fantasied chair not found. This newcomer was still feeling intensely sensitive to loss, still acutely aware of all she had given up in making her move. "I can't decide what I want," she continued. "I want the furniture to be an expression of me, and right now I don't know who I am."

Her anxiety was intense but not unique. Another newcomer who bought a house several months after her move to the area could hardly force herself to go and look at it, let alone think about interior decoration. That empty, featureless house seemed to mirror her inner state. "How do you express yourself in a house when you have no sense of self, when you don't know who you are?" Her question was tinged with despair. Her separation from family, friends, and the other connections and roles that confirmed her identity, had deeply threatened her self-constancy—the ongoing sense of "this is who I am" that sustains us through the continuous changes of our lives.

"Home is an expression of yourself," movers had said. Self-expression did indeed take place. But for most of these women, it was a very gradual process, delayed by temporary living arrangements, lease restrictions, financial limitations, depletion of energy, emotional distress. Yet, ironically, it was during the first months of transition that the validation of self emanating from a compatible milieu—a house painted "our color," for example— was most needed.

The close connection between home and identity did provide some women with a positive impetus toward getting settled. It did for Reni, who was still depressed and anxious 11 months after her move.

"Somehow I can't make a commitment to the house I'm living in. My way of putting my imprint on a house is visual; it has to do with the way I make things look, and the final refinement is hanging pictures. Somehow, I just can't get myself to hang those pictures."

Two months later she had hung the pictures, but not primarily for her own satisfaction. "I really did it to show Jim [her lover] that I'm feeling more together." And the pictures did help her feel more together. Now an upward spiral was set in motion. Feeling more together allowed her to invest more energy in recreating home, which then helped her feel more together.

A number of women were spurred on by the expectation that others would visit. Is not a housewarming really a house-showing, and a declaration of "this is who I am"? When that was an expected ritual (before U.S. mobility became frenetic), the structuring of expectations it offered may have given many movers an impetus toward reintegration.

CONTINUITY

Home expresses the self, and by embodying personal and family history, home reinforces a woman's sense of continuity.

"My husband and I both keep things," a young newlywed admitted, explaining why it had taken six weeks to pack up their household accoutrements when they moved from a temporary apartment into a house. "I still have mementos from grammar school days; so does he. We're not sure why they're so important, but we can't throw them out." She acknowledged with a hint of embarrassment that she had saved only the schoolwork she was proud of, the papers that got good grades. As she had confided her doubts about her capabilities, her fears of failure, it seemed likely that those school papers provided this young woman with a touchstone of accomplishment. And they sustained connection to her girlhood; in fact, they sustained connection to the home she had lived in until her birth family made the first move she remembered—an intensely disruptive move when she was 12.

We reflected together that in times past there were family homesteads with huge attics in which yellowing bridal gowns and musty books and outgrown toys and packets of faded love letters were stored. Many have succumbed to the rising tide of mobility. Lacking a family repository, countless movers have had to carry with them the artifacts that pull past into present and provide links to the future as well.

"When I moved I took boxes of toys and books that had belonged to my children. Someday I want my grandchildren to have them,"

an older mover told me, expressing just this need for transgen-
erational continuity.

But time must pass before there is a history; experience must
accrue before the history has meaning.

"The house is still a disappointment," Polly told me after two
years in the Northland prefab she thought of as a shack, "but
we have made every effort to make it feel like home. And it does
now, in a way, because of the things we have in it from our years
of marriage. Did you notice the stenciling I've done on the walls?
And my husband built that large hutch for our china. We've both
expressed ourselves here." Polly's "shack" was gradually being
transformed into an embodiment of her married life. A conjugal
history was being recorded.

Most movers have had to leave behind special possessions. New
objects will be acquired, new stencils painted, new hutches built.
Gradually they will acquire special meanings, they will represent
special relationships and experiences. As the contents of a dwelling
acquire that patina of continuity, they help a dwelling to become
a home. At best, that patina develops slowly. And, ironically, the
very process of fostering the sense of continuity can itself be dis-
continuous. An almost unnoticed aspect of relocation is that a move
from one community to another is likely to involve several moves.

REPEATED MOVES

When movers have the time and financial means to make househunting visits, and succeed in finding a pleasing house or apartment
before they move to a new community, the images of that new
dwelling can be sustaining. Because these movers can begin to
envision themselves functioning in their new place amidst their
special possessions and special people, their images help bridge the
abyss of psychological homelessness. There was a handful of
Northland movers who were this fortunate, and who also expected
that their new dwelling would be permanent. These women could
mentally begin recreating their homes even before they moved,
and could anticipate carrying on that process with reassuring
continuity.

Most could not. Most moved into rental housing of variable desirability. Some who felt keenly disappointed in their quarters lacked either the money or the energy to make a change. Like Polly, they needed to allow their fantasies to yield to reality—another loss—and come to terms with compromise.

Among more than half of the newcomers, the urge to create a new home was initially stifled by the awareness that they would have to move again soon when their leases expired. Their moves to Northland were in fact multiple moves. A few could only move from one rented dwelling to another. Most of the shifts were from rented to purchased houses. To be sure, these were considered moves of betterment, wanted moves. Yet these women had to work through the disruption of leaving one dwelling and settling into another at least twice during the two-year time span of my study, and some endured it three or four times.

There were exceptional women for whom the repeat move was easier than the first. "This is the first move we've ever made that has been free of anxiety because there are no unknowns," reflected Ellen, whose life was centered in the work of affiliation. After 10 months in Northland she enjoyed a strong network of support—interested, encouraging acquaintances—a network she had worked energetically to create. And this network set in motion, through their own friends, an active outreach toward Ellen from within her new neighborhood.

Literally and metaphorically, Ellen was fed. On the first chaotic moving day, an acquaintance from across town brought supper already cooked; the next day another couple invited the family for dinner. A neighbor came by and offered to take the children so Ellen could have quiet hours to get settled; two days later, another neighbor gathered five adjacent families for coffee and conversation.

These contacts grew swiftly into a helping network of neighbors who borrowed each other's tools, pitched in with the chores and formed a child-care cooperative. Through her willingness to expose her needs and her warm responsiveness, Ellen acted as a catalyst in this new neighborhood, extending and enriching those re-lationships that already existed.

Although she didn't enjoy the affluence of several older women who happily set about creating their retirement "nests," Ellen's second move did share common elements with their first. She, like they, had familiarized herself with the area and formed ideas about locations that would feel compatible; she, like they, had time and energy available for house hunting; she, like they, had friendly acquaintances to act as sponsors and gather her in. And—at least as important— she, like they, expected this new house would become her permanent home. It felt safe to allow her energies and her feelings to flow into it freely. Painting the house red, as she did, seemed an act of celebration. (Yet two years after this move, because of professional difficulties encountered by her husband, she would sadly have to leave her red house, leave Northland, and rebuild her life once again.)

Ellen mobilized extraordinary external support. Joan experienced the support internally. Joan's move to Northland immediately followed her marriage to a man already committed to law school here. Home currently meant "where my husband and I have our private life together," she told me, and that matrix was undisturbed by a second move within Northland. She and her husband had not accumulated a large number of possessions (their conjugal history was just beginning to be lived); he felt able to move them with help from a friend, and to set his own comfortable pace.

Although each of their Northland apartments seemed to be a nascent home, Joan's attachment to her mother and to her childhood home was still close. There she still had a locus where memories of her past life were centered, a repository for mementos that represented her girlhood and family history. Joan's sense of connection was reminiscent of the mover who suggested that "home is a familiar place you can go away from, confident that it will be there, unchanged, when you return." Like many young women setting foot on the paths to adulthood—college, job, marriage— Joan had left, but not lost, her original home. Its image was vivid and sustaining.

Barbara was not sustained through her second move by such a cord of connection, nor by the hope of permanence, and her experience was more typical than that of Ellen or Joan.

"It was a heller," she told me vehemently. "It was a heller, not so much emotionally because we weren't leaving the community, but physically." The packing up after 10 months in a rented house felt overwhelming. "We'd never really organized things because we knew we wouldn't stay here. There were piles in the closets, under the beds, everywhere." It took her husband much longer than they expected to move all the cartons into the new house. And that was another rental, so they faced moving once more. Barbara again "made it mine" by vigorous cleaning, "but only up to a point, and then I gave up. I feel somewhat indifferent now, because I know it's only temporary."

Others were as severely stressed by the repeated relocation— a euphemism for dislocation, it seemed. When I phoned to make an appointment with another mover settling into a house she had bought, she quipped, "I still can't find the pencil sharpener!"—her metaphor for disarray. "The move was awful," she said. It took six weeks to pack up their things, those mementos that she had told me embodied her personal history and her husband's. Like Barbara, she created her repository wherever she currently lived— modern nomads uneasily carrying their life story in a crate. And she had been required by her lease to dismantle all the changes she had made in their rented unit, all the expressions of self intended to create the illusion of home. She had constructed a study for her husband in the basement. She was proud of her workmanship and he liked it immensely. Pulling that down dragged her spirits down with it.

"Why don't the movers find it challenging?" Rose had asked. This young woman had risen to the first challenge, and was now engaged with another. She was moving into a purchased house that she intended to remodel with her own hands, both as an adventurous occupation for herself and as an investment. But she knew that would be temporary too; she faced yet another disruption within several years when her husband finished his training. How many times would this spunky woman be able to search for the pencil sharpener? How many times would Barbara be able to "possess" and then lose a new habitat before her indifference became chronic?

There were many others who felt pushed to their limits by the need to move again in Northland, or away from Northland, long before they had recovered from the stresses of the move into Northland, long before they had recovered from disappointment, disorganization, confusion, frustration, and loss of control and competence.

And yet, during their temporary tenancies, linkages had been growing. "I love the fence posts outside our house and the way they lean under the snow as though they're bearing the weight of their memories. I like to walk down the country lanes, and we can see mountains all around the house." This lyrical voice belonged to a mover whose growing attachment to the physical surroundings was soon to be ruptured. The owners of her rented dwelling reclaimed their home, and she was forced to move again.

For almost all of those who moved again in Northland, it seemed that the fragile strands of familiarity, competence, self-expression, and continuity that were developing during the first months were unraveled. The physical and psychological work of homemaking had to begin again.

One third of all the movers felt at home in their dwellings within two years. It could be stated that *as many as* one third felt at home, or that *only* one third felt at home. Both emphases would convey truth: The first attests to the power of the urge to recreate home in spite of impediments; the second, to the power of the impediments thwarting that urge.

Although not all the women fully engaged in domestic life were able to recreate home, all those women able to recreate home were (with one exception) engaged full-time in domestic life. It was engrossing work.

ENVIRONS

Goods and Services

This complex work of recreating home extended outside of the actual dwelling. "Feeling at home means knowing how to find things and make them work," a newcomer had explained, and she was referring both to "things" in the dwelling and to needed goods and services in the community. The others concurred.

"Sometimes I have a terrifying image of endless supermarket aisles," admitted one of the very frequent movers. "I think of the numerous supermarkets I've had to find my way through, finding how and where the food is arranged, over and over again. It seems like a metaphor for having to discover and master a new environment over and over again."

The metaphor is apt. Food is a basic provision of care, care of self and of other. Whether or not identified with a particular ethnic group, every individual and every family prefers foods that symbolize emotional states of safety and comfort, that represent special relationships, that invoke memories of family rituals and tradition. Locating those foods in a new community is a significant element in feeling at home, but one that may require a diligent search. And if the newcomer seeks foods not commonly sold, her sense of marginality is heightened.

The newcomer has many new realms to fathom. The dry cleaner, shoemaker, plumber, and electrician have limits to their clientele. Which one is available? Which one is the best? Who will come if the roof leaks, a pipe bursts, the septic tank backs up? The library, school, gymnasium are institutions with their own technology, space, rules, and customs both overt and covert—their own interpersonal systems. Each is an inside, one that the mover must tactfully penetrate from outside.

Finding out where things are and how they work can invoke friendly and helpful responses. In Northland, many movers discovered local repositories of information in the country stores, village post offices, small garages—all traditional gathering places as well, although more often for men than women. These, particularly the stores, were the counterparts of the urban neighborhood shops in which the storekeeper functions as "a communication center and local banker as well as a vendor of goods around whom people coalesce to receive services and information" (Schorr, 1975, p. 107)—shops, which, ironically, are themselves becoming victims of mobility.

But the mover also encounters those who release information grudgingly, volunteering nothing, so that the mover must ask another question and another, revealing her ignorance, feeling foolishly like a pre-school child whose incessant questions exhaust and exasperate those around her. There may be shame associated with her ignorance and with her inquisitiveness as well. In the past, there have been constraints against women seeking knowledge. For example, it was deemed "unladylike" and impolite to be "nosey," to ask "too many questions" (how many was that?), and young girls were admonished that "curiosity killed the cat"—that very expression equating an inquisitive attitude with forbidden aggression. Vestiges of such taboos still linger.

Investigating the unfamiliar aroused anxiety among these intelligent movers who were so competent in their accustomed spheres. "It took me six weeks to get to the gym to find out about swimming," said a newcomer who lived near the pool. And she hadn't explored other facilities either. She feared that she would "make a fool of myself," making mistakes, exposing herself to criticism. Her anxiety signaled the danger of humiliation if she were perceived by outsiders, and by her own internal critics, as incompetent.

Her hesitation to go to the gym would have seemed more exaggerated had another mover not gone to that gym to swim, and asked an official where the women's locker room was. "Go right out the back of the building and turn left and go in the green door," he said. She went. There were four unmarked green doors. The first one opened into a dark, empty recess and she drew back. The second one opened into a foyer, and an inner door swung open. She glimpsed a leg bare to the groin, a thickly muscled, hairy leg—no woman, that. She pulled open the third and there were three people with racquets. "Do you possibly know where the women's locker room is?" she asked, quelling the impulse to say, "my name is Alice, I'm lost in NorthWonderland." The woman began to give directions and broke off, as though it were inexplicable. Or she sensed the mover's bewilderment. "Come," she said kindly, "I'll show you." Feeling very, very young, the mover allowed herself to be led—not quite by the hand, although she might have welcomed just that.

To feel momentarily so helpless and dependent was unsettling, yet her observing self was amused by her plight, and by the gym official's apparent ambivalence toward women (this had been a male facility until recent years). For others, such states of confusion, helplessness, and dependence were difficult to tolerate; at risk was the mover's self-esteem.

In different situations, movers feared the helplessness of isolation. "It took me quite a while to feel familiar with the surroundings," a usually self-possessed newcomer confided. "I'm frightened when I have to travel the country roads. I have a fear that the car might break down and there would be nobody around to help. I'd be stranded. I'd be all alone."

"I love to explore. If you get lost there's always someone to ask." This contrasting voice belonged to a woman who enjoyed deep trust in the good intentions of others and in her own capabilities, and easily forgave herself for making mistakes. She was exceptional among the stressed movers. To be sure, others found exploration to be zestful and new discoveries to be exciting, but it was a rare mover who enjoyed the process without a companion to share the risks.

So for women with a vulnerability to embarrassment, or with anxiety about separation and abandonment—and there are many such women—investigating new places alone felt hazardous. And in some circumstances, it was in fact hazardous. Whether in rural lanes or city streets, women are preyed upon. (After "Alice in NorthWonderland's" adventure, she suggested that an identifying sign, Women's Locker Room, be painted on the correct green door at the gym. But that could place women at risk, she was told. Molestors might go in.) For psychological or physical safety, the newcomer seeks a companion. Yet during those early months of exploration, a companion may be difficult to find.

On the average, becoming familiar with the surroundings—learning to locate and use the needed goods, services, and facilities—took the movers half a year. Enjoyable for some, worrying for many, and necessary for all, the process helped to restore the mover's sense of mastery and was a significant element in beginning to feel at home. And since the newcomer was so actively exploring and inquiring, she was likely to make discoveries that could be shared. There could be a surge of delight, a glow of competence, associated with saying to a long-settled resident, "Come with me and let me show you . . ."

Neighborhoods

It has been suggested that "Attachment to place refers to *individuals' commitments to their neighborhoods and neighbors*" (Gerson, Stueve, & Fisher, 1977, p. 139), and is directly proportional to the length of residence in a particular neighborhood. Although one third of the Northland movers felt at home in their dwellings, fewer than one sixth felt positively connected to their neighborhoods two years after their moves. Neighborhood was not a primary object of attachment for most. This may have been influenced by the fact that half the newcomers made second, third, or fourth moves within Northland during the time span of the study. Yet those movers who became most attached to neighborhood were also among those who had made such repeated moves, so attachment was not proportional to their length of residence.

When it did occur, the linkage could happen unnoticed. "We were going away on a vacation, and I realized that there were three houses on our street where we could leave our dog!" a newcomer told me with a laugh, for the first time recognizing the lines of connection that she had developed.

More often, the connections were purposefully developed, the neighborhood being regarded as an essential resource by some of the movers with young children. Here there is agreement with Gerson et al (1977), who observed that having children influences their parents' needs for neighborly involvement. Such was the case with Ellen during her second move, and with Ruth, whose sense of neighborliness was an experience of personal growth.

Having moved out of her rural counterculture realm into the cultural mainstream of town (Chapter 2), and as a member of an ethnic minority, Ruth felt exposed and frighteningly isolated. "I'm afraid of annihilation." "In what sense?" I asked, thinking she spoke in metaphors. "I mean literal annihilation, being killed." This was not projection. Recently, she reminded me, there had been a Ku Klux Klan gathering in a town not far beyond Northland, a rally that rekindled the deep feeling of vulnerability that Ruth had absorbed from her family history, her racial history.

"When we rented this house, we had to apply for a zoning variance so my husband could have a home office. Most of the neighbors have been antagonistic. Some don't speak to us at all. I'm worried at the survival level. If there were a medical emergency, who would I call? Who should I tell the school to call if my daughter gets sick and my husband and I aren't available?"

For many months, Ruth endured these worries. As she developed other lines of connection, new families moved nearby, diffusing the neighborhood homogeneity that had excluded Ruth and her family. Then, toward the end of her second year in town, with a national holiday approaching, she initiated and helped organize a neighborhood cookout. Her timing was right; the neighborhood was responsive, people turned out in number, mingled, and talked freely, and the party brought about a dramatic change. Neighbors began to greet each other openly and go out of their way to help each other. They began to watch out for each other's houses. Ruth felt safer now. If there were an emergency, she would know whom to call.

The painful feelings of alienation, aloneness, and awareness of antagonism that earlier made her so anxious were assuaged, and largely through Ruth's own efforts. She had recognized her intense need for neighborly connection in order to feel safe, and realized that she would have to act energetically to fulfill it. She had, however, needed close to two years to mobilize herself in that way—two years during which many of the other psychological challenges of moving had been worked through, releasing energy for this one.

Ruth's accomplishment, as well as Ellen's, highlighted the potentiality of the newcomer to serve as a catalyst for change in a settled neighborhood or a neighborhood without cohesion. But these were extraordinary movers who invested extraordinary thought, time, and energy to fulfill their goals.

REPRODUCING THE PAST

Unconsciously, people tend to recreate their past, reproducing relationships and circumstances that have had special meaning. It was through that process that movers experienced some of the most powerful feelings of psychological reconnection.

Some found, at first unnoticed, that they had reproduced elements of the homes they had left behind. They felt strongly drawn toward particular characteristics of a house—its orientation to the sun, an open layout of rooms or a sense of snug enclosure, an enfolding forest or a view of distant hills—often without understanding why. Through ensuing months, a sense of feeling right, a "good fit," developed, illuminated when old friends noticed the similarity to the house that had been left behind or when a flash of memory brought this into focus in the mover's own awareness.

For many movers, the first intimations of reconnection between past and present, bridging the abyss of homelessness, came through momentary sensory signals. Ten months after Donna's move from France, and a month after her return to a house she couldn't yet recognize as home ("we came back from a trip and we didn't know where we were"), she went to a gathering of scholars where someone was smoking a pungent Gauloise cigarette. Her friends in France had smoked them. "Smelling that, and looking around at the assemblage, I had the happy feeling, we're home." For Donna, this was a premonition, a fragile strand of connection, yet it gave her encouragement that more secure attachments would develop.

Reni came out of a shop one day, 13 months after her move, and noticed the tantalizing aroma of Mediterranean food—a spicy, sun-drenched mélange of garlic, oregano, pepperoni—and her thoughts flew back to Italy. "I had a wonderful trip there two years ago. That whiff stirred such gladness that the sky seemed brighter, the grass seemed greener." And that gladness crept under the cloak of depression that had shrouded Reni, her house invaded by bats and mice.

Perhaps olfactory experiences were most frequently described by movers because the sense of smell is among the most rudimentary. It forms an early linkage between mother and baby, and throughout the animal world it signals safety or danger. Perhaps in a newcomer—a stranger sometimes feeling at the margin of safety—the awareness of scent is heightened.

But there were other sensory experiences as well. When her first spring came, Ellen saw lilacs blooming in a nearby garden.

"I had lilacs in my childhood house—my mother loved them. So I asked my neighbor if I could have some and I brought them inside. It gave me a wonderful, warm feeling to see them here."

"Last Saturday night it began to snow," another mover told me. "We went for a walk, feeling the flakes come onto our cheeks. It was completely quiet. We walked up a lane and there were tall fir trees, their branches sagging with their burden of snow. And I remembered a weekend in the Sierras with some dear, dear friends. We walked with them through snow like this. It felt the same on our cheeks, and there were tall evergreens there too. I remembered that happy weekend and I felt happiness here." That happiness became intermingled with the deep anxiety that this young woman was feeling about her transition.

One rainy day in April, four months after her move, an older mover's husband phoned. "Come into town if you can, and walk past the white church. There's something I want you to see."

She did. "The rain was gentle, coaxing up the earthsmell from newly thawed ground," she remembered. "And next to the church there was a sweep of cobalt blue, hundreds of Siberian Scillas freshly washed and teased into a dance by the falling raindrops. The beauty entranced me and I was transported to an English woodland where, 25 years ago, I walked in the early spring with my husband and infant daughter. The ground was carpeted with bluebells as far as we could see. And the joy of that day welled up and infused this moment."

For all the movers who experienced such moments, it was as though the sight, touch, or smell of the present stirred forgotten images of the past, images of place that were associated with loving people—parent, friend, lover, husband, child. Then the glad feelings infusing those memories flowed into the present and permeated the new surroundings. With those emotional connections, the sense of home began to be rekindled.

Such happenings were typically adventitious. Yet some movers had purposefully fostered them as well.

The autumn before she left her home, an experienced mover snipped a score of pachysandra cuttings. Through the long winter they grew tentative roots in a mug until the earth was warm enough to receive them. One day there were young green shoots amidst the mature foliage. The plantlings had accepted and were accepted by their new earth home.

During an advance visit on a wild, stormy October day, another mover planted an armful of bulbs wrenched from her Rhode Island garden. In May the first golden daffodil from that home displayed a shining trumpet to its new world.

Such here-there, now-then links sharpened grief because they confirmed that the *there* and *then* were in reality gone. But alongside the grief were upwellings of hope because the past was again coming alive in the *here* and *now*. In reality it was gone, but psychologically it was again present, and there was validation of the continuity of existence.

*   *   *

Attachment to place, defined as neighborhood, has been found to be multidimensional, composed of multiple forms of attachment (Gerson et al., 1977). Similarly, feelings at home among Northland movers involved multiple linkages, including but extending beyond the dwelling and the physical surround:

"Feeling at home means the house has become an extension of yourself. It means a sense of familiarity, knowing where things are in the house and in the community too, knowing how to find them and make them work," a mover had summed up. And then she added, "It also means recognition of people in a widening circle— both being recognized and recognizing, feeling familiar."

Such statements were echoed often.

"Feeling at home means going into town and meeting people who know you, going to the store and having them call you by name. It's a sense of belonging."

"Feeling at home has to do with knowing people and feeling accepted by them—having a network."

"There's the physical move, and then there's the emotional move. I'm settled in my house now with my cat and a huge dog and I'm very lonely."

"Having friends would make it feel like home."

Thus movers targeted the next major realm in the work of moving, making new friends.

RÉSUMÉ

Home had been experienced by these movers as maternal—a warm, strong, enfolding shelter in which a woman felt safe. Furthermore, home expressed her talents, tastes, and history. And it was a domain in which she enjoyed competence and influenced relationships.

Moving meant experiencing psychological homelessness. There was a disturbing absence of the sense of belonging. There was an interruption of the sense of continuity, and a loss of feelings of mastery. This limbo kindled anxiety in the present, and rekindled anxiety from the past.

Movers made intensive efforts to recreate home, carrying out personal rituals of possession and self-expression in their new dwellings. For some, these rituals were joyful. But the efforts of most were impeded by practical constraints (such as financial limitations, or the need to move repeatedly within Northland), and by psychological disarray (especially the confusion, loss of the sense of competence, and lowered self-esteem associated with inevitable disorganization and unpredictability). One third of the movers were able to transform their new dwellings into a home during the two-year time span of the study.

The sense of home involved not only the dwelling, but the neighborhood and community as well. There was an urge both to recognize and be recognized. Exploring the unfamiliar environs was a pleasant adventure for some movers, especially when a companion was available. But it felt hazardous for many because of the risks of embarrassment, helplessness, dependence, or isolation. Yet, of necessity, these women persisted.

In spite of the movers' purposeful efforts, it was through random sensory experiences that linkages between past and present were most powerfully experienced. Scents, in particular, could evoke memories of situations associated with loving people. The glad feelings permeating those memories could then flow into the new surround, enhancing the sense of reconnection.

FOUR

Friendmaking

Among the longings that newcomers expressed, none were more intense than the longing for friendship. Most of the women, single or coupled, had separated from close friends when they moved. Persistent efforts were made to keep those friendships alive, either through eager visits or through heartfelt letters and phone conversations that were difficult to end. There was comfort from those efforts to sustain connection, to recapture an intimacy becoming elusive, but there was poignancy as well. Visits and phone calls made the separation feel real. Over time, those relationships underwent transformation, and the changes were experienced as grievous loss.

The movers' intense focus on their new milieu could mask the sense of loss. But sooner or later, with only a few exceptions, they began to grieve for lost intimates. They felt sad, tearful, lonely, and irritable. They felt upwellings of painful longing for reunion and for new friendships to fill the void.

Trying to understand what the movers had lost, and what they needed to regain, I encouraged them to explain what they meant by close friendship. They spoke not in abstractions, but with reference to particular people of great importance in their lives. Out of the mélange of their descriptions, tumbling out at the juncture of loss and need, certain qualities—related but distinct—could be distilled.

THE MEANING OF CLOSE FRIENDSHIP

Mutuality is the bedrock of close friendship, the movers told me.

"There's a shared value system, you share a common interest you can build on, there's a sense of empathy—maybe you both feel passionate about nuclear disarmament."

"I took a long walk with a woman I'd just met, and we talked about the ethnic homogeneity here and the influences that might have on our children. We had such a warm sense of shared concern." She experienced a premonition that close friendship might develop, based on the commonality of ideals.

The word spoken over and over again was *shared*. These women were not describing relationships in which a friend would simply serve as a mirror, reflecting back an identical image—identical ideas, attitudes, and feelings. Friendship allows room for differences between two unique individuals, they believed; the relationship can absorb and be enriched by differences and the partners can each be expanded by another point of view. But the empathic bond— the capacity to understand and resonate with each other's thoughts and feelings—is sturdy and sustaining through both joyful and troubled times. The movers describe a bond familiar to clinicians— it fosters the deep sense of being understood that soothes aloneness from the first time a baby's gesture evokes a comforting response from her caregiver, the feeling of being understood that helps one feel "held" through a lifetime.

Mutuality embraces interests and values, and life experience as well.

"While my husband was in medical school, I had an awful job that I hated. It paid well and we needed the money. My main emotional support came from my friends, wives of other students. Maybe I'll never have friendships like that again because we helped each other through such dismal times—we shared so much."

"My best friend and I used to wheel our baby carriages together almost every day, and we'd talk about our lives and what we dreamed about. We brought up our babies together."

"A best friend wants to share the special moments of everyday life."

So sharing refers also to a living-through-together that gives continuity to the experience of self and of other. It would be unsettling if life moved ahead in small, segmented jumps like the restless leaps of a digital watch face or a sequence of lantern slides, each unit disconnected from what came before and what will come after. Most women need continuity that feels gradual and smooth, like the sweep of the second hand or the flow of a well-edited film. The living-through-together with a close friend, as well as the recapturing in memory of that shared experience, pulls past into present and strengthens the reassuring sense of going-on-being.

* * *

There is spontaneity. Close friends can depend on each other's responsiveness at the very moment of need.

"She's someone you can call up on the spur of the moment and tell about something special, something you've just done or seen, something that really matters and the way you feel about it, and your friend will care."

"It's someone you can call on in an impromptu way to help you out—maybe just raising the garage door if you have a sore shoulder."

"You should be able to drop in on an impulse and know you'll be welcome." This was a Western voice; regional differences in attitudes about spontaneity were apparent. Westerners, it seemed, were least concerned about the boundaries that protect privacy. To the contrary, a hallmark of close friendship was the expectation of informality, confidence that dropping in would be well received, and a wish that friends would reciprocate in the same impromptu manner. Easterners, especially Northeasterners, felt more hesitant about showing up at the door without an invitation, although they valued spontaneity in their telephone contacts and their spoken communications.

"When it's still a potential friendship, if you *happen* to be together because of circumstances it's okay to express your thoughts or feelings. But if it's a close friend, you can call up and express a need." This interesting distinction seemed related to the risk involved in making a spontaneous claim, even on the phone. In asking for attention and interest if circumstances had placed her in the company of another woman, a mover was making a lesser claim, a safer claim, since the responsibility lay in the circumstances as much as in herself. In taking the initiative to phone and express her need, a woman had to accept the responsibility for asking. Only in a close friendship, a well-tested friendship, could such spontaneity feel legitimate and safe.

* * *

There is authenticity in close friendship, the movers explained. A friend's responsiveness can be depended on. It is genuine, not simulated, and it communicates a concern that nourishes self-esteem.

"If you go over and she's busy she'll tell you that, but hopefully she'll also make space for you just because she cares about you."

"A friend is someone you can call up and say, ' I'm feeling really down today,' and the friend will be truly interested and she'll try to help."

"The warmth of your friends helps you feel like a worthwhile person." The movers attest that there are few, if any, women whose feelings of worth are so secure that they need no replenishment from others. Being loved (and a close friend's affection is a form of love) reassures a woman that she is lovable.

* * *

In close friendship there is trust. Whereas a friend's responsiveness is genuine, one can also be genuine with her. Repeatedly, women used the word "expose" to convey the experience of opening up, revealing the inner core of self.

"You can speak from the gut." Whatever unconscious meanings this metaphor might have, to speak from the gut is to speak from the core of one's being, allowing words to emerge uncensored.

"You feel you can take your shoes off, let your real self show." Another bodily image is used here to convey trust. To be unshod is to be safely vulnerable; it is also to feel familiar and at ease.

The podiatric defects, like the psychic flaws, can be allowed to show.

". . . she's someone you can be completely honest with about your feelings."

"You don't have to be on guard, you can be yourself."

What is it that one does not need to be on guard against? Harsh criticisms, the movers suggested—criticisms, judgments, and attitudes that would be bruising to their self-esteem.

"You can really expose yourself. A close friend knows you, good and bad, and totally accepts you." This is the unconditional acceptance that is accepted as an entitlement of young children, yet the movers suggested that it is a touchstone of security throughout life.

* * *

And there must be reciprocity.

"A friend is someone you can expose yourself to and appeal for help—but you can't be just the receiver, you have to be the giver too."

"She cares about your needs, and the other way around."

"It's someone you care about deeply and who cares about you."

Some women who felt emotionally depleted by the stresses of moving longed at moments for a one-way flow of affection and care. But most of the movers thought of true friendship as a two-way relationship. To be sure, a woman gives back to avoid feeling greedy or guilty about asking and receiving. That is the giving of conscience. But she also gives back because she feels genuine concern for the other. That is the giving of love. She is both active and passive, giving and taking, nurturing and nourished.

"An acquaintance is someone you go places with or recognize on the street and wave to. But a close friend is someone you can count on, someone you really care about and it goes both ways. It takes a long time to develop that."

Indeed, the images of intimate friendship the movers portrayed not only defined its complexity but also suggested how slowly it may develop. Mutuality, the foundation, is built through repetition and continuity of shared experience, thought, and feeling.

Authenticity, spontaneity, trust, and reciprocity develop through countless trials, risky trials, involving disclosures and gestures that may as often result in wounding and withdrawal as in affirmation and continued approach.

The movers' images also helped to clarify what they felt they had lost by moving. To be sure, when close friendship has been established, there is confidence in its continuity. "A best friend is someone you can talk to about private things, and you can start right up again after a separation." Yet the sharing of "the special moments of everyday life," as well as the possibility for impromptu contacts and immediate responses, were important elements that were greatly diminished, if not altogether lost, when moving separated close friends.

The longing to share very private experiences and the readiness to trust that those confidences would be received respectfully and treated kindly was evident in the openness with which almost all of these women disclosed to me their inner worlds of thought, feeling, and wish. Even without their explicit expressions of need, this candor alone would have demonstrated their readiness for psychological intimacy with another woman, the intimacy disrupted by their move and so slowly and painfully to be regained—if it was, in fact, regained.

Friendship and Gender

Almost invariably, close friendship was defined in relation to another woman. One of the coupled women spoke of an outside-the-family man as a confidant; a handful spoke of their husbands or lovers as best friends. But each of these women sensed that something was missing; they longed at times for an intimate woman friend as well.

One mover pondered this: "When I communicate with a woman, I can be open—up front—about my feelings, my experiences. The other woman will respond by sharing something of her own experience and a dialogue develops. But if I talk personally to a man, his response is likely to be 'you poor thing.' Then we're in a hierarchical relationship with each other" (she gestured, holding one extended hand above the other, the upper one representing the man). "And, too, so many men aren't even aware of their own feelings—they just aren't able to talk about them."

Her comments about ways in which men distance themselves in emotion-laden communications were akin to the subtle observations of a male therapy client of mine, himself a mover and the husband of a mover. "Women are more skillful at relatedness," he reflected. "They convey an interest in the whole person, not just the topic. There is more reciprocity. There are postural differences. When you stand face-to-face, men seem more nonchalant, they seem to be pulling back, their eyes are moving around as they talk. Women seem to lean toward you; they keep eye contact." This man longed for intimate friendship but feared it deeply.

"I'm afraid the boundaries between myself and the other person will become blurred—I'll feel overwhelmed, subsumed by the other." His words almost echoed Erickson's observation that men

> find it hard to empathize, especially where empathy makes it necessary to see the other in oneself and oneself in the other, and where therefore the horror of diffused delineations is apt to kill both joy in otherness and sympathy for sameness. (1985, p. 293)

Yet my anxious but insightful client went further; he soon discovered that parallel to his dread of losing the self there was a wish. "Sometimes I have a longing to be overwhelmed, taken in. It's as though at moments I really want to go back to the womb."

There is much evidence that men shrink away from the intimate friendship that women seek, perhaps because of its regressive dangers. Levinson, studying male development in adulthood, observes that "in our interviews, friendship was largely noticeable by its absence. As a tentative generalization we would say that close friendship with a man or woman is rarely experienced by American men" (1978, p. 335). His speculation is supported by Rubin (1985) who observed that three-quarters of single women she interviewed identified a best friend, whereas only one-third of single men could do so. She distinguishes, however, between intimacy and what she terms *bonding* (an atypical usage): intimacy, prevalent among women, is dependent on the verbal sharing of one's inner life; bonding is an unarticulated but deep relatedness that can occur among men, especially in threatening situations such as war. Indeed, movers in my study observed how much their mates appreciated relationships with other men grounded in shared activities if not in shared confidences.

Intimate friendship among women is not only a contemporary phenomenon. Studying the experience of American women from the late 18th century through the middle of the 19th, Smith-Rosenberg (1975) found that richly textured relationships of emotional and sensual intimacy were the norm between women. There was a female world in which men made only a shadowy appearance.

Psychological Roots

Nearly two centuries after the subjects of Smith-Rosenberg's study lived, emotional intimacy among women is still prevalent, even among women coupled with men. The need seems to be embedded deeply in female psychology. It has roots in infancy and in the vicissitudes of the child's developing self, as well as in her relationships with those closest to her. Since moving imperils close friendship, it is important for the prospective mover and those who counsel her to understand the depth of this need. It can be best understood by taking another look back to the early years of life.

Whether or not the infant is merged in symbiotic union with the mother during the early months, as Mahler et al. (1975) believed, or whether a sense of bounded, separate, and cohesive self begins developing at the time of birth, as Stern (1985) believes, the central task of infancy is to negotiate the path between connection and individuation. There must be growth toward a consolidation of the sense of self, related to others yet also distinct, and the infant's gender identity is integral to this.

In some respects, individuation may proceed more readily for the male infant, whose characteristically greater size, activity, and muscular vigor help to propel him away from his mother as his first year advances (Barglow & Schaefer, 1977). Furthermore, his growing sense of maleness, the core gender identity developing during the second and third year (Galenson & Roiphe, 1977; Stoller, 1968), heightens the toddler's awareness of his difference from his mother as well as his separateness from her. This recognition is likely to be reinforced by his caregivers, especially the father. Yet his development is complex, because the consolidation of his sense of maleness requires that the toddler "disidentify" from his mother (Greenson, 1968); that is, there must be a repudiation of those maternal qualities that have been internalized.[1] Although masculinity is reinforced by the secondary identification with the father (when one is present), it is often brittle and subject to the lure of a regressive union with the mother (Stoller, 1974). It may be for just this reason that emotional intimacy threatens many men.

The girl infant, who is likely to be smaller, less active, and less aggressive than the boy (whether this is inborn or a result of the gentler way she is handled), seems less inclined to pull away from the mother as the first year advances. As a result, she is less likely to be perceived as an antagonist by her mother. For this reason, and also because she is female like mother, the mother may be more attuned to her daughter's needs than to her son's (Barglow & Schaefer, 1977; Bernstein, 1983). She may be more empathic and have a greater capacity to soothe her baby, and this in turn enhances her own feelings of effectiveness. So the early girl-mother attachment may be more harmonious and longer-lasting.

In the second year, another strand of attachment develops as the girl's emerging awareness of self-as-girl (her feminine gender identity) includes dawning recognition that she is like mother. The mother's sense of being like daughter begins to be paralleled by the daughter's sense of being like mother. Through conscious imitation as well as unconscious identification, the little girl takes within her developing self many of the attributes of her mother.

In the ordinary family, the daughter-mother attachment scarcely remains blissful nor does it continue to develop smoothly. There are rivalries and hostilities that may continue through life. There are the intrusions of brothers and sisters and of father, who becomes a significant person to his daughter at least by the end of her first year, if not before (Abelin, 1971; Kleeman, 1977), and then later becomes the focus of her erotic stirrings and romantic daydreams. But the mother is not excluded. The little girl does not give up or turn away from her deeply rooted relationship with her mother in favor of her father. Rather, she gradually draws him into the alliance, developing the triangular relationship that is likely to continue in some form throughout her lifetime.

There are interludes, of course, when the scenario changes. There are school years when girls seem intertwined in their pairing, arms around each other's shoulders, stroking each other's shining hair and disdaining the company of males (as they are in turn disdained). But in adolescence, the energy of the triangle is rekindled and flows into adulthood. Most heterosexual women stay in a triangular relationship through much of their lives. They turn to a man as the primary object of erotic love but as a somewhat less important emotional object, whereas the affect-laden daughter-mother bond may be recreated in a women's relationship with her own child, especially her daughter (Chodorow, 1978; Deutsch, 1945; Kestenberg, 1956).

Chodorow (1978) has argued that women's longings for intense emotional relationships tend to be directed toward daughters rather than other women both because of taboos against potential homosexual attachments and also because of isolation—women today are likely to be physically separated from their mothers and close kin, and live in households apart from other women. But the voices of the movers do not concur. To be sure, apartments and single-family dwellings are isolating. To be sure, the sexual interest of all the women movers was directed toward men (this was by chance, as there had been no intentional exclusion of lesbians). And, indeed, two among the older women explained that because of close relationships with adult daughters their need for a special woman friend was not urgent. But among the rest, longings for emotional intimacy with other women were repeatedly expressed, and seemed as intensely felt among women with children as those without.

All relationships include displacements from the past. In all relationships there is an effort, often unconscious, to reproduce gratifying elements in the service of pleasure or frustrating elements in the service of mastery, or to provide what was not provided before. Most of the qualities identified by the movers as central in intimate friendship—mutuality, authenticity, spontaneity, and trust—are qualities that characterize a young child's relationship with a devoted and empathic mother. It would have been understandable that these stressed women would have longed for motherly nurturance. But more was involved, as they emphasized reciprocity as a central quality of the wanted friendship. Reciprocity is scarcely childlike; it is a quality of more mature affection, a quality that develops as the mother is appreciated as a separate being with qualities and needs of her own. It seemed that these women strove to reexperience daughterly needs and fulfillments, but also to transcend them. They strove to be care receivers and caregivers as well. They strove, it seemed, to experience the sense of "self-in-relation" that Miller (1976, 1984), Jordan (1984), Kaplan (1984), and Surrey (1985, 1987) have identified as a core of female development throughout the life cycle—self both influencing and influenced by other, self both responding to other and responded to by other.

The movers' longings may have been heightened by the losses of moving. Past friendships may have been idealized somewhat. Rubin (1985) reminds us that friendship is rarely free of envy and competition. The struggles around control, boundaries, and intrusion that beset many mother-daughter relations can be transfered into a friendship. Although free of many of the imperatives of kinship, friendship undergoes vicissitudes even in settled life. Yet to have reminded themselves that friendship is imperfect would have afforded these women little comfort.

Awed by the intensity of their longings, I listened closely to what these movers were telling me about how new personal contacts occurred and how relationships developed. Were newcomers welcomed? Were they expected to take the initiative? What were their strategies for meeting new people? How long would it take to make new friends?

WELCOME

Welcoming Gestures

Most of the movers had expected that they would be welcomed by neighbors, their own colleagues, their husbands' colleagues, and their churches. They had imagined that these first gestures would lead to wider connections and then to the friendships they longed for. There were such gestures, but they were sparse and inconsistent. A minority of movers were supported through their transition.

All the women in my study had been visited by the Welcome Wagon representative (who informed me of their presence). That woman was warm and kind, the visit was informative, and it assured the newcomer that her arrival had at least been noticed. But its purpose was to acquaint the newcomer with goods and services in the community and to provide local businesses with new customers. The ritual was not intended to initiate a personal relationship.

Connection to the workplace was the next most common conduit through which some welcome flowed. Nine of the 35 coupled women were welcomed through the linkage of their husbands' colleagues; two coupled women and one single one were welcomed through collegial connections of their own. There were annual, institutional parties in which some of these newcomers were included. Such gatherings were appreciated as acknowledgment of the newcomer's presence, yet in a large and noisy group it was difficult to sustain conversations that might lead to recognition of potential friendship. So these rituals, too, were single happenings frozen in time, leaving the mover with the question, "What next?" They made clear that welcome and incorporation are not the same.

A few wives were targeted for other institutionalized welcomes. An outreach from a well-organized network of wives within a medical facility was the most exemplary form. Initiated by mail even before the newcomer was on the scene, it conveyed the promise of community and continuity. Four movers were personally welcomed by their husbands' colleagues, or the colleagues' spouses, through invitations or practical help (one imaginative resident couple brought a list of sources for all the goods and services the newcomers might need).

After they had expressed a wish for this, three movers were gathered into the fold by their churches—they were called on, introduced to other members, and invited to participate in church affairs. One who had hoped to be greeted thus was not. Her welcome awaited the coming, much later, of a new pastor.

Half a dozen movers were reached out to by neighbors. Three enjoyed isolated and sporadic gestures—the gift of a clump of perennials, for example. They signified a cautious welcome, a welcome that left space for privacy and held no promise of continuity. But for three others, the welcome conveyed a readiness to incorporate the newcomer. Dorothy and Jennifer, who already had personal connections to the close-knit neighborhood into which they moved, were warmly greeted and absorbed into the social life of their microcommunity as quickly as they would have wished. For them, in fact, the need was to establish boundaries around the solitude they needed to recover from the stress of transition.

Jan's experience was both similar and different. The day her van came, Jan's neighbor from up the street walked over with coffee and bagels. A neighbor from down the street came with introductions. A lad was sent from across the street to find out what help Jan needed. The neighbor from the house behind came, too, within a few days, and the couple next door invited Jan and her family for dinner. There was a convergence of welcome from strangers, and it extended beyond an isolated gesture into a process of incorporation. This might, in fact, have set in motion the restructuring of neighborly relations that Ruth and Ellen had experienced after many months in Northland. Yet, whereas Ruth and Ellen had regained enough psychic energy to participate in their neighborly interactions, Jan was not ready. She was appreciative, yet so aggrieved by the losses involved in her move that she could not maintain a momentum with neighbors.

Jan's plight illustrated two more of the newcomers' dilemmas. Whereas gestures of welcome are likely to occur soon after the mover's arrival, this may be just the time when newcomers have little energy available for reciprocity. Furthermore, Jan was among the many who soon moved again within Northland. Whatever strands of connection were developing with neighbors would be ruptured anyway, so reciprocity scarcely seemed worthwhile.

Seven fortunate women moved under an umbrella of welcome. Relatives or friends already living in Northland took on the role of sponsor. They entertained the movers, acted as escorts, introduced them to people with kindred interests, acquainted them with the community and explained its customs. Although sponsorship couldn't spare newcomers the pain of their losses, it did relieve many uncertainties and anxieties about their gains.

Ironically, those very movers who were actively welcomed at all enjoyed simultaneous gestures of greeting from several different sources. But, altogether, these included only one third of the newcomers.

Absence of Welcome

Two-thirds of the movers were not actively welcomed to Northland. How did these women feel?

For some it felt unsafe. Ruth, a member of an ethnic minority who moved into a settled, homogeneous, and apparently hostile neighborhood, felt the most at risk—physically as well as psychologically. But other newcomers without Ruth's sense of ethnic vulnerability also echoed some of her fears. In the event of fire, accident, illness, who would help? Like Ruth, their worries were "at the survival level."

So the absence of welcome was frightening. It aroused anger as well.

"I've had moments of absolute fury," another newcomer told me. "I could actually imagine myself going down Main Street with a machine gun! We're the only newcomers in a settled neighborhood, an interconnected neighborhood. There are 'block parties' but we're not included. None of the adults have reached out to us. One day a neighbor drove by while I was out at the mailbox. She paused for a moment and said, 'we forget about you up there.' She didn't mean to be hurtful, but it made me feel terrible. We're just not in the neighbors' consciousness."

As I listened, I was reminded of a wise comment made at a professional meeting: "The opposite of love isn't hate. Where there's hate, there's at least some involvement. The opposite of love is indifference."[2] This newcomer had experienced the chill of just such indifference in Northland. She was reminded that she simply didn't exist in the thoughts of others, and there can be no deeper wound to a person's self-esteem. Such a profound narcissistic injury can arouse rage and stimulate fantasies of retaliation such as this mover described.

Most women either didn't feel, or didn't admit feeling, rage as profound as this, or anxiety as intense as Ruth's, even when they felt unnoticed. But most did express worry and a longing to be reached out to, especially in moments of sorrow, loneliness, or emotional depletion. "Nobody invited us out," I was told sadly, "just when we needed to feel looked after." "Welcoming arms are comforting arms," said another mover in a wistful mood.

"I don't really believe there's such a thing as a cold community," a frequent mover, ever fair-minded, declared. Why, then, were so many movers not welcomed?

Were there seasonal cycles of welcome? "We came in the winter. We didn't see anybody outside. It's as though they were all in hibernation," recalled a newcomer who had endured a lonely season. Indeed, in a northern climate those who ventured out in the long, cold winter are purposeful, in haste, enshrouded in protective and concealing garb. There is less sauntering about, fewer casual encounters than in warmer months, and even recognition is more difficult.

But, in the movers' experience, the summer weather doesn't necessarily foster a welcoming ambiance either. Especially for families whose rhythms of activity are connected to the school year, summer is vacation time, time for impromptu comings and goings. Settled householders may not provide a stable presence with which the newcomers can feel connected. The visibility of community life—the barbecues or tennis games in which the mover is not included, the lakeside clusters of mothers and young who fail to reach out to the stranger—can heighten the newcomer's poignant awareness of being an onlooker, an outsider.

Whereas regeneration in nature begins in the northern spring, human regeneration seems to begin in the autumn, perhaps linked to an upsurge of energy after the lassitude of summer, perhaps simply associated with the school year. Autumn seems a time when various institutions experience an annual "beginning," a time of receptions, ritualized welcome. It seems to be then, if at all, that newcomers are formally absorbed into an institution or a community.

So to some extent, the date of moving influences the welcome extended to the mover. But as important, or more so, the settled residents are deterred by their own fear of loss. "Peter and I befriended a number of newcomers in Bradford Village and we became very attached," explained a Northlander who joined in the group discussions. "But then, one by one, they inevitably moved on and left us, and we felt awful. So we decided we wouldn't risk that any more." She was an informal spokeswoman for others in Northland who protected themselves similarly from painful separations. Mobility means loss for both the leaver and those left behind.

Indeed, a number of movers, uncertain of their tenure in Northland, sensed a recoil from settled residents if it was suspected that the newcomers might leave in a few years. "People don't seem to feel that it's worthwhile getting to know us," they reflected. Ruth, with her strong wish for the nearby connections that would help her feel safe, noticed a shift in the neighbors' attitudes when she and her husband bought their rented house and then painted it. "I think that signaled to people that we weren't transient so it was worthwhile to make an investment in knowing us." But that was close to two years after her move.

There is fear of loss and there is also inertia, the force that resists change among those already settled into personal networks and careers, the force that resists finding time and energy and carving space out of busy lives for new people.

And there are changing customs. Packard (1972) has suggested that rituals of welcome have succumbed to the high mobility of United States society, and the experience of Northland movers confirms that they are indeed uncommon. This has left a disturbing legacy of ambiguity. Where, when, and how does the newcomer start making those connections that could develop into the friendships she needs? Are the first gestures up to the settled residents or up to the newcomer?

If the mover has friends or relatives who act as sponsors, or if she is quickly absorbed into an existing network, or if strangers who welcome her provide her with ongoing connections, then she is supported and guided and doors are opened even before she knocks. But if there have been no sponsors or networks or ongoing expressions of interest, then the initiatives must come from the newcomer.

INITIATIVE

Taking the initiative proved to be surprisingly difficult for Northland movers. For many, it felt like another realm of work in a time of depletion. For some, it was linked with forbidden aggression.

"As students you're all sharing space, living quarters, study space. You're all together. Your paths keep crossing and the relationships just grow out of that. It's informal and spontaneous," recalled a newcomer with nostalgia.

In contrast to the inevitability of encounters such as those, inevitability that relieves the participants of purposefulness and responsibility, most newcomers must take intentional action.

"You have to keep working at it," many observed, and this intentionality was disturbing.

"It's hard to be planful and calculating about making friends."

"It seems absurd to have to make an appointment because you need someone to talk to."

It would seem easy for a capable, intelligent woman to make friendly gestures—to strike up a conversation in the library, at the pool, in line at the supermarket (perhaps complimenting a shopper on her attractive haircut and asking the name of her hairdresser, a favorite gambit of one experienced mover)—or to walk from house to house in a new neighborhood with a winsome preschooler and gentle collie and introduce herself (the strategy of another). And it did seem easy for a minority of the movers.

The majority found it hard. Initiatives required energy-fueled, time-consuming, persistent action during the period when women felt drained by the physical and psychological tasks of moving.

"When we moved here," Ruth explained, "I was at a low ebb. I would have enjoyed being reached out to, although I wouldn't have really expected it. But I didn't feel ready to take my own initiatives. It's not hard for me to do, but the time has to be right." Ruth's dilemma was common. Because of her depletion, the newcomer intensely needs emotional nourishment from others; because of her depletion, she feels unable to seek it.

Initiative, Aggression, and Anxiety

Depletion was not the only deterrent. The prevalence of anxiety about social initiative among competent women of all ages, women who were experienced in business and professional life as well as in the complexities of family life, was impressive. The anxiety seemed to stem from a deeply felt linkage between initiative and aggression.

"I've never been so aggressive with people before!" This mover, who spoke as though she was confessing wrongdoings, told me with embarrassment that she had been starting conversations with strangers at the lakeside (populated with parents and children), and making phone calls to new acquaintances to propose they join in some shared activity. It was such benign, friendly actions that she experienced as aggression within herself.

"I don't like to worm my way into other people's lives," said another, revealing her view of initiative as potentially harmful. She worried about being intrusive in her new relationships. "I've known the other side, people who suffocate you because their emotional needs are so great." She feared invading other people's private spaces because she had felt invaded in the past. Yet her fear seemed also to reflect an inner struggle against the temptation to be intrusive, because now her own needs felt so great.

Ideas of acting toward others in potentially harmful ways (pushing, worming, invading, penetrating other people's boundaries) generated guilt. Ideas of acting at variance with the mover's own ideals generated shame.

A woman's mental representations of her ideal self reflect the attitudes of family and society. In the first half of the twentieth century, classical psychoanalytic thought both embodied and articulated sociocultural taboos against aggression in women. Core feminine characteristics were believed to include passivity and masochism, in contrast to the activity and aggression central to masculinity (Deutsch, 1944). By implication, the "truly" (or ideally) feminine woman was passive and masochistic, the "truly" (or ideally) masculine man was active and aggressive. Such sociocultural ideals, and their gender-linked dichotomies, were surely communicated to most of these movers in their childhood and internalized as personal ideals in their developing selves—and they have lingered.

One of the younger women, for example, spoke of initiative— "pushing myself on others, being aggressive about contacting people"—as a male trait. "It's a value my father inculcated in me," she said. And she was uncomfortable about the initiatives she forced herself to take, because this internal "maleness" felt in disharmony with her ideal of femininity.

It was common for movers to justify their "aggressive" initiatives on the grounds that they were acting on behalf of their children, not "just" for themselves (indeed, many of their initiatives were actually in the service of establishing parenting and child-care networks). Their attitudes were consistent with a contemporary psychoanalytic observation that

> when aggression is expressed on behalf of the protection of their children or their homes, it is approved. In every other circumstance, "aggressive" as an attribute of a woman is a pejorative. Clinically, we note that tremendous anxiety emerges [in women] when aggressive fantasies are touched on, or aggressive behavior stimulated. (Bernstein, 1983, p. 190)

Sociocultural tolerance of child-related female aggression is curiously paradoxical, because it is the very fact of maternal power that underlies dread of the aggressive woman. Men especially, but some women as well, recoil from the image of that all-powerful mother from whom they struggled to differentiate in order to achieve their selfhood (Dinnerstein, 1976).

Paradox notwithstanding, the anxiety many newcomers felt about "aggressive" behavior can be understood as revealing internalized sociocultural prohibitions. It is less easy to understand that behavior that was no more than friendly and outreaching was deeply felt as aggressive and therefore dangerous and forbidden.

But the ambivalence about initiative was fed from another source as well. Some movers feared retaliation.

"I hate phoning people I don't know or speaking to them on the street. It seems like supplication and you risk feeling humiliated if you're rebuffed. I have the impression that people here see reaching out by a newcomer as being intrusive." This mover's self-esteem was particularly precarious, yet her fear of rejection was voiced by others as well. The position of a newcomer as an outsider revived memories of childhood vulnerability, of wounds inflicted on her self-esteem, and fears that such wounds could be experienced again.

"I've been remembering how it was in junior high," Barbara the photographer reflected thoughtfully. "There were new kids and I was very shy. I can remember the misery of waiting at the bus stop and being told that if I stood next to one particular girl nobody would like me. I wasn't sure what to do. Now, wanting to make friends here, it's like I'm that child again. I'm afraid people won't like me and then I'll feel destroyed. That makes it very hard to take the initiative, it's too much of a risk. I wish it could all come to me."

Reminiscing about her previous move, another newcomer recalled being told she would have a lot in common with a neighbor who shared her interest in old maps. One day she walked past that neighbor's house and saw the top of her head over the enclosing fence. She passed through a gate and introduced herself. The two immediately "clicked"; they talked nonstop for two hours. It seemed likely that they would become close friends. They planned to go on an excursion together the next week, a bus tour of special gardens.

"When I got to the meeting place, my new friend was there already. I suggested that we sit together on the bus, but she was planning to be with another friend of hers and she didn't make me feel included. So it ended up that everyone else was in pairs and I was alone. It was lonely, embarrassing, and hurtful." It reminded this mover of how she had felt as a twelve-year-old when there were often jealousies and rivalries among close friends, and painful moments of exclusion.

For many women, the fears and wounds in the present caused resonances from the past, from those childhood years when there were inevitable experiences of feeling rebuffed, left out, at the margin of the group, unsure, unattractive, unworthy, and unwanted.

The expressed fears of rejection and humiliation arose in part from the psychic interiors of these women. But their worries were reinforced by experience in the present—hurts heedlessly inflicted by settled residents protecting the boundaries of their privacy, safeguarding the equilibrium of their lives.

"People here have been awfully pleasant," said Barbara, whose relatives had at first "sponsored" her and introduced her widely. "But I wonder how you move to the next stage. When I was in high school, there was a group of boys who told me that I was really very nice but nobody would know it because I didn't let it show." So here Barbara tried to let it show. "I walked over to see one of my neighbors. She came to the door but she didn't ask me in. She stood there and talked to me through the screen door. In the South, you would have people come in and you would feed them!" Barbara sounded appalled. The mesh of the screen door was both a physical and psychological barrier signaling "don't come too close." It was a barrier confirming that taking initiative made the newcomer vulnerable to feeling held apart.

"I gave three dinner parties during my first year here," another mover said sadly in a group discussion. "The guests were all people I'd met here and thought I'd like to know better. Everyone seemed to have a good time. But not one of them asked me back in return."

Extreme as this seemed, unreciprocated hospitality was not unusual. It caused bewilderment. Was the newcomer being tacitly reproached for her initiative? Was she not seen as a likable person? How could the reality be known?

Timeliness of Initiative

In spite of the risks to their self-esteem, in spite of their often justified anxieties, all but a few of the newcomers did in fact extend themselves outward. The drive toward making connection was powerful. But the moment for their gestures had to be carefully gauged.

"You have to give it time," declared one of the older movers, well aware that the hazards of initiative were real. "People wouldn't like it if you were pushy." She had joined a circle of women who enjoy needlepoint. After six months or more she might consider inviting one or two over for tea. They might then reciprocate, or maybe not. "How do you gauge the timeliness of that invitation?" I asked. She wasn't sure. "It's somehow like having good taste," she mused.

Dorothy, another socially experienced woman, expressed similar thoughts. "A personal relationship grows out of a working relationship. You can sense when it's time to make an overture, gauging it by the response you're getting."

Having good taste, sensing the right moment—neither woman could articulate clearly the subliminal cues she responded to and the judgments she subconsciously made. They were uncertain about the basis for timing their initiatives even among women they would see regularly. Yet many movers faced the more complicated challenge of judging the timeliness of overtures toward people they encountered only occasionally. Without traditions to guide them, they were confronted with ambiguity.

STRATEGIES

Yet the drive to make connection was powerful, the hope that connection would deepen into close friendship was sustaining. A variety of strategies was employed, some well practiced, some newly learned, all engaging so much energy that the accuracy of the phrase "making friends" became obvious. It was clear that friendships do not just happen, they are indeed made, and the making is a

challenging job in its own right—an unrecognized realm of work
that women do.

Collegial Connections

"I'll begin inviting people. I'll cook Italian dinners at first, and
then when I know them better, I'll call them up to come sit on
the deck in the sun and talk. You have to be responsible for all
of it, they won't come to you. It's very hard because you have
to sound lively and interesting. If you're lonely and depressed they'll
hear that and they'll say 'watch out for her, she'll drag you down.'
You have to play a part," said Susan, the "modern gypsy," now
fully involved in professional work.

Susan had soon understood that the daily contacts with
colleagues would not suffice. To allow for the private conversations
that might reveal some grounds for friendship, special situation,
or even a special mood needed to be created. There was none
among the professional women who found it otherwise; some
learned through the doing, some by failing to do.

"I'm somewhere in between the early contacts and forming deep
friendships." One of the women who moved to advance her own
career told me this five months after she arrived. Colleagues had
welcomed her warmly, but, like Susan, she had not responded to
their gestures with initiatives of her own. She recognized the need
to do that if relationships were to develop further. This bright,
independent, professional woman was among those who found
social initiative uncomfortable: "I suppose it's left over from
childhood. I'm really afraid of being rebuffed; I'd much rather wait
and let people approach me."

People did, in fact approach her. She was invited to special
discussion groups, but was preoccupied with her work, anxious
to prove herself professionally, and unaware that the meetings
provided rich opportunity for social connections. She failed to attend
and also failed to reciprocate other invitations. Then they began
to dwindle. Clearly, there had been a critical period for her to
make her own approaches, and she had let that pass. Then it seemed
too late. Her colleagues' personal interest had waned. Two years

after her move, she was keenly aware of lost opportunities for making friends.

None of the movers intensely involved in professional pursuits found that close friendship was a by-product of collegial associations unless they created situations in which personal disclosures could develop. Whereas the men affiliated with women in my study had spouses committed to support their careers and to reconstruct their social ties, the reverse did not apply. Women did this work for themselves (and for their families) or it was not done at all.

Affinity Groups

"Volunteer," suggested staunch Dorothy. "Join some group working toward a goal. The personal relationship will grow out of the working relationship. You have to be ready to give 75% and get 25%." That was seven months after her move. But four months earlier, Dorothy had felt hesitant to get involved in community affairs, even church affairs, although church had been important in her life before. She recognized that involvement would create expectations (in others and in herself) that she felt unable to meet. "I find it very hard to say 'no.' I feel guilty when I do and I can't delegate work. I have to do it myself. Right now, I don't have the energy to do much." Right then, giving 75% and getting 25% would have been too great a skew.

Religious experience had been important in the past lives of 10 newcomers, but most were as hesitant as Dorothy about church affiliation. Their concern about being met with expectations difficult to fulfill—such as taking immediate responsibility for a Sunday School class—was a major barrier. Indeed, with their membership eroded by contemporary mobility, some churches have become vigorous in recruiting newcomers to assume active roles in church affairs (Rossi, 1980). Such efforts are sometimes premature, the movers' experiences suggested.

Yet, to make the contacts that can relieve loneliness and ignite purpose, a newcomer must somehow mobilize energies that are already sapped by the other tasks of moving. The activities the Northland movers engaged in, as they sought the mutuality that is the bedrock of friendship, were extensive: Women's Network, Women Against Nuclear Development, Women's International League for Peace and Freedom, political parties, Support Group for Parents of Children with Special Needs, Parents and Teachers for Social Responsibility, Amnesty International, Parents Without Partners, Sierra Club, Garden Club, Herb Study Group, choral society, handicrafts groups, college courses, Lamaze class, After Childbirth Transition class, Newcomer's Club, church, concerts, sports, and lectures. Strategically, this was relatively easy because there is open access in Northland (memberships and admissions are open to all). Psychologically, it was complex.

Newcomers became involved in spite of the imbalance between investment and return that Dorothy had pointed out and in spite of another hazard. Whereas most salaried work includes delineated expectations, voluntary work often lacks boundaries. It is unclear what is enough to fulfill the sometimes limitless needs of the organization, or even enough to meet the standards of the volunteer herself. The propensity for feeling guilty about declining to help that Dorothy described is shared by many women. Yet the drive toward personal connection was so strong that movers pushed through these uncertain territories. Some movers went even further and formed their own affinity groups—groups united by common interests or values. All these activities were in addition to paid jobs and family commitments. The outpouring of both physical and psychological energy was extraordinary.

Newcomer's Club was started in Northland by one of the movers in my core population, one who longed for closeness to other women and was ready to work toward it. The initial response was small but enthusiastic. Women came "looking for instant understanding," and validation of their troubled feelings, the founder told me. But the network was difficult to sustain.

"I'd rather meet people who are settled here," explained a mover who dropped out, wanting to become integrated into the permanent community. "I don't like the idea of going somewhere where everyone's purpose is just to meet people," said another, suggesting that such a strategy would seem contrived. She preferred relationships to develop spontaneously through repeated contacts and shared interests. Although the very experience of being a newcomer provides a shared interest, too direct a focus on that interest felt uncomfortable for some. It seemed to confirm and make visible their marginality in their communities and marginality felt like a flaw.

Yet under the umbrella of Newcomer's Club, special interest groups did form, and several developed continuity. A shared purpose, whether it was gourmet cooking, literary criticism, or bicycle riding, could neutralize a little of the emotional intensity that may arise in a gathering of people feeling lonely or anxious. It could allow the focus to flow back and forth in an easy rhythm between the people and the activity.

"We have really meaningful conversations about our lives. Working together makes it less self-conscious," explained a mover who drew together a small group of women interested in Scandinavian knitting, and noticed the ways their activity could foster intimacy. The women's hands were busy and that provided an outlet for the release of tension. Their gazes were focused on the intricate patterns, so they avoided eye contact that might be prematurely intense or emotional. And pauses in the conversations didn't need to be too quickly filled with words, as the rhythmic motions allowed the silence to be natural. The women's disclosures could follow a relaxed and spontaneous pace.

"But you have to be available," advised one of the very frequent movers, who used her athletic skills to make connection. "Our first house here was near the golf course. I began to be called to fill in when a fourth was needed, sometimes at the last minute." Several of her golf partners did gradually become close friends. But she had to muster time and energy to respond at just the moment when she was wanted. Being so available is possible only for a woman whose children are in school or older, possibly only for a woman who is not committed to scheduled work outside the home. It is an effective strategy, but a luxurious one.

Connections Through Children

Movers with children had expected that adult contacts would develop around their children. For mothers of school-age children, this hope was not necessarily realized. Efforts to arrange after-school play proved discouraging. One mother repeatedly invited her child's classmates over after school, even offering transportation. Some did come, but her child was not invited back in return. "Nancy can't understand it. How can you explain to a six-year-old that other children don't need her in their lives?" wondered the mother, feeling painful bewilderment of her own. "The parents seem to find it too troublesome to alter their usual way of doing things. I've gone as far as I can go with that." Had her experience been unique, it might have raised question about the personality of her child. But it was not. "The children want to choose their own friends," another mother commented philosophically, "and you may not have much in common with the parents anyway."

Elementary school children begin to form cliques, supporting each other in their early striving for independence from the adult world. There may be strong resistance against adult manipulation of those spontaneous joinings, resistance that can exclude the new child. Further, the contemporary middle-class child, guided into every available program to develop potential skills and talents, has little time for unstructured play after school. Movers could appreciate such realities. Yet not only did the lack of response to her child thwart the mother's own quest for connection, but the child's apparent difficulty in making new friends could also cause a mother to doubt herself. Mothers need evidence of a child's healthy and successful development to affirm the effectiveness and significance of their mothering (Ornstein & Ornstein, 1985).

Preschool children provided for their mothers a more effective entry into the new community. Nonetheless, energetic efforts were needed for movers to search out existing networks, ease their way in, or form new ones: baby-sitting cooperatives, mother-child play groups (in which mothers socialized while their children played), or child play groups (in which mothers alternated as caregivers). Adult conversations were fragmented in the bedlam of child play, but the networks did lead to friendship when the mothers created opportunities for other encounters in which there could be private, woman-to-woman conversation.

Special Issues

The need to make new contacts was intense enough so that most movers couldn't risk turning away from any avenue that looked promising. Settled life has a familiar, predictable rhythm. Choices have been made, priorities set. There is time for replenishment, time for doing nothing at all. For movers, the choices are unclear, the priorities blurred. The untrodden paths must be walked. So a number experienced a sense of fragmentation and overstimulation—"being under a strobe light, confused and anxious," as Susan described it.

"With new people you're always trying, always having to prove yourself," Jan observed sadly, four months after her move. "I miss my dear friends so intensely. They accepted me just as I am, good and bad. I want to find people here who will accept me just as I am." Such a longing was widespread, yet newcomers felt cautious about exposing just who they were. Rather, they felt a need to be discreet about disclosures of taste, preference, value, or belief. Some felt the need to conceal some significant aspect of their being, perhaps political views or passionate beliefs about population control, lest they be rebuffed. There were few who felt so confident of their value and goodness as to say, "Here I am. Take me or leave me." These forthright movers, who favored candor over discretion, were forced to accept some bruising of their self-esteem when those being approached expressed aversion or, often worse, indifference.

In many realms, movers needed to be alert to the sensitivities of the established residents. Recalling the times she was called to complete a foursome, the golfing mover confided, "I often felt nervous because if I wasn't good enough for the foursome they wouldn't want to ask me again, but if I was too good that would embarrass them and so they still wouldn't want to ask me again." So this accomplished golfer had to calibrate her effort and her skill to just the right level to be accepted. Through frequent moves, she had learned how threatening a newcomer can seem to the established ones if her abilities surpass their own.

It has been said in jest that if a millipede had to become consciously aware of how to walk, its legs would become hopelessly entangled and it would be immobilized. As the complexity of making new friends became apparent, the newcomers seemed to share the plight of a self-conscious millipede. Their moves had made them aware of having a thousand legs, and they had to find out anew how to synchronize those legs—showing good cheer, sensitivity, good judgment, taking enough initiative but not too much, being talented enough but not too much, having bountiful time and boundless energy, and having money as well.

"I don't know how people without money can handle it," a despondent mover wondered. "My husband and I've been trying to raise our spirits by giving ourselves a treat. Every Sunday we go to the Northland Inn for brunch. We love their blueberry pancakes, and maybe we'll see someone we know."

The core population included some affluent women. But more were, or their husbands were, engaged in work commanding more prestige than income. Those who were on tight budgets were keenly aware of how limited their participation in community life had to be. Sports require athletic equipment. Concerts, plays, and movies require tickets. And participation in voluntary or recreational activity requires time free of economic demand—time not occupied by paid work. The heightened participation of the newcomer can be expensive.

Traveling in Pairs

"Women seem to travel in pairs," observed a newcomer curiously. Many did seem reluctant to go to any happening alone—a discussion group, an art exhibit, a lecture—even where there was the likelihood of meeting others with kindred interests. Some felt quite anxious at the prospect.

To go alone was to risk humiliation. The newcomer might not know enough, might not be articulate enough, might not be skillful enough. Enough for what? Enough to meet the unknown expectations of others. She might "make a fool of myself" and be judged by others as flawed. As bad, or worse, she might experience herself as flawed at a time when her self-esteem was already under siege. Having a companion deflected attention away; it shielded her from the spotlight in which her flaws might become visible.

Having a companion could also protect against the loneliness of feeling like an outsider. "I don't really know how to start up a conversation among strangers," explained a shy mover. "The other people at a meeting might already know each other and then I'd feel left out. That happens at big parties, too. With another woman, I'd at least have someone to talk to."

These were not sheltered women nor inadequate women. They included women experienced in orchestrating family life, competent business women and professionals who had had their worth and likability affirmed through work (in the home or the marketplace) and through past friendships. But the prospect of standing alone seemed to kindle a latent fear of experiencing their helpless selves, their imperfect selves, and perhaps sliding into depression in this time of vulnerability. Yet their reluctance to "go it alone" also reflected long-lived sociocultural attitudes about solitary women.

"I was brought up in a traditional family," a 51-year-old mover told me. "My sister and I were raised to be ladylike, and that meant not to be forward or conspicuous." In moving to Northland, she had eagerly looked forward to the plethora of concerts, yet she had attended none. She had found no companion, and the idea of going alone was intolerably uncomfortable. She would feel conspicuous, awkward, and self-conscious, she told me. She would believe that people were having critical thoughts about her because she was solitary.

Indeed, in her generation, when women were being reared to be "ladylike," they were defined primarily in terms of their relations to men. A solitary woman was viewed as a failure or a predator. Movers learned that such attitudes are still thriving in Northland today (and, perhaps, in much of the nation as well). Such attitudes are even aroused by women in pairs.

Two outgoing, confident movers went together into a local restaurant one evening to enjoy a quiet drink and conversation away from the clamor of their young families. But they were challenged. "Just what," asked the hostess, "are you girls doing here?" Her reluctance to offer them a table was obvious. Rather than make a strident demand but unwilling to leave, the women perched uncomfortably on bar stools, having a less than private talk. Once again, their sense of marginality was heightened.

RHYTHMS

"I've been surrounded by friendly people and I've felt intensely lonely," a perplexed mover told me. She was among the women most comfortable with initiative—outreaching, friendly, involving herself with affinity groups. Her seemingly contradictory experience was authentic. Weiss, exploring the meanings of loneliness, has concluded that:

> Different forms of loneliness are responsive to different remedies. . . . A form of loneliness that appears in the absence of close emotional attachment, which we characterize as "the loneliness of emotional isolation," can only be remedied by the integration of another emotional attachment or the reintegration of the one that had been lost. (1973, p. 18)

For this mover, as for most, the sharing of common interests was important but insufficient. It was discouraging to wait for the trust, genuine caring, and easy spontaneity of intimate friendship.

"I'm very disappointed that making friends is so slow," confided a disheartened newcomer nine months after her move. "I knew it would take a long time, but I hadn't expected I'd feel so badly about it." A steady progression from the first "click"—the recognition of mutual interests and values and concerns—to felt intimacy was unusual. This did happen for a few. The "click" was experienced within a few months of moving and most usually in a chance encounter. Then the women persistently created opportunities for shared experiences and dialogues while there was a gradually deepening trust.

For most newcomers, the choreography of friendship was erratic, marked by advances, pauses, retreats, and by some painful falls.

Molly's experience told just such a tale. A professional woman herself, she moved to ease her husband's professional life at a time when he was finding his job too demanding. Whether he could have changed the circumstances was unclear; he preferred to change the location and found an opening in Northland.

Molly had had misgivings. Her balance was poor, so she feared the winter's icy pathways, and her hands swelled painfully in the cold. Southern climates were her preference, but Jake felt he hadn't time to investigate distant prospects thoroughly. Having moved many times (including during his boyhood), he felt an urgent readiness to put down deep roots.

Jake's job had priority, Molly believed. Because she didn't take her own work as seriously as he took his, she had no right to make claims for herself. Northland seemed acceptable enough— they had had friends who loved it. "It didn't seem like a gut-wrenching move," she told me, because it was close enough to maintain ties to her friends. Connection was intensely important to Molly, who had also moved often in childhood and who had energetically preserved friendly attachments since high school days. So Molly, like so many others, set aside her misgivings and consented to her husband's choice.

Six weeks after she arrived, Molly told me, "Losing friends is the worst of moving. I felt very sad after we came here even though I keep in touch by phone." Trust in new people develops slowly, she believed—it develops through a lot of trial disclosures and a growing sense that the other person will really help. "It takes one and a half to two years before you can speak from the gut."

Molly was pregnant and expected to make friends through the Lamaze preparation for childbirth classes, through a part-time professional job, and through her husband's colleagues. She was both sad and optimistic.

Three and a half months after the move she said, "I've been working for a month. At least that gives me someone to talk to." She didn't yet see her job as a source of friendship since she had found little in common with others in her office. She hoped that when she started the Lamaze classes she would find out about the mother's network she'd been hearing about. She thought the baby would provide the entry into new relationships. Hopefully, she and her husband would make friends among other newcomers who were having similar feelings. She kept hearing it would take two years.

She'd met two women she'd done things with, and maybe they would become friends. "That's the way it works. First you share an activity, then you talk about it." But Molly's confidence that she would be a desirable friend was faltering. She saw herself as having "nothing much to offer—no special skills, I'm not good at sports." I pointed out how readily she communicated; wasn't that something to offer? "Yes," she said, "but you don't do that with someone you've just met. You can do that with someone who's researching a book about moving."

"I asked a woman with her baby over for lunch, but something came up and she couldn't come. She said she'd call but she hasn't. People have their own lives established; they have all the activities and relationships they have time and energy for." Molly's observation was realistic, but there were undertones of stark self-deprecation. Feeling unwanted in Northland seemed to have rekindled feelings of being unwanted in her early life, and memories spontaneously emerged. She had been the oldest child in a large family, she explained. There always seemed to be another baby absorbing her mother, and Molly often had to fend for herself. "I sometimes think of myself as the forgotten diaphragm," she told me wryly, revealing the depth of her hurt.

Six months after her arrival the Lamaze classes had begun, but hadn't yet been the source of friends as Molly hoped. One couple seemed very interesting, but the wife became depressed and the couple dropped out. Molly and Jake then developed a feeling of kinship with another couple, but they would be leaving soon for Ohio. Hopes had been raised and dashed.

Molly was disappointed they were not making friends through her husband's job, but his was a small, rather isolated engineering office. His few colleagues were absorbed in their own work and not outreaching. Molly often had lunch with several women in her own small physical therapy unit. They were friendly enough, but their interest in each other hadn't carried over outside of work.

She and her husband spent Christmas alone. For the first time, they didn't have a Christmas tree. "When you're alone there doesn't seem much point in that." During the holiday, they wallpapered the bathroom.

"If things don't change, I'll go bonkers and they'll find me in the cellar." Molly's story was tinged with wry humor, but the cellar seemed a metaphor for the depth of her discouragement and the barrenness of her loneliness. Yet she communicated a resilience. She'd been able to tolerate the aloneness so far because she still hoped it was going to change. Her hopes were strongly focused on the baby as a means of entry, maybe through an after-childbirth support group. "I really don't know how it will happen otherwise."

Nine months after her arrival Molly wasn't yet "in the cellar." To the contrary, she enjoyed her new baby and the After Childbirth Transition (ACT) class, a mother-infant support group. Molly had become friendly with the one local woman in the group, and another who lived way out in the hills had promised to call when the weather was warmer and the roads more passable. The woman who canceled her lunch date five months before came to see her and explained that she had been feeling depressed at the time of the lunch. That was why she canceled, and that was why she didn't call afterwards. Her energy was sapped, and she was unwilling to reveal her blue mood. "We both admitted how we all hide our hard times from each other and pretend everything's wonderful," Molly recalled. By concealing their needs, these women had withheld from each other their comfort.

Now Molly had a weekly lunch date and someone to go into town with, both wheeling their babies. She had gone back to her part-time job, less for the work than for the companionship.

Sixteen months after the move, the couple Molly and Jake really liked from the Lamaze class had left for Ohio. "Now we're feeling pretty leery" (of more disappointments).

The relationships from the ACT class hadn't developed any further. But Molly had met two other women at a reception who might become genuine friends.

Two years after the move those two friendships had not developed either. One woman started full-time professional work and the other lived quite far away, so neither was very available. There were two colleagues at work Molly could confide in about her job, but they didn't have enough in common for the relationships to carry over outside.

Outside of work, Molly and Jake were alone most of the time. Her expectation that "it will take two years" was unfulfilled. To be sure, Molly was among the women who felt anxious about taking initiative, "worming my way into other people's lives," as she put it. But she was very responsive to overtures from others and she went comfortably into new situations with a companion.

Since school days she had nurtured close friendships, and with me she was trusting, candid, genuine, and humorous—a woman one might expect to enjoy as a friend.

She had walked a tightrope between hope and disappointment, attachment and loss, and these polarities permeated the two-year experience of the study population.

"She said she'd call but she hasn't." Many movers told me this— it seemed a metaphor for the lift of feeling appreciated, the plateau of temporary fulfillment, and then the fall of feeling unwanted. Incipient friendships were interrupted when an apparent mutuality was revealed to be illusory because either woman, or both, disclosed aspects of her being that felt alien to the other. Incipient friendships were interrupted when one partner succumbed to an interlude of depression. Incipient friendships were interrupted when one partner took a full-time job outside the home and no longer had free time, when one partner moved further away in Northland and was harder to reach, or when one partner left Northland altogether. To be sure, the polarities of hope and disappointment and attachment and loss permeate all people's lives. Yet, when a woman is settled, ongoing friendships allow loss to be absorbed; affirmation allows disappointment to be absorbed. All is not in flux at once.

Like Molly, movers suffered grievous wounds to their self-esteem in their quest for friendship and endeavored to soothe themselves. Many tried to attribute their apparent failure to external circumstances.

One newcomer who longed intensely for a best friend doubted after two years that she would find one. "Maybe it's something about me," she said, revealing her wound. "Or maybe it's because I'm home with the children full-time and I don't have time to do things with other women that would lead to friendship," she suggested, trying to rationalize away the hurt.

"Maybe it's because I'm home only part-time and working outside part-time," Molly had said.

"Maybe in young families people don't have the time and energy for close friendships," said another.

"Maybe you only develop close friends when you're bringing up your babies together," thought another.

OUTCOMES

For almost all the movers, the work of making friends involved narcissistic risk—ruptures and wounds to their sense of self. It could also involve narcissistic gain—a clearer sense of self, clearer and more purposeful choices about how and where time and energy should be invested. For Andrea, this was a new possibility. Her repeated moves to advance her husband's career had exhausted her capacity to master the pain of separation. To avoid further loss, she began avoiding further attachment. Withdrawn and lonely, without intimate friends, she could only cling to her birth family from a distance, and they were unable to supply the nourishment she needed.

Anticipating the eleventh move in her married life, she succumbed to immobilizing depression and sought psychotherapy. As she grappled with her feelings of hopelessness and futility, the guilt related to unconscious fury and the shame related to her incapacity to be endlessly adaptive were relieved. Her energies were freed to flow outward—aggressive energy to assert her own wishes and participate actively in the choice to move to Northland (where she had lived before) and pleasure-seeking (libidinal) energy to make new personal connections.

"I'm very happy we came back here; I feel quite content," Andrea told me at the end of two years. What had made it work out? "Mostly people," she said. "I now have two close friends I feel very comfortable calling up when I want to talk, or calling on for practical help, and I don't feel I have to reciprocate right away. It's the first time I've ever had friends like that. I don't think people are different, I think I'm different. Before, I was always facing another move, so it didn't seem worthwhile putting out enough to make friends. Now, when my mother and I can't communicate the way I'd wish, or when I'm disappointed in my sister, it doesn't matter as much. That's because of the closeness I feel to my friends."

Peck has suggested that the "ability to redistribute emotional investment in relationships appears to be very important for the maintenance of emotional well-being and a clear self-definition" (1986, p. 279). In finding a new equilibrium between her conjugal, maternal, and natal relationships and her friendships, Andrea seemed to be doing just that. Ironically, it was fortunate that she had become dysfunctional enough to need professional intervention, because it was then that the tide began to turn as she was helped to assert her needs and rights.

Gains such as Andrea's were experienced by the minority, however. Among the core population, fewer than one third made new, close friends within two years. Among half of those who did, separation had again occurred, or was going to occur, because the newcomer was intending to leave or the friend had already left. So only a sixth of the movers developed deep friendships likely to endure. Only a sixth had recaptured the dependable intimacy they had lost.

These were primarily women whose lives were centered in their homes. Theirs was the work of affiliation, and friendmaking was a crucial part of that work. They used significant amounts of time and energy developing networks to support their interest in domestic life, to share the experience of mothering, to find the affirmation of their worth and their work. Their friends were truly their colleagues. These movers strove to transcend the barriers we, in the United States, have erected among ourselves. From their separate homes, with their separate faucets or separate wells, their separate larders and separate freezers, separate kitchens, separate laundries, and separate nurseries, they tried to recreate the flowing connections that pre-technological societies have never lost.

Two thirds of the movers were unable to make new, close friends within two years. Many were women who combined mothering and professional work. Their lives seemed too fragmented, their time and energy too dispersed to persistently coax the embers of acquaintanceship into the warm glow of intimacy. Except for chance occurrences—having a landlady or neighbor with whom there was the "click" of recognized affinity—women such as these needed a time span far longer than two years for close friendship to develop. Yet, just because of the fragmentation of their demanding lives, they needed that sustenance just as urgently as women at home full time. They were caught in a paradox.

In judging a social phenomenon, society readily blames the "victims," imputing to them some flaws that have brought about unwanted results. Although movers are victims, in a sense, they were no more flawed than nonvictims. They were not seclusive; all were actively involved with networks or affinity groups. They did not fear intimacy; all but two had had close friendships in recent years.

The persistence of their efforts revealed their powerful drives toward bonding with other women. But it was clear that time, energy, availability, and the emotional resilience to absorb rejection and disappointment were needed—and sheer luck, as well. Gathering places were needed where casual conversations could develop in a spontaneous and easy flow, where fragments of connection could grow, deepen, and become imbued with warmth, interest, and recognition of shared concerns—and with trust, the core of close friendship. Clearly, that can take years.

In making their choice to move (or declining to choose), most of these women had failed to take into account the strength of their need for attachment, or the pain they would experience before new connections would be made. On what were these denials based? Was it that the movers unconsciously felt unworthy of such fulfillment and therefore minimized or disregarded their needs? Or did they heroically overestimate their capacity to muster time and energy, and to absorb hurt, sadness, and loneliness? It seemed that both tendencies may have been at work. It seemed that the contradictions many women revealed in their sense of self had diminished their capacity to care for themselves thoughtfully and lovingly. They had not realistically appraised the importance of close friendship or the complexity of making new friends before committing themselves to a move.

RÉSUMÉ

Movers grieved intensely over the loss of intimate friendships with other women and longed intensely for new bonds permeated with mutuality, authenticity, spontaneity, trust, and reciprocity. Their needs seemed to arise from special characteristics of female psychological and social development.

Movers expected that welcoming gestures from the new community would open pathways toward new relationships, yet only one third were offered an active welcome. In its absence, movers felt painfully unnoticed and uncared about. At a time when they felt depleted by their moves, they were faced with the responsibility for taking initiative. Yet initiative needed to be exercised with extreme discretion and aroused deep anxiety in many women.

Extraordinary investments of time and energy were involved in the work of friendmaking. Movers persistently developed collegial connections and parenting networks, and joined special interest groups. Such affiliations were supportive, but did not replace close friendships. In their search for new intimacies, movers recurrently experienced hope and disappointment, attachment and loss, and absorbed many wounds to their self-esteem. New bonds deepened slowly. At the end of two years, only one sixth of the movers had formed new, close friendships likely to endure.

NOTES

1. The understanding of this process has been considerably enriched by examining the development of male gender identity in other cultures. Among Melanesian cultures, for example, internalized maternal qualities are rejected both symbolically and physically through prolonged and painful rites of passage into manhood (Lidz & Lidz, 1977, 1984; Stoller, 1974; Stoller & Herdt, 1982).

2. The unidentified speaker was a participant in a symposium on "Women and Psychoanalysis: Today and Yesterday," sponsored by the Boston Psychoanalytical Society and Institute, February 1984.

Working

WORK AND THE SENSE OF SELF

"I have felt very dispersed," Barbara the photographer was saying. Her searching lens was turned inward as she tried to understand the malaise she was feeling three months after her move. "That inner voice in me—a male voice that represents my critical father who used to tell me I was lazy, not accomplishing anything—that voice has been berating me. I shouldn't be so dispersed, it tells me. Like a man, I should be focused—a brightly focused beam should burn through the page!" There was only a tinge of irony in her voice.

"I doubt that I'll go back to professional work," another newcomer told me, also three months after her move. "I'd have to read the journals, keep abreast of new findings and techniques. I don't feel that focused, my interests are more dispersed. I really feel a total sense of dispersement. I wonder if any other women are that way too."

Among the movers, many were "that way too." The word "dispersed" was used repeatedly, and by competent women who were accomplished in their chosen realms of work. They described a state in which their energy seemed to flow out into myriad different directions, a feeling of being pulled in response to inner pressures as well as external demands, a feeling of having

163

"permeable walls" in their psychic structures. And they saw themselves in contrast to men who seemed focused, not dispersed, and with "clear divisions" rather than permeable psychic walls.

Dispersion was both valued and devalued. It was appreciated as an expression of resiliency and flexibility that allowed women to respond to diverse and often conflicting claims. Yet women also spoke of it uneasily, as though it were a deficiency in contrast to the sharply delineated commitments that they perceived in men. In so doing, they mirrored the widespread view that women have less career commitment than men (Markham & Pleck, 1986), or show a motivational deficit in the workforce (Laws, 1976), and they disregarded their own awareness that their commitment reflects a different arrangement of priorities. Attributing a higher value to the focused professional life of men, many women had allowed it to become the central factor in a decision to move. Yet it was not a quality that many of these women sought for themselves.

Their sense of dispersion seemed central in their subjective experience of self. It was intensified by their move, as though a fragile integration had been disrupted. And in turn, their sense of dispersion shaped in important ways their experience of moving. It greatly complicated the necessary process of realigning their priorities and reengaging in their chosen realms of work.

How could this state of dispersion be understood? Once again, it seemed, the answer lay in the development of self—the body self as well as the psychic self. Many feminist scholars are wary of attributing any aspect of human development to biology, because such ideas have been distorted and misused in the service of political ideologies about sex as well as race. Yet, from the moment of birth there is an inevitable interaction between organism and environment. There is mutual stimulation and mutual response between the infant with her or his genetically and perinatally shaped potentials, and the caregivers with their physiologically, psycho-logically, and socioculturally shaped behaviors. To acknowledge our biology is not to subscribe to myths of biological determinism.

Dispersion and the Body Self

Male or female, an individual's sense of self is grounded in the body. Infants develop mental images of their bodily selves from the feel of their bodies in motion—kicking, turning, reaching, arching, rocking; from the sensations of their skin exposed to cold and roughness, enveloped in warmth and softness, encountering firmness or even the nothingness of empty space; from the sight of their exploring fingers, their curling toes, their face gazing back from a mirror. They feel sensations from deep within—the gnawing ache of hunger, the soothing gush of warm milk—as well as sensations aroused by the caregiver who carries and cuddles and joyfully flings the baby up and then down into a snug embrace. From myriad sources, the earliest sense of body self develops, even, Mahler and McDevitt (1982) have suggested, the very sense of being alive.

Sensations emanating from the sexual organs play a special part in the developing body self, and contribute specifically to the awareness of self-as-girl or self-as-boy that is being shaped from birth onwards. Those sensations are aroused by internal biological functions as well as caregiving, and by the ordinary activities of daily life.

There are deep pressures against the walls of the infant girl's vagina when her food wastes gather in the adjacent rectum, pressures that may arouse inchoate pleasure. And her vagina is stimulated from outside as well. That occurs because her clitoris is exquisitely sensitive to touch—the touch of her inquisitive fingers, the touch of the caregiver who cleanses and diapers her, the brush of her clothing, even the pressure of the walker or rocking horse or grandparent's knee on which she bounces in delight. There is a flow of exciting sensations traveling inward from her clitoris to her vagina and beyond. The sensations are diffuse, spreading, lacking precise contours or exact limits. The infant can scarcely, if at all, find with her fingers or see with her eyes the sources of those sensations. She can scarcely know where in her body they are happening or whence they come. So from babyhood onward, the female experience of self includes intense bodily pleasure that comes from mysterious sources and is diffuse and boundless (Bernstein, 1983; Kestenberg, 1956b; Montrain 1983).

In contrast, the boy's sexual organs allow him to experience sensation that is clearly localized, focused, within boundaries. Furthermore, he can locate with his hand as well as his eyes the source of his pleasure—his penis.

Sexual experience in infancy and early childhood is powerful and helps to shape the developing mental representations of self— bodily self and psychic self. So the boy's sense of self is likely to include the qualities of clarity, boundary, and focus that characterize his sexuality. The girl's sense of self is more likely to include qualities of mystery, diffusion, and boundlessness— qualities which she will reexperience again and again in the womanly orgasm that spreads outward from deep in her pelvis, flowing in successive waves throughout her whole body. In fact, "feminine sexuality may have remained an unknown continent precisely because we have not wished to recognize that it is under the sway of intense forces and gives rise to sensuous experience that does not have exact limits" (Montrain, 1983, p. 169).

It seems likely then, that the mental images arising from a girl's sexual development comprise one source in the sense of permeability and dispersion that women experience in themselves. And this sense of dispersion significantly influences their experience of work and of moving.

Dispersion and the Interpersonal Self

But even though shaped by bodily experience, the self develops primarily in an interpersonal realm. The core is the interaction and communication between infant and mother (or motherly caregiver). Because the girl is female like mother, and mother like girl, and because their empathic attunement may be smoother, the differentiation between them may remain hazier than between mother and son, and contribute to the feeling of having "permeable walls" through which energies flow in and out.

To attain what our culture defines as masculinity, the small boy must experience himself as different from his mother. In renouncing his sameness he must renounce those of her qualities and roles that he has incorporated into his developing sense of self, and deny some emotional connection as well. The father replaces the mother as his foremost object of identification.

In contrast, the little girl can more comfortably maintain her deep linkage with her mother as her development advances. She need not renounce her earliest identification even as it is gradually transformed into a more mature awareness of being both separate from and the same as mother—a "secondary" identification. But the girl is likely to form a secondary identification with her father as well. The wish to please father, the wish to be like father, the incorporation of some of his qualities, roles, and expectations into her ideal self and her conscience, often provide the seeds of aspiration for a career in the marketplace. (If his expectations have been very high, as they were among fathers of many of the movers, his influences on her ideal self will be powerful and her conscience— the critical inner voice—will be severe.)

Sociocultural values and attitudes are at first transmitted through the family, and later through a host of others—friends, teachers, all those who interact with the developing child in a meaningful way. In addition to expectations communicated about their roles as student, teammate, and date, girls have traditionally been exhorted to be nurturant caregivers, responsive to others. Single-minded pursuit of a professional goal has only rarely been encouraged. More likely, the girl has been encouraged to experience herself in a multitude of relationships, roles, and situations—a state of dispersion, which is sometimes integrated, sometimes not. Her vision of her life's work is usually one of diversity, encompassing the work of affiliation as well as the work of the marketplace— perhaps being like both her mother and her father. This duality expands her realms of aspiration, but it can also create tension. It, too, can contribute to feelings of being pulled towards different aims.

For all these reasons, then—the mysterious, spreading, diffuse quality of the girl's sexual experience from babyhood onward, the sense of oneness with her mother from whom she feels differentiated by somewhat permeable boundaries, the additional identification with her father (as well as the pull towards him as the longed-for but forbidden object of nascent erotic love), and finally the diverse expectations and communications of teachers and friends and even the mass media—for all these reasons, a woman can scarcely avoid feeling dispersed. When life is stable, her capacity to tolerate dispersion allows her to respond to diverse needs and claims that many men would experience as chaotic. Her capacity to sustain multiple roles, rather than depleting her, can enrich her sense of self and secure her self-esteem (Pietromonaco, Manis, & Frohardt-Lane, 1986; Sieber, 1974; Thoits, 1983). A woman's dispersion can be a strength, but it can be a vulnerability as well.

Dispersion, Work, and Moving

A woman's sense of dispersion can make her move far more complex than a man's. This arises from the fact that our experience of self becomes deeply embedded in the work we do.

A woman (or a man) develops enduring images of herself over time. Whenever she scans her mental "cassette" of memories of herself in varying experiences and situations, she recognizes familiar and common elements. That recognition contributes to a feeling of self-constancy that is deeply reassuring. It allows her to experience inner sameness through external change—a sense of going-on-being that is sustaining (Tyson, 1983).

But this enduring, stabilizing sense of self must be replenished throughout the life cycle. That happens when a person's identities, the outward expressions of self, are recognized and responded to by family members, friends, colleagues, or associates in a variety of special relationships. And it is through work that identity is most widely, and perhaps most seriously, affirmed in our culture.

Their roles of affiliation (as son, husband, or father) have not usually been viewed by men as their work. Rather, the occupation in the marketplace is a central organizer of their ongoing sense of self and of their identity. Even husbands and fathers tend to define and label themselves first as a doctor, professor, carpenter, musician, or accountant. It would seem to be this professional core of identity, and the energy bound up in it, that women perceive in men as focus. Men who move for career development experience a continuity in this. The man's identity as a lawyer, merchant, or engineer is perpetuated and mirrored back by the new milieu. His self-constancy is reinforced.

Some women, too, develop a single-minded, focused commitment to professional careers akin to that of the traditional male commitment. But for most women the story is more complex. Their realms of work are various, and rather than being inwardly experienced in a stable hierarchy of importance, these realms may seem to be of parallel value or of changing value as the hierarchy is restructured.

For example, about three quarters of the movers had earlier developed professional careers (the remainder had been absorbed in domestic life and in the complex and disruptive work of repeated moves). Yet there were only half a dozen who arrived in Northland firmly centered in their professions. Their professional work allowed them to express their capabilities and to enjoy their competence, as it does for men, and it provided continuity of identity. But not for long. By the end of my study, four had left Northland, primarily because of the pull of love relationships and a new alignment of their priorities.

Such pulls were powerful. Only three women remained continuously centered in their professional work in Northland through a two year time span. One mover, divorced, was not currently involved in a love relationship. The primacy of her work in the marketplace represented financial necessity as much as choice (as it does for many women), and she struggled against loneliness. The second was a coupled woman who had come to pursue her professional career, followed by her lover. She was steadfast in her professional commitment, even though her lover experienced the serious disruptions in his career advancement that wives so often experience. After they married, she accepted prolonged intervals of separation in order to concentrate on her work. Her priorities seemed the mirror image of the traditional priorities of a married man. Her anxieties, like those of traditional men, were centered around proving her mettle in her professional career.

The third was Chris, whose husband had come with her to support her professional training, and whose choice to move to Northland seemed to express the ideal of interdependence. But Chris yielded to her husband's career goals when her studies were completed after two years. She left feeling pulled between her marriage, her professional future, and a rising longing to have a child. She felt dispersed.

In contrast to the half dozen who arrived in Northland as active professionals, 26 newcomers had interrupted their professional work, some in anticipation of this move. Responding to a melange of "shoulds" and "wants," they had chosen not to sustain these careers as the primary organizers of their lives. Like the women who had never developed professional careers, they had diverse commitments through which their identity was expressed. Enmeshed in a variety of work roles and associated relationships, they needed to loosen many more attachments than their men, and they lost more sources of affirmation. Their dispersion made them highly vulnerable.

The psychological threat could be deep. For a few, there was an interruption of the reassuring, stabilizing feeling of internal sameness, of continuing to exist unchanged through external change. That interruption was experienced as a profoundly anxious interlude expressed as "I don't know who I am." Others expressed their anxiety as "others don't know who I am," and spoke of being "nobody," being unrecognized by others, being "invisible." These were coupled women. In the anxious limbo of transition, the affirmation of their husbands and children was insufficient. With varying degrees of intensity, almost all of the movers admitted their need to be visible outside the family, their longing for recognition in their new community.

Only a few, their ages varied, expressed the traditional expectation that they would gain recognition through the achievements of their men. A woman's fulfillment through a man, expressed in the idea, "He is great and I am part of him," was viewed in classical psychoanalytical theory as intrinsic to normal feminity. But in contemporary psychoanalytical thought, such vicarious fulfillment is recognized to be hazardous. It predisposes a woman to disappointment and anger if her man's "greatness" is seen to be flawed (Fast, 1979). That was to become a painful issue for several women whose husbands were unsuccessful at the jobs that had lured them to Northland.

In contrast to the traditional position, many women felt hurt and indignant if they were identified in Northland as nothing more than an affiliate of their spouse. "I was invited to a tea," said Mildred, who had developed a professional career precisely because she wanted to be "more than a wife and mother." "The guests were mostly older women. Not one of them asked me what I do. They just asked me what my husband does." It was as though, among these traditional older women, her doings didn't deserve notice; it was as though she was assigned the dreaded position of "being nobody."

Jan's lament, "Nobody knows who I really am," spoke for many others. The mover is challenged to disclose to the new community who she really is, primarily through her work (paid or not). To do this, she must first find out for herself who she now really is. She must regroup her dispersed energies, realign her priorities, redefine her work goals (which may have been obscured by the primacy she has given to the needs of her loved ones before and during the move), and then find new opportunities to engage in the work she chooses.

OCCUPATIONAL CONFLICTS

For many women, a move rekindles occupational conflicts that have seemed to be resolved. Most common is the tension between wishes to become absorbed in intimate relationships and wishes for a professional career. "That's a choice men don't have to make," one newcomer wryly observed. Indeed, it has traditionally been assumed that men can, men should, men will have careers in the marketplace and wives as helpmates to enhance their capabilities. They will have children to mirror their accomplishments, fulfill their thwarted aims, transcend their mortality, and perpetuate their lineage (a heavy burden for their progeny—the very burden that some of the women movers carried within themselves). That has been a hierarchical image, with man and his needs at the top, although for many men the psychic costs have been high (Ehrenreich, 1983).

Out of necessity, African American women have also traditionally assumed that their lives would include affiliation in the home and work outside (Wolfman, 1984). Until recently, many Caucasian women have not.

Contemporary young women do expect that their lives will include marriage, motherhood, and work in the marketplace (Laws, 1976). But women's visions of how and when these realms will be integrated vary greatly. And when their expectations are at the threshold of fulfillment, realities change, and unanticipated conflicts well up from deep within a woman's psyche. Choices have to be reworked and solutions redesigned throughout life in response to the vicissitudes in a woman's development, and changes in her loved ones. At best, the most need-fulfilling resolution is found for each phase of a woman's life. Moving is a powerful disruptor of such resolutions.

Frances's move overturned the phase-specific equilibrium that she had achieved. Her story told of tugs and pulls between affiliation and the marketplace, tugs and pulls intimately connected with fluctuations in a woman's sense of fulfillment and of worth, tugs and pulls that were greatly intensified by moving.

From the outset, Frances revealed striking contradictions in her sense of self. In our first interview she seemed shy and anxious, urgently sipping tea to moisten her dry throat, her large grey eyes at once trusting and wary.

"I don't have any confidence in my judgments, I often don't know what I really think," she told me as we talked about her part in the decision to move, and other decisions as well. "I usually prefer not to make choices. It's hard for me to make up my mind because making a decision is a risk. If someone else makes it and things turn out badly, you can blame them." Blaming others allowed Frances to avoid the pain of self-blame, which was usually severe. "I'm prone to feel very guilty about things."

Her self-doubts were repeatedly reinforced by her husband. "I often feel put down by Peter. It's the way he listens to me, avoiding eye contact when I talk. Or he doesn't listen, he simply goes on reading his newspaper. I take it that he doesn't find what I have to say either valuable or interesting."

Frances had had a voice in each of the four moves she had made with her husband as he climbed his career ladder. Northland, where she had lived 12 years before, had been her own second choice this time, although it was an appealing choice because of the energizing change of seasons, the beauty of the surround, the rural privacy, the cultural facilities, and the access to her birth family nearby. She would have preferred being close to the sea, she told me, but the job her husband was offered in Northland seemed the better one and his career had to be the deciding factor. Why was that? Because she wasn't now active in her profession. "I can be a wife and mother anywhere." So she, too, subscribed to the "myth of the transportable homemaker."

She, too had an heroic image of herself. "It's my responsibility to make the move work out, especially in relation to helping the children, but also taking care of my husband, encouraging him, listening to him." "Who takes care of you?" I wondered. "I do. I do it by withdrawing occasionally to read the paper or treating myself to a mystery." She was the caregiver for all.

Trying to fulfill her high standards in family life, Frances soon felt depleted. "I got depressed last week," she told me three months after she arrived in Northland. "I got depressed because everything seemed out of my control." Living in inadequate, temporary housing with no outdoor play space for the children, working frantically to finish the house she and Peter were building, Frances felt a disagreeable degree of dispersement. The disorganization and uncertainties of moving had threatened her capacity to "make the move work out," and her spirits plunged. No longer feeling powerful, she felt debased. "Sometimes I feel like the servant mother. What I do isn't even noticed."

At this low point, Frances began to consider resuming professional work. Trained as a nutritionist, she had enjoyed her profession, especially her effectiveness in helping patients solve complicated dietary problems. But she had willingly set that aside to stay at home with her two children during their preschool years. It was a phase-specific choice. The idea of turning back to nutrition was incompatible with her primary commitment to the family, but it expressed her need to recapture her feelings of competence. And it reflected her longing for her competence to be noticed.

Three months later, Frances and her family moved into the house they had built. Her joyful fantasies about it were overshadowed by frustrations and disappointments. "This was a happy move, a move we looked forward to and wanted to make, but after we got here it was an anticlimax. It was like the day after Christmas," she told me poignantly.

She felt alone. Her husband was obviously discouraged, but unable or unwilling to allow her into his inner world. Frances knew he was waking up during the night, she suspected he was worrying about his performance in his new and "better" job, but he didn't welcome her expressions of concern or her ideas about how he might be more effective. So her aim of making the move work out for him, encouraging him, listening to him, was thwarted. Her ideal of nurturant power was unfulfilled. When Frances tried to express her own sadness, confusion, and anxiety, Peter would sometimes walk out of the room in mid-sentence. "He hardly knows he's doing it," she realized, but she felt disparaged and criticized.

She had made energetic efforts to make new contacts that would enhance her domestic life, becoming active in a baby-sitting cooperative, inviting a new acquaintance in for a glass of cider, taking part in a mother-child play group. But the group was large and without cohesion; there were different people each time so conversations seemed fragmented and superficial. "I don't have anyone yet to talk to about real things—there's nobody who would really listen to me, who would be honest. People I've met seem to be putting on fronts, trying to impress each other. But I guess I do that too.

"I feel that many of them look down on someone who stays at home, but maybe that's just because I'm feeling that way myself." Even while knowing that she was an affectionate and effective mother, Frances realized that her children were becoming more independent, needing her less.

She strove to understand the bleakness she was feeling. "Maybe I can't value myself as a homemaker because I'm not earning any money," she confided. "Other women at home are doing things: one bakes and sells fruitcakes, another is offering group day-care, another is giving art lessons. I enjoy weaving, but it's not cost-effective. My husband disparages my spending the time that way." Although earned money would have been useful in practical ways, it seemed even more important as a symbol of recognition from outside the family—recognition that Frances was painfully missing.

Ten months after returning to Northland, Frances was still depressed and asked for names of experienced therapists. Gazing around at the exposed beams, the unfinished partitions in her house, recalling the enthusiasm with which she and Peter had shared their vision of building their home, she told me sadly that she could scarcely gather the energy to saw, nail, plaster, and paint. It seemed so meaningless. She vividly remembered the fulfillment of her past professional life, and her thoughts were turning towards finding a new career. Jobs were scarce in her own field, and her commitment to being a nutritionist was not intense. But her need to be noticed and approved outside the family was urgent indeed.

In spite of her depressed mood and the tensions in her marriage that continued to deepen, in spite of shyness—anxiety about taking initiative and fear of not being liked—Frances persistently searched for support and friendship. She was active in a variety of networks, enrolled in courses, and formed a handicraft group of her own.

But within two years after her move, still struggling to restore her feelings of effectiveness, she had turned away from her full-time domestic life and immersed herself in a demanding and responsible position in business—a position requiring the organizational and integrative skills that were exercised unnoticed at home. She received swift and positive recognition in the workplace, and proudly represented her firm in the community.

"I've grown a lot," she told me happily. "I feel more competent and self-confident, I have more energy."

The contradictions in her sense of self were still apparent. "Now I feel that I'm looked down on by women who are at home," she admitted ruefully, seeming to recognize that her devalued self had to find expression. Predominantly, though, she felt an exhilarating awareness of success and power. "It's hard for me to delegate at work because I feel I can carry out the functions more effectively than the people I would delegate to."

This conviction operated at home, too, in dividing up domestic responsibilities with her husband. Voydanoff (1988) has observed that:

> At the present time, women are sharing the provider role to a greater extent than men are sharing family work. . . . Our understanding of men's and women's resistance to developing a more egalitarian division of family work is extremely limited. (p. 277)

Frances's stance contributes to such an understanding. As much as she needed Peter's help, she had trouble giving over the control of the hearth. She had trouble believing that he would do the laundry with judgment as good as hers—the navy socks would surely end up in the hot wash with the white shirts, she imagined. She was aware that her negative expectations would contribute to Peter's reluctance to do the job. Yet, subject to painful feelings of debasement, she held tight to those realms that expressed her competence and her power.

But for the present, and with the help of a therapist, her depression had lifted. "I love living here now," she declared.

Frances's conflict between affiliative and professional work wasn't created by the move. But she had reached a resolution, related to the developmental needs of her children, which was then disturbed. Her conflict was re-ignited by the move—a move that disrupted her familiar, predictable and controllable lifestyle, causing anxiety and a plunge in her self-esteem; a move which disrupted her personal bonds and exposed her to uncomfortable judgments in a spectrum of new relationships; a move that made her husband less available and less receptive because of his own transitional anxieties; a move that made it more difficult to tolerate her children's increasing independence because she had lost other sources of validation.

It might be argued that Frances's move had served as a catalyst, bringing a latent conflict into focus and propelling it towards resolution. That did happen, but at great personal cost. The two year period of my study was an interval of considerable suffering for Frances, and it seemed likely that her depressed moods and her precipitous and deep immersion in the business world affected her husband and young children also. Had the other elements in her life had continuity and stability, there would have been opportunity to progress gradually and with less suffering towards achieving a new, need-fulfilling balance between family and professional work.

Frances had moved to support her husband's career advancement four times before. She had experienced loneliness and anxiety, and the stresses had had cumulative effects. The full impact of those moves had been unexamined. Clearly, Frances was not prepared for the complexity and pain of this wanted move back to Northland. But at the end of two years she felt so aware of the pain that she doubted she would move again. If her husband didn't "make it" in Northland, if he needed to find the next rung on his career ladder elsewhere, she doubted she would go with him. "I just can't imagine going through such a struggle again." And the elements in her struggle were typical for many movers.

OCCUPATIONAL TRANSITIONS

The moves of many women are caused by or coincide with a transition from one life phase to another, from one predominant identity to another. Women pass through entrances and exits as well, changing from the single state to the coupled state, from the coupled state back to the single state, from student life to employment in the marketplace, from the marketplace to motherhood, from the marketplace to retirement. Each life phase or identity is connected to certain realms of work. And each realm of work is shaped in complex ways by a move.

Daughterhood Into Wifehood

In our virilocal society, marriage has commonly occasioned a woman's move—almost always away from her natal home, and quite often away from her community as well. There is a skew in both losses and gains—whereas the man's identity will be perpetuated, the woman's will be unraveled; whereas the man's work will be furthered, the woman's will be transformed. And the interplay between the marriage and the move is likely to reverberate in a woman's self-esteem, imbuing work in the marketplace with unexpected meaning. It was Joan's story that best illustrated this.

It was a recent marriage that brought Joan to Northland, marriage to a man who had already committed himself to moving here for postgraduate training. The place where they would live together had felt less important to her than how they would live together. Earlier, there had been hints that her lover might not ask Joan to come as his wife, but only as his companion. "I wouldn't have come without the feeling of commitment and the sense of my place in the relationship that came from marriage. I wouldn't have trailed along behind him," she said with dignity.

Joan had been sad and worried about leaving her family. Feeling close to her widowed mother, Joan dreaded the separation. She confided in her mother, felt cared about and taken care of in special ways. To free Joan to live her separate life with an easy mind, her homemaker mother had begun preparing for a new career in landscape design. In turn, Joan felt a special concern for her mother; through her encouragement and interest in that new realm of work, she took care of her mother. In moving away, Joan feared losing that precious reciprocity of caring and being cared about, a reciprocity that allowed each woman room for growth. Joan had little need to wrench loose in order to find her adulthood; rather, she and her mother designed a transformation in their relationship that preserved its continuity, a transformation that many young women hope for but find difficult to realize (Kaplan, Klein, & Gleason, 1985).

After she moved, Joan longed at times for the security of home. She worried that she might have trouble making friends—"people I could have real in-depth discussions with"—because she had been disappointed in people in the past. It felt good to be able to go on confiding in her mother by long-distance phone calls. Her husband was her best friend, she asserted. Yes, she wanted to let him into her inner world, but not to burden him with her troubled feelings. Those she could share with her mother.

It was a traditional vision of domestic arrangements that this young woman had brought with her to Northland. Joan was trained in occupational therapy and had worked in her profession. "But I guess I'm old fashioned," she declared with an edge of defiance. "My marriage is my top priority." She was worried about learning to keep house, do marketing, and cook for Russell. "I'm a perfectionist and I really get down on myself if I don't do things as well as I think I should." It wasn't Russell's criticism she feared but her own. If she hadn't left her home city, her mother might have helped her achieve her aims.

But her move made Joan aware of other needs just as compelling as being a perfect homemaker and a nurturant wife. And they caught her by surprise. When I phoned to arrange the first interview, she said, "I haven't been able to find a job and it's been bleak. My whole attitude about the move hinges on that." Two months after her move she declared again, "I know my attitude about the move is going to be colored by whether I find a job or not. I know my qualifications are good, and I've had experience. But when I've met other wives who found jobs right away and I haven't found one, I've felt worthless. I've cried a lot at night."

"I've been very aggressive," she told me the next time we talked, explaining how she had finally found a job. "I'd go right into professional offices and introduce myself and ask about the occupational therapy field here and any possibility of openings. People were very friendly and made suggestions. And when I took my résumé into personnel offices I'd ask if I could talk with someone. I thought if they could connect a smiling face with the résumé it might make more of an impression."

Joan's manner was well modulated. "In what way did your strategy seem very aggressive?" I asked. "Well, maybe that wasn't quite the right word. Maybe I mean assertive."

"You took the initiative. Wasn't that comfortable for you?" "Well," she reflected, "it would have been lovely to have been very passive, to have sat back under my husband's protection and waited for a job to come to me." "That would have been lovely," I echoed, "but do you think you would have felt the same about yourself?" "Certainly not." Joan described the self-respect and self-confidence she had gained from the search, now that she had found a job. "I did it all by myself." Her vision of a traditional marriage was, it seemed, undergoing change.

Joan's wish for professional work was not primarily financial. Nor was there pressure from her husband. Russell would support her in any career undertaking she wanted; she felt the choice was hers. Nor did it seem to be a response to societal pressures, as she had suggested earlier. Heatedly she had exclaimed, "Society makes you feel you should want a career!" as she described the priority she wanted to give her marriage.

Rather, the urgency of her wish to be professionally active was fueled by her dual move—into a new community where she was not yet recognized and respected as she had been at home, and into the new state of marriage, a state in which her own dignity had felt crucial ("I wouldn't have trailed along behind him").

"It's my need to have my part in the scenario. Russell is growing, he's intellectually stimulated, he talks to me about what's happening to him. I want to be growing and experiencing and to have something to bring to the relationship." She was reaching for a feeling of reciprocity akin to the reciprocity she experienced with her mother.

Joan worked in her profession but she soon began to feel she had reached a dead end. In Northland she was not finding the sophistication in her field that she had experienced in her home city. She felt she was lagging behind her husband. So she left her job with the plan of beginning postgraduate study in a new realm. In that interval there was a keen awareness of the difference between his status and her own, an awareness that bruised her self-esteem. "Especially when we visit our relatives, there is so much focus on Russell, the lawyer," she told me indignantly. "He's put on a pedestal, and in contrast I certainly don't feel very good about myself." What a change this seemed in a young woman who had told me she was old-fashioned, intending to give her marriage priority over all else!

My thoughts turned back three decades or more to the center where my own professional life developed—a distinguished center steeped in classical psychoanalytic thought. In my memory, I could hear the voices of men and women whose names are hallowed in the field, defining the central goal of therapeutic intervention with a woman: "to help her accept her feminine role." And what was her feminine role? It was to be the glowing hearth at home—to nourish, comfort, encourage her husband and children, subsuming her own aims to theirs, incorporating their aims as her own. It was, in fact, the role that many movers expressed as their ideal of nurturant power.

At first, as she defined the ideals she held for her new marriage, Joan would have appeared to be fulfilling that "feminine role." But as her professional goals took shape, Joan would have been seen as competitive with her man, expressing her "penis envy" through her own aspirations. Should she equal or surpass him in accomplishment, it is likely that she would have been viewed as a "castrating woman," intent on diminishing his manhood.

There has been cautious change, selective change, arising not only from the chorus of outraged women's voices but also from deeper understanding of the development of self. To be sure, feminist scholars and feminist activists alike have prompted serious questioning of the assumptions long held about woman's nature and woman's destiny. But psychoanalytic clinicians and theorists have also rethought their own conclusions. Those clinicians who have studied young children—"normal" young children in homes and nursery schools as well as child patients—and those who have probed the earliest childhood experience of their adult patients have helped us understand that there is a compelling drive towards fulfillment of innate capabilities. From the first gestures, the earliest struggles of the infant to roll over, sit up, take his or her first unsteady steps, to grasp, to throw, to take apart and put together, to speak and sing, there is a surging forward to express and activate all that lies dormant as human potential. Those clinicians and theorists have helped us understand that throughout life there is a persisting need for response to those gestures and struggles, a persisting need for recognition, encouragement, and approval.

So Joan's strivings can be understood differently now, not as a distortion of "normal" femininity, but as expectable needs for fulfillment and recognition in her work—needs that her marriage and professional frustrations in the new community had brought into focus. The convergence of marriage and move had caused an aspect of her self to emerge that she had not fully recognized. When she began her new studies, she now predicted, she would be growing and learning like Russell; her self-respect would be enhanced. In time she, too, might decide to earn a doctorate— then there would be a parity, then Joan would enjoy recognition such as Russell was enjoying. To be sure, there was a competitive tinge in her aims. Yet it seemed a constructive competition, spurring her towards full development of her potentials. And it was linked to a view of marriage as an alliance that both partners would enhance from their professional lives.

But Joan's aims didn't have a single focus. When Russell finished his professional training she would want to start having babies. "I feel clear that when we have children I'll want to be home full time, and put my career on the back burner for a while." Joan's friends were having babies, and she noticed that her own maternal longings were being kindled. Another of her potentialities was pressing towards fulfillment. And it seemed likely that her professional accomplishments would enhance her parenthood, allowing her to respond to the uniqueness of her children rather than guiding them to fulfill her own thwarted aims.

There are similarities between Frances's and Joan's stories. For both women, the move caused pain which catalyzed change. It spurred the two to shift their priorities and pursue professional work with unexpected urgency. However, the emotional cost to Frances and her family seemed much higher than for Joan. Frances needed professional help to resolve her dilemmas, Joan did not. Joan was warmed by a joyful new marriage, Frances's marriage was significantly flawed and strained by the move. Joan was emotionally supported by her mother as well as her husband through the bleak period of feeling unrecognized in the new community. Frances's mother and husband could not provide such support. In fact, as commonly happens, both young women had been drawn towards men who had many of the essential qualities of their mothers. Whereas Frances's husband, like her mother, was critical and derogatory, Joan's husband, like her mother, encouraged her to develop along whatever lines felt fulfilling. He encouraged her to be herself and to grow, and Joan was able to accept that encouragement.

Joan could explore the possibilities of Northland unencumbered, whereas Frances was responsible for the well-being of two young children who both needed her intensely and at the same time were beginning to push away her care. The equilibrium Frances had struggled to develop between her various realms of work had been disrupted four times in previous moves. This move was Joan's first.

Studenthood Into Profession

A woman's entrance into the marketplace is so often linked with relocation that the significance of the move is usually unexamined. Yet it may propel the mover across the fine line between challenges that stimulate growth, such as Joan experienced, and those that overwhelm.

Liz appeared to be coming into Northland poised at the threshold of shining opportunity. Yet the convergence of transitions associated with her move felt like a frightening entrance into adulthood. "I'm giving up my childlike roles and becoming one of the grown ups," this insightful woman told me. Although she had moved out of her natal home some years before, it had remained her home psychologically, and sustained her through a sequence of temporary living arrangements. But soon she would become a homeowner herself, and in that sense step into her parents' shoes. And not long before moving, she had given up her role as single woman to become married—it was her husband's new job that prompted the move. But most threatening of all, she was giving up her status as student to become a teacher. Feeling no assurance about her capacity to fulfill the new roles, she felt profoundly anxious about the loss of the familiar ones. At stake was her self-esteem. "Up until now I've always been preparing. Now I'm expected to be able to give. I can't seem to take that last developmental step."

At first it seemed uncertain that she would have the opportunity for that last developmental step, since she could find no work in her field of Oceanic art. It seemed likely that she would have to live away from Northland, separately from her new husband, and she wondered if the conjugal bonds were sturdy enough yet. Then, after months of searching, a professional door opened. Liz's delight mingled with her dread.

"I can't visualize making the major commitment I need to be successful in a very small and competitive field. I'm afraid you have to be selfish to make that commitment. Miles, my husband, sometimes seems quite selfish when he shuts everything out to concentrate on his research. I don't want to wall myself off. I want to be able to respond to people, to give to people." Unknowingly and unerringly, Liz confirmed the observation that:

a woman is engaged in a constant process of monitoring her own growth and change against their possible impact upon the relationships she values. This need . . . seems to be a central dynamic in women's self-definition." (Peck, 1986, p. 281)

Liz expressed the conflict between the ideal of achievement, linked to "self-serving male" focus, and the ideal of emotional provision, linked to "altruistic female" dispersion, that was alive in almost all the movers engaged in professional work. Her aims were not organized in a hierarchy, but were experienced in parallel importance.

"I want to have babies quite soon and I want to breast feed them. But I want to finish my writing, too, and start a job, and I don't see how a woman can do all that!" Liz's outcry revealed her painful state of dispersion, and she felt uncertain whether her husband would help her fulfill her aims as well as his own.

"I'm afraid Miles would find reasons not to share the baby care. He would probably have to give a lecture just when I needed him. I'm the memory in our household just like my mother used to be in hers. My husband forgets and I have to nag him, and I resent doing that."

As Liz described those fears, it was unclear whether she more greatly feared that Miles wouldn't do his share, or that she would have difficulty asking him decisively for help. Nursing her babies was to be her realm. As much as Frances, Liz seemed hesitant to give over her nurturant power.

But the need to demonstrate her professional competence was intense as well. "Even though I have doubts about the commitment, I have to prove to myself that I can be successful in my field. It's not enough to be loved and valued by my husband. He accepts me no matter what, just as I am. I have to earn the outside recognition."

Liz connected this need with her father. He had dropped out of high school and was locked into a drab, dead-end job. Liz was chosen to live out his private scenario, to fulfill his thwarted aims. Like many children whose parents can only experience their young as extensions of themselves, Liz became burdened by his hopes and needs. Her education was of prime importance to him. "Every day when I came home from school he would ask how many A's I had gotten." "And now," I commented, "it sounds as though you ask yourself how many A's you've gotten." "That's true," she said. "I hadn't made that connection before."

Her speech flowed out in lyrical images ("I love the fence posts outside our house and the way they lean under the weight of the snow, as though they're bearing the weight of their memories," she had told me, describing her rented farmhouse). Yet her writing was tortured; she was her own severest critic, laboring over every phrase. When her thoughts were on paper, she was accountable, subject to judgment (would she get an A?) Now faced with a job, she was tormented by worry about her professional performance. People would find out she wasn't as good as they thought she was, that she didn't know all that she'd been trying to convince them she knew. "They'll discover I'm really a fraud." And those worries were to plague her as long as we were in communication.

Liz's anxiety about adult competence was not caused by her move. Her ideals were unusually high, her critical conscience unusually severe. She brought within her to Northland the potential for her struggles. But her anxiety was surely aggravated as the move confronted her with new and major challenges to her feelings of worth. Paramount was exposing her professional competence, risking that she would not earn the A's that her father—and the internalized paternal critic within her—demanded of her. It was required that she expose herself, not to those accepting scholars who were already familiar with her capabilities as a student, but to strangers she might have misled into believing her more gifted than she really was.

This fear of being exposed as a "fraud," less knowledgeable than others suppose, is prevalent among women and men alike as they begin new work. For Liz, the threat of exposure felt particularly intense. It included not only the threat of repudiation by new students and new colleagues, but repudiation by her severe internalized critics as well, and an inevitable plunge in self-esteem. Those threats coincided with the task of creating a new home ("I want the furniture to be an expression of me and right now I don't know who I am," she had told me desperately), and the work of making new friends. And her marriage was still young. Her move had separated her from trusted fellow students, teachers, and friends whose affection and respect might have supported her through these multiple passages.

Moving to begin a new career, taken for granted in contemporary United States life, is thought of as exciting opportunity. As indeed it may be. It can also be painful, frightening, and conflict-ridden psychological work. It was all of that for Liz. Yet, within a few years, she was to face another move when insurmountable administrative problems developed in her workplace.

OCCUPATIONAL CONTINUITY

Striving for Professional Continuity

For movers established in their fields, work in the marketplace can be a sustaining strand of continuity, giving shape to the first exciting but bewildering and lonely weeks in a new community, affirming the mover's sense of continuity, validating her identity, and providing collegial connections. Such things can happen when work is available.

Even if they were not primarily centered in their professional lives, many movers felt certain that some professional work was as important to their well-being as their intimate relationships. Yet only two of the coupled movers had confirmed that professional opportunities were available before deciding to move. The remainder committed themselves to the move with little or no information about the prospects for work in their fields, simply assuming that such work would be available when it was wanted. In almost every case, the search for appropriate work was prolonged, and marked by disappointments and compromises along the way. A number of movers who resumed working outside their homes found it necessary to change their fields. Two were so frustrated in their quest that they left Northland in deep discouragement. To the extent that a job search could have been carried out before a decision to move was finalized—and that was usually the case—these obstacles were self-inflicted. Had they learned that the prospects were bleak, some might have chosen not to move, or to move to another area (all but two of the husbands had opportunities elsewhere). Or they might have come to terms with their disappointment while their networks of support and affirmation were still available. These movers had not taken good care of themselves.

In exploring choice among movers, I had concluded that such an absence of self-care reflected the "paradoxical self"—expressed feelings of inferiority and lack of entitlement on the one hand, and fantasies of empowerment to triumph over all obstacles on the other. As I explored work among movers, another influence became clear, namely the conflict between the ideal of nurturance and the ideal of achievement in the marketplace. They questioned whether they could focus their energies sufficiently to attain success in a profession; they questioned whether they should make a single-minded commitment. Depending on the lens through which women are viewed, such a conflict can be seen as reflecting a flawed commitment to achievement, or as expressing a wish to preserve the nurturant self. Movers experienced it both ways. Their ambivalent commitment to professional work (as traditionally modeled by men) seemed unconsciously to influence them not to find out what they needed to know to perpetuate that work.

Consciously, some movers were fully committed to their fulfillment, both in the marketplace and in love relationships—committed not just to the prospect, as college students are (Freedman, 1987), but to the actuality. Yet, since they arrived in Northland without job prospects, it took determined effort to reestablish their professional identities. And they were expected, and expected themselves, to be responsible for the psychological and logistical integration of their various realms of work. Because it is complex to balance multiple needs and fulfillments, a state of equilibrium is hardwon.

Barbara was exceptional among the movers in achieving an integrated equilibrium within two years. This young woman had left a particularly nurturing milieu to come to Northland. "I was involved in a caring network of people who related to each other intensely and very supportively. We turned to each other with every kind of need. The support among women was intense. We saw ourselves as better people and stronger than the men (though we ended up marrying them," she interjected humorously). "We tried to find broader ways of being women. We used fables and stories to find ways of thinking about unwanted work—cleaning or laundry—so we wouldn't feel diminished by it. That would be ant work, but doing that didn't make you less of a person, it wasn't demeaning." Barbara described a women's culture, akin to that which has operated powerfully in the past (Bernard, 1976).

Now Barbara had lost that supportive, affirming matrix. "When Martin comes home full of excitement and accomplishment, I feel angry." Barbara held up her hands in a gesture of warding off, as though to push away her husband's satisfaction. "What have I accomplished? I have to remind myself of my accomplishments. I've been feeling a little depressed."

In important respects, Martin's professional situation threw into bold relief the challenges that Barbara faced in reintegrating her work: finding lifespace for creativity, developing a new work structure, finding colleagues, finding clients, and absorbing and mediating their responses. Martin's work was protected by a schedule, the structure was provided, it had a central focus, he was supplied with an instant community of colleagues and mentors.

In a new milieu, with myriad new stimuli impinging on her awareness, Barbara struggled to find coherence in a day of repetitious, tiring, distracting, frustrating, fragmenting and sometimes urgent household tasks, some typical of isolated life with a baby, some imposed by the move. She strove to find a new rhythm, to reconcile conflicting wishes and needs. "When I'd go down to the darkroom, I'd be reproaching myself for not doing the laundry or playing with my baby. So I planned a schedule of tasks that I had to confront and make a decision about. I may decide not to do the laundry, but I face it. It takes a long time. When I'm rich and famous, I'll pay someone to do those things."

Through her photography, Barbara interpreted and transformed realities. Until now, she had been exploring her potential as an artist. Just before her move, she had felt ready to communicate to others through her art: "It's time to begin moving my work out to other people."

That effort was both practical and psychological. Month after month, Barbara made contacts and followed up leads in the hope of participating in an exhibition. Yet the effort felt laden with risk. "Suppose people don't like my things? I'd have to convince myself that I'm still a good person, and even that the work is still good." Barbara feared that the external criticism would activate the severe internalized critic that she identified with her father—an introject that caused her to "feel like a hellish worm."

There was a mounting need for affirmation. At a luncheon meeting of apparently traditional, conventional women, Barbara had to quell a mischievous impulse. "I had an intense urge to say something outrageous like, 'did you know I used to be a Go-Go girl?' I needed them to know I'm not normal, I'm different." Barbara's uniqueness was unrecognized. Her impression that "nobody knows who I really am" was isolating and frightening.

But after eight months of risk and struggle, Barbara was accepted into a critique group of photographers and other artists; she found understanding and kinship. Soon afterwards, her new acquaintances helped her arrange for exhibitions.

"I'm excited, and now I'm known." Now, when she tells new acquaintances she's a photographer, they will connect her with work they've read about or seen. The establishment of her professional identity has helped her feel rooted. "I'd like to stay in Northland," she told me, almost exactly echoing Frances's jubilant cry, "I love living here now!" after she became successful in the business world.

Barbara's professional fulfillment was sustained. The structure of the critique group forced productivity, and the members were helpful to each other in sharing reactions and ideas about contacts for exhibiting their work. Out of that network, friendships began to develop. So, for Barbara, a supportive milieu was created anew. She was given encouraging but realistic appreciation that could help modulate and stabilize her fluctuating self-esteem.

With her artistic career in ascendancy, and a prior experience of severe morning sickness, she had felt conflicted about another pregnancy. But 15 months after her move, feeling established professionally, she became pregnant again. Secure in her professional commitment, she could risk extending her affiliative commitment—her maternal and artistic energies seemed mutually reinforcing.

Barbara manifested "female" dispersion at its most constructive. Her energies flowed from role to role, her work embraced and integrated the realms of profession, wifehood, motherhood, and intimate friendship as well. It embodied the aims that Nellie, the single mother (discussed in Chapter 1), articulated as she developed professional work for the first time in her life: "I want my work to be an expression of all I am—my experience, my interests, my values. I don't want it to be encapsulated, a split-off part of me. How could I sustain interest if it were?"

Barbara was among the very few movers who were able to achieve a reintegration of the various realms of their work within two years. She recurrently faced conflicts concerning her priorities and serious challenges to her narcissistic equilibrium, as did most others. But unlike others, Barbara had assured herself of professional opportunities and of the presence of facilitating "sponsors" before deciding to move. Unlike others, she came to Northland with a high level of self-awareness (enhanced by earlier psychotherapy). Although the lability of her self-esteem was a source of suffering, she had a well-developed "observing ego" (if ego is understood as the organizing, integrating, modulating aspect of mental life). Even as she suffered, self-observation could ameliorate the suffering by allowing her to understand it, gain some distance from it, and act to relieve it.

"I'd like to stay in Northland," Barbara told me. But two years after her arrival, to advance his own career, her husband needed to move again.

Striving for Affiliative Continuity

Just as some movers, like Barbara, were clear about wanting to continue their professional lives, others were just as certain that they wanted lives centered in the development of their families. These women were so committed to their choice of work that it could legitimately be considered their career. They imagined it simple enough to transport that work through a move, along with the furniture and clothing. "I can be a wife and mother anywhere" was their refrain. But their experience told a different tale. The search for the new connections needed for affiliative work to be fulfilling was every bit as taxing as the hunt for professional opportunities, and the field of search was far less well defined. Donna's search, carried out with unflagging persistence and ingenuity, could serve as a model for many a bewildered newcomer.

Donna's life in France had become centered in domestic roles. Contemplating her return to the United States, she felt misgivings about expected pressure to develop a professional career, pressure that might ignite an inner conflict about her priorities. She wanted to stay at home, but knew that she needed appreciation from outside the family as well.

"I'm very ambivalent about working outside. In France, the side of me that wanted to stay home was supported. I was afraid from what I've gleaned through the media that wouldn't be the case here."

In Northland, Donna undertook to reconstruct the supportive connections she had enjoyed in France. She energetically gathered information about play groups, for her children's pleasure and for her own. Methodically, she got a listing of nursery schools from her town library, phoned several and asked the registrars for information about play groups as well. She was given names and persistently phoned.

"It wasn't easy to make myself make those calls to strangers because I'm rather shy," she confessed. But the responses were friendly, easing Donna into the next stage of visiting play groups that had openings. Noticing in one that other mothers handled their children much as she cared for her own, she became a regular member. She began to arrange lunchtimes and coffeetimes with several women she wanted to know better. Ten months after her move, the play group began to feel like a network, and four months later that feeling was secure. "It's nice to know that every week I'll be among a group of women I'll be glad to see, and they'll be glad to see me."

As much as any professional, Donna had gathered around her a group of colleagues. It had taken over a year of energetic effort, but she had successfully reconstructed one of the important strands of her identity. As in France, she was noticed and valued in her work as a mother.

But there was still a void. "I'm still the wife of a linguist, the mother of young children," she reflected. "But I'm reaching for something else." Nothing yet replaced the active role she had played in France in an organization supporting the Leboyer techniques of natural childbirth—a role that was an extension into the community of her interest and effectiveness in domestic life. "I thought perhaps I'd feel more a part of the community here if I had an outside job." So she undertook a temporary project that helped her feel connected to the academic world in which her husband worked. But it still seemed not enough. She reached some more.

"There's been a turning point," she told me four months later. She had interviewed for an administrative position. "I didn't get the job, and I was really relieved because I didn't want to give up taking care of my children. But I presented myself well, and the interviewer treated me with respect. It made me feel good to present that self—that part of my being—that isn't a wife or mother, and to have it noticed."

That recognition seemed pivotal. Donna had started some graduate studies in France, but discontinued them when she realized she didn't want the focused, specialized work of a scholar. Soon after moving to Northland, groping to find meaning in her new life, she considered publishing the studies she had done of women's lives in rural France. But she admitted, "I'm not excited about finishing the book. It's tedious. I would enjoy the recognition, though." It was soon after she enjoyed the recognition of the interview that Donna turned with renewed interest to her writing, and was further spurred on by an invitation to share her observations at an international meeting about women in rural societies.

That interest was to continue through her second year in Northland. Clear that she wanted to be home with her children, affirmed by her mothering network and her special place of leadership in it, "I felt quite free of guilt about having my own time to write. I'm not a supermom. I simply told the children I had to work. They find ways of playing on their own." Donna had reproduced elements of her own childhood: "My mother was always there for us, and that was neat. But she would encourage us to do things on our own." And Donna had also recreated crucial elements of her satisfying life in France.

Among these movers, as among all women, the wish to be at home with children could represent either a positive or negative identification with the mover's mother—being similar to the mother or being opposite from the mother. Some recalled the warmth of enjoying a mother's presence when they got home from school— "She was there for me"—and a wish to reproduce that presence for their own children. Others, consciously or unconsciously, needed to provide for their children a nurturance that their own mothers were unable to provide—a nurturance that they could vicariously experience. It was doing for the child what the mother wanted and needed in her own childhood, but didn't receive.

But every mother at home with children echoed Donna's wish for "something more," a wish that expressed several needs. There was a wish for something more to provide relief from housework that most women at times experienced as tiring, tedious, repetitious, and boring, as well as relief from childcare that at times felt frustrating, fragmenting, incessant, and depleting.

"I do love my children," said Nellie, the single mother, with quiet conviction, "but how can one person meet all those needs, play all those games? I love my children very much, but with them I'm always putting out. I get a little back, but not a whole lot right now."

"Something more" would offer a respite. It would offer companionship and support as well. Mothering networks, as Donna observed, were like an extended family. Women shared problems and solutions, comforted, encouraged, recognized, and validated each other. They supplied each other with the "refueling" essential to the healthy narcissistic equilibrium of a parent (Ornstein & Ornstein, 1985).

In other ways, "something more" would supply the "getting back" that Nellie missed. Women needed more "getting back" than children could (or should) be expected to give. Childcare is somewhat regressive. To be empathic, a mother must be able to release the childlike, playful elements in her personality. Childcare does not necessarily fulfill the need Joan described—to be learning and growing as an adult.

Whereas slightly over half of the movers endeavored to reorganize their identities around the parallel cores of affiliative work and professional careers, just under half the movers were centered in affiliative work by the end of my study. These women had redefined their identities as homemakers. But most were also committed to developing productive activity outside of their homes, activity that would allow expression of their talents, earn recognition in the community, and perhaps have the potential for future financial gain. In reaching for connection between hearth and marketplace, they could be seen as reconstructing conditions that existed before the industrial revolution. Then, before the recognized "workplace" was separated from the domicile,

> The women had become manufacturers, producing fabric, clothing, candles, soap and practically all the other family necessities. . . . They had been productive workers within the home economy, and their labor had been no less respected than their men's (Davis, 1981, p. 32).

Those movers who did feel content in full-time domestic lives were creative, they were accomplished in some form of craft or art that commanded attention from outside the home. Their products were exhibited, published, or sold. They were appreciated as women of significance outside of the spheres of motherhood or marriage.

It was an intricate tapestry of attachments, recognitions, affirmations, and opportunities that enhanced these women's capacities to find fulfillment in domestic life. This tapestry was unraveled by their moves, and had to be slowly and painstakingly reconstructed. The idea that a homemaker is readily relocatable is indeed a myth, perpetuated in the minds of women as well as men.

Among all the movers, homemakers, and professionals, the development of a realm of work (paid or not) commanding recognition outside the home was a crucial factor in the degree to which they felt at home in Northland two years after their moves.

RÉSUMÉ

A subjective sense of dispersion, perhaps arising from biological as well as psychological and social influences, was prominent among the movers. In contrast to their male partners, only a minority had sustained professional work as the primary organizer of their lives. The identity of most was expressed and affirmed through a diversity of roles and relationships, and this diversity comprised their work.

Moving ruptured myriad lines of connection, and caused an unraveling of a complex integration of roles. Even women with partners and children initially felt "invisible" in Northland. Their anxiety was expressed in the idea that "nobody knows who I am," or (more deeply disturbing) "I don't know who I am."

The reintegration of their identity required a realignment of their work priorities. Loss of accustomed roles, feelings of insignificance in the new community, and a partner's preoccupation with his own work contributed to painful internal conflicts between the mover's commitment to affiliation and her commitment to work in the marketplace. Such tensions were further heightened when the move coincided with a major role transition such as marriage or the initiation of a career.

Surprisingly few women had assured themselves of opportunities in the marketplace before deciding to move. Therefore, many who did wish to maintain continuity in their professional work encountered an unexpected paucity of opportunities. They struggled through frustration, disappointment, and depression until their work could be resumed, or until a new realm could be developed that allowed for personal growth and visibility in Northland.

Women committed to full-time homemaking engaged in intensive effort to reconstruct the supportive networks they needed for "refueling." It was apparent that homemaking was far from the readily transportable realm of work they had assumed it to be. These women also became aware of their need for some productive activity outside the home that would allow expression of their special abilities and earn recognition in the community.

S I X

Moving and Marriage

Some couples contemplating a move accept the opportunity to look together at their lives, and to look at their life together, and to consider how the move might shape their lives as individuals and as a couple. That scrutiny is especially fruitful if they can free themselves of the traditional fixation on the man's career as the over-riding concern, if they can spur each other to think about the full range of their capabilities and limits, hopes and fears, dreams and fulfillments, and if they can think about themselves as woman and man as well as a melded twosome. Some couples do just that. My study suggests that many do not.

Coupled women had considerable difficulty in considering themselves as individuals, related to but also differentiated from their loved ones. That became clear through exploring the issue of choice. It also became evident that few couples had examined the effects of previous moves, and few had seriously considered the impact this move might have on their relationship. Most of the women, and perhaps the men as well, seemed unprepared for the marital strains they experienced in Northland.

SOURCES OF TENSION

Inevitably, the stresses of moving were carried into the marriage. Thus inevitably, the relationships among many couples were seriously challenged by their moves. Separated from familiar and trustworthy sources of comfort and validation—friends, relatives, colleagues, clergypeople, health professionals—the couple needed to seek within their dyad the fulfillment of needs for recognition and nurturance that were intensified by the taxing transition. And in the absense of other confidantes, powerful emotions aroused by moving needed to be expressed and absorbed within their partnership. Furthermore, in this time of heightened need, the equilibrium in the relationship was disturbed; the availability of each partner to the other was altered by psychological states, external realities, or both. The distribution of time, energy, and interest between the marriage, the marketplace, and the development of new roles and connections needed extensive renegotiation. Only when both partners felt nurtured and affirmed themselves, could they comfortably offer nourishment and affirmation to each other. Yet when that did happen, there was the potential for constructive change and growth in two individuals and in their coupling.

Troubled Wives

Women were distressed by their moves, some briefly and most prolongedly, some mildly and most intensely. Since women were the direct focus of my inquiry, the effects of their distress on their husbands or lovers could only be partially understood, inferred from the perceptions of the wives as well as my own clinical experience with other couples. It would be expectable that the interludes of sorrow, depression, and anxiety that women described would reduce their responsiveness to their men; it would be expectable that those states would arouse concern, sympathy, anxiety, guilt, resentment, or anger in those husbands who allowed themselves to notice. Such expectations could not be confirmed.

However, the emotional states that stirred primary concern among women, insofar as those states could affect the marriage, were those of envy, resentment, and anger. There was a convergence of causes for such disruptive feelings. First, the losses of moving were painful, and women felt anger at the cause of that pain—

often the husband who needed or wished to move. Second, women experienced wounding invisibility during a time when men experienced apparent fulfillment, and this contrast generated envy. Third, women experienced heightened needs for recognition and comfort during the same period when men became less available, and this imbalance generated resentment. Finally, anger kindled by the disappointments and frustrations of settling into Northland was at times displaced onto the husband, the only available target.

"Every move we've made has resulted in a year of fighting between John and me," said Caroline, candid, forthright, accepting of her needs and her emotions, and among the few movers who seemed aware of the impact of moving on their conjugal relationship. "That's been largely a result of the cost. It's been about $5,000 per move above the transportation costs. It's getting the new home just the way you want it to be. John complained about the cost and I resented his complaints. Half jokingly, this time I said I'd have him sign a contract! But the fighting's also been a result of the strains. I've had to give up my friends and career three times." Getting the new house just the way she wanted it was the compensation she expected, and was even ready to demand. It was compensation for the ordeal of dislocation. But it seemed that Caroline accurately targeted the deeper cause for the fighting. "I've had to give up my friends and career three times."

There was further cause for anger as well. "John complained about the cost," Caroline said. Through his complaints, he covertly denied the legitimacy of Caroline's claim for compensation. He thus seemed to deny the profound effects the moves were having on her life and to show a disregard for his wife's well-being that intensified her resentment.

Caroline's acceptance of her anger, of her right to feel it and to express it forthrightly to her husband was unusual. Among movers such as Andrea—women with unattainably high expectations of themselves—resentment, anger, or even fury smouldered silently until something gave way, either the conjugal bonds or the wife's mental health.

"If you had talked with me before I had psychotherapy, I wouldn't have known how I really felt about moving. I might have said, 'It's no big deal'," Andrea said thoughtfully. She was among those women who had repeatedly moved to advance their husbands' careers and experienced no conscious sense of choice. Her self-confidence and motivation to make new friends had been eroded. She had become increasingly lonely and withdrawn, and she gradually succumbed to depression.

It was not until Andrea explored the sources of her depression with a therapist that she had become aware of fury at her husband for causing the repeated disruptions, fury that had been repressed. "Everyone moves this much," her husband had told her, thus disconfirming her painful experience. Andrea expected herself to comply—to be his superwife. She was unable to tolerate any hatred of him because such a negative emotion was dissonant with her ideals, but she was able to hate herself for failing to fulfill those ideals.

In such ways, the painful losses experienced by movers resonated powerfully through their marriages. And the women's pain was heightened by the common experience of "invisibility"—the interlude of narcissistic loss they endured before their identity was newly confirmed. The plight of the newlywed brought this into focus with special clarity.

Marriage is often linked with moving. But on the threshold of marriage, many women become more urgently concerned with questions of whether they will live with their mates, and how they will live with their mates, rather than where they will live with their mates, and what that place will be like for themselves. This can be true even of women who have visualized marriage as an egalitarian partnership. It was true of the newcomers whose moves to Northland coincided with marriage. These young women, each of whom had already embarked on a professional career, allowed aspects of their own being to be eclipsed. In the nuptial passage, they seemed to experience themselves as melded into an undifferentiated oneness with their lovers. They felt sheltered within the cocoon of their newly confirmed intimacy.

But this was temporary. This would change. Within a few months, there was growing awareness that marriage, warm and loving as it might be, was both too much and not enough. Marriage was too much in that the woman felt primarily, or totally, defined in the new milieu by her husband's identity. She needed to separate out of the conjugal melding and reclaim her own individuality. Marriage was not enough in that she needed a realm of work in which to express her own uniqueness, distinct from her husband and commanding recognition from a broader community. An experience of being perceived only as an extension of her husband's selfhood kindled outrage or pulled her into depression. Those feelings were intense and unexpected.

One might wonder whether those feelings would have welled up as intensely if the newlyweds had not moved. It seemed unlikely. Moving had ruptured connection with the familiar and sustaining sources of validation. As one mover observed, even if she had changed her status in her former community, her identity would have stayed continuously alive in the consciousness of those who knew her both before and after the transition. It would not have felt lost. It was the conjunction of moving and marriage that imposed special strains on a relationship already undergoing complex transformations.

Yet the plight of the newlywed was to some degree shared by all the wives who came to Northland without a "public" identity— those many women who had set aside their realms of work, paid or not paid, that commanded recognition outside of the home— and who had lost the affirmation of their friends as well. They felt invisible, and the emotions aroused by that state pervaded their conjugal relationships.

The state of invisibility felt like an unbearable contrast to the husband's state of fulfillment in his move. While the women movers were losing, their mates seemed to be gaining. While these women were trying to reconstruct their identities, their husbands were enjoying the continuity of their own. The men were entering a workplace that enhanced their self-esteem (by affirming their identity and their value), a workplace that enhanced their sense of mastery (by structuring their time, energy and skills), a workplace that provided nurturance (through those persons available to inform, support and facilitate—those persons such as administrative assistants and secretaries who are usually women).

"For several weeks after we moved," Liz told me, "I felt intensely crabby and irritable towards Miles. And I felt a loss of interest, a coldness, sexually. I've been really angry at him. Here he is in a fine job and goes off to his office every day. I don't have that yet." What this woman did have just then was an experience of oceanic anxiety, a loss of her sense of self.

"Nobody has asked me about my own interests or work," another mover confided wistfully. "They ask how my husband's getting along, not how I'm doing. That's made me feel terrible—very sad and very resentful of my husband, too."

Almost every woman mover felt surges of anger, resentment, and of envy as well, when their men came home emanating excitement and feelings of accomplishment while the women were experiencing their own lives as kaleidoscopic confusion.

Unavailable Husbands

Being assimilated into their own workplaces and concerned about demonstrating their own competence, many of the men were less available than usual to their wives—physically, emotionally, or both. Furthermore, this was during the time when the woman was grieving for her lost home, friends, and workplace, and experiencing an anxious sense of disconnection. It was the time when her need for him was likely to be heightened and perhaps more intense than he felt able to absorb.

To maintain her psychological equilibrium, a woman needs flexibility in her most significant relationships. That is, she needs to be able to redistribute her emotional investment among them in order to receive support and affirmation as needed. Disappointment in a love relationship may spur her to turn with heightened intensity to a friend (Peck, 1986). Moving thwarts such a flexible redistribution. The very time when a husband's unavailability might have prompted a turn towards a woman friend, no such friend was readily available. Ironically, it was the loss of the women friends that prompted the turn with intensified need towards the husband, and he was not available.

This was a time when existing faultlines in a marital relationship were likely to widen. Wives (such as Frances) who already felt devalued by their mates—taken for granted, unworthy of special attention or authentic communication—experienced their husbands' emotional or physical unavailability after moving as salt to the wounds in their self-esteem.

But the months after moving could also have profound effects on relationships that were sturdy. The experience of two couples highlighted the strains imposed by the husband's absorption in his professional work. In significant ways, these couples were similar. In one relationship, the outcome of the move was disastrous. In the other, there was recovery.

Jane and Derek's move contributed to the breakdown of their marriage. That marriage, occurring two years before their move to Northland, had been the culmination of a relationship that had grown and deepened over a five year interlude of sharing their inner worlds, examining together their life goals, their needs, and their wishes. Their marriage seemed to have been founded on self-knowledge and deep knowledge of each other.

Jane was a skilled artisan, a cabinetmaker. She had intentionally chosen a profession she could easily set aside when she had children; "It wouldn't ever become obsolete," she explained. She felt clear that she wanted wifehood and motherhood as her central roles, although she was confident that her husband would have supported whatever career choices she made. But now it seemed that he was so intensely involved in his training that he could scarcely support her in anything at all.

"Nobody knows what it's like; they wouldn't believe me," she exclaimed four months after their move.

"Can you tell me what it's like?" I encouraged.

"Well, Derek is up about 6:00 a.m., the same time as the baby, and he's out of the house soon after that. It's rare that he's home before seven. Sometimes it's six, but often as late as eight. Every third night he's gone all night. We were lucky to have a part of Christmas day together.

"When he comes home he's so exhausted and drained that he only wants to go to bed. At first Derek felt too tired to play with the baby, but I strongly encouraged him to and he found that it was actually relaxing. We almost never go out in the evening. We've gone to a few concerts and by intermission we're falling asleep." (One reason they had chosen Northland, she had told me, was to enjoy its cultural offerings.)

"There's so much I don't tell him about because he's too tired to deal with it. I also had to come to terms with his not remembering things I had told him. At first I felt hurt because it seemed as though those things weren't important to him. Other medical wives have told me they had the same experience, so I began to understand that his not remembering was a result of his exhaustion."

"I try to be there for him, to encourage him, to comfort him. I think he values me and sees me as his equal. In fact, one day he was at home feeling sick, and he was amazed at what a typical day is like for me. I was even doing less than usual so I wouldn't disturb him. He got an idea of how boring and tedious housework is, how repetitive it is, and the isolation of being at home with a baby."

"I'm proud of the work my husband does, and I'm proud of the way I support him," Jane had earlier told me with conviction. She had actively involved herself with a network of young mothers for encouragement and understanding as well as problem-solving. But after seven months in Northland, there was an ominous imbalance. In spite of some problems with her health, attention and care were continuously flowing from Jane to her husband and infant. But she was not feeling cared for in return. In her new community, still developing her mothering network, still developing untested friendships, she had too little replenishment to maintain her equilibrium.

Jane had left her husband and left Northland when I next tried to contact her. She had so emphasized her pride in her domestic life, her resourcefulness, her emotional strength, and her likeness to her strong, adaptable mother who had moved in the wake of her own husband's career and "always seemed confident it would work out," that the risk that Jane would become depleted had been disregarded. Jane was another woman who needed to experience herself as invincible; she was another woman whose ideals were unattainable. Needing to be both superwife and supermom, she overstretched her adaptive capacities to the point of collapse. Jane's life in Northland collapsed.

Jane and Derek's relationship had seemed unusually sturdy, but their experience was extreme. The stresses of moving were compounded by the rigor of Derek's training program which made him unavailable to his wife, as well as by her full-time domestic life with an infant (Had this baby been well-timed?), and by Jane's health problems. The stresses were extreme, yet they were only an exaggeration of what many other couples faced.

Ellen's tale was an interesting contrast to Jane's, especially because of similarities in the women. Like Jane, Ellen was committed to her central role as homemaker and expressed pride in her nurturant capacities. "Feeling competent is very important to me," she explained half a year after her move. "When I don't feel that, I'm uneasy and anxious. I like to have things under my control. Feeling competent means being confident that I know how to find and use the goods, services, and facilities that our family needs. Most of all, it means that I've successfully supported my husband and children through the transition." Ellen saw herself as the matrix of the family, responsible for their well-being.

"My husband was absorbed in his teaching, that was his role. He needed extra support from me until he began to get good feedback from his students. My role was childcare, and I was absorbed in that. Then it was time to turn back to each other."

"It was a heavy weight, but I knew from past experience that it would only last five or six months. I was confident it would pass. If it continued indefinitely, I would become very resentful."

Experiencing her power as the emotional provider and feeling responsible for making things go well for her family, Ellen showed considerable resemblance to Jane and to those women who experience themselves in the extremes of power or helplessness, heroism, or worthlessness. She, too, seemed to be at risk of overtaxing her capabilities or, if she could not fulfill her high ideals of competence, plunging into depression. But there also seemed to be crucial differences. Ellen recognized her limits: "I knew it would only last five or six months." She comfortably accepted her limits and her right to protest: "If it lasted longer, I would become very resentful." Furthermore, she expected and enjoyed emotional reciprocity in her relationship with her husband, Bjorn.

"Who nourishes you?" I had asked. "My family does." It was clear that by nurturing, Ellen felt nourished. Like Jane, she seemed to be one among those women who unconsciously identify with the objects of their care, so that in giving care they also receive it. Having grown up in a warm, close family, perhaps she also unconsciously reexperienced the loving care she had received as a child. But Ellen was nurtured from outside as well as from within. "Now Bjorn is very interested, concerned, and sympathetic," she told me nine months after she came to Northland. In contrast to Derek, who became exhausted, Bjorn could again provide nurturance as well as receive it. He could validate the importance of Ellen's work by concerning himself with it. There seemed to be three factors working together that helped Ellen and Bjorn's marriage to recover from the strains of moving: her recognition that her power as emotional provider was not limitless, her acceptance of her own right to receive care, and Bjorn's renewed capacity to give it. Ellen responded to her own needs as well as those of her family.

There were husbands other than Bjorn who were interested, concerned, and sympathetic, who cared about their wives' fuilfillment and happiness. Yet it seemed that they were captured by their focused commitment to their work in the marketplace. The social and psychological work of moving was primarily left to their wives, and was undertaken by their wives.

Most of the married women who had moved to advance their husbands' careers expressed sadness, loneliness, envy, and resentment—mild or intense, transient or prolonged—in response to the absorption of these men in their new professional lives. This absorption, coupled with other stresses of moving, stirred deep doubts in some women about their primary commitment to their marriage. This had happened to Jane, who could find no other resolution than to leave her husband and turn to her parents. In some women, the "loss" of their husbands stirred longings for other satisfactions. Some sought solace in alcohol, food, or even in love affairs outside of marriage—covertly punishing their husbands for their abandonment. Some women searched for a new realm of accomplishment. Terry's search told such a tale, as she explored one pathway after another.

Terry had acquiesced to the move to Northland in recognition that it allowed her to evade an entanglement of uncomfortable conflicts—conflicts disturbing to many contemporary women. The wish to please her boss by excelling in the laboratory was opposed by the wish to cut back on her hours there and be a pleasing wife. The tug of profession was opposed to the pull of marriage. The tug towards performance vied against the pull towards intimacy. The urge to please herself opposed the urge to please others. She set aside her career as engineer when she moved, in part because her interest in the field was not intense, but also because she feared it would threaten her marriage. If she and her husband, Brad, were both committed to full-time professional lives, they would have too little of themselves left for each other. Not sharing with Jane and Ellen a desire to make homemaking her central role, Terry nonetheless gave primacy to the care of her marriage.

But once in Northland, with Brad immersed in the new career that pulled his time, energy, and attention away from their marriage, Terry lacked a satisfying object of her care. This woman who, from early childhood, had enjoyed her power to provide for others, felt a loss of meaning in her life.

Terry turned to the marketplace to recapture that meaning. "I like to please people through my work, to win that pat on the head," she confided. "And the influence of the Women's Movement has made me feel that I should be representing my gender out in the world." Through her outside work, she could provide satisfaction to a business firm and support women as well. But, within months, and through circumstances beyond her control, her job lost its funding.

Now her wish to be a pleasing wife surged up with fresh intensity. With winter coming, who else would sustain the household, who else would stoke the woodstove? Yet Brad was still engrossed in his own effort to be successful, and within three months, Terry's drive to nurture was seeking a new object.

"We had decided that there were no unselfish reasons to have children, and we didn't really want them. But when my mother died—the last surviving parent between us—we couldn't bear the thought that the family line was shrivelling away. We needed a sense of continuity. We decided it was okay to be selfish. And since I might not develop a career right away, this would be a good time for a baby."

Terry stayed at home. She was creative, a talented weaver. She was proud of her skill and could keep herself well occupied. But now a need parallel to her wish to please began to reveal itself. It would be risky to exhibit and market her weavings, Terry said. People might not like them, or might not pay enough. Financial needs weren't pressing, but she wanted to be paid for her work. "I keep score in life with money, that's a value I learned from my father. I can only value my work to the degree that it is paid." That pay was the tangible equivalent of the pat on the head from her colleagues, the smiling approval of her childhood playmates when she served them cocoa. It was public recognition of her effectiveness as a provider.

With the wish for a pregnancy not yet fulfilled, with her effectiveness as a wife not yet validated, Terry felt a rising urgency to find some sphere of accomplishment. Brad had found the arena in which he wanted to prove himself, but Terry was still searching— a plight typical of the movers who were wives.

"I really enjoy studying," she explained, telling me that she had applied to a graduate program in a new field. "I enjoyed being a grad student before, spending evenings and weekends in the library. I often had to work in the lab until 4:00 a.m., but I'd work all day too, because I didn't want a late arrival questioned." Her vision of study was of being taxed to the utmost. Terry demanded as much of herself as the father she described as perfectionistic had expected of her—she had internalized his high standards of performance. But as she thought of immersing herself in study, the impact on her marriage was much in her mind.

"Brad has always complained when I'm working and he's not, even if I'm just working in the kitchen. That comes from his father calling him lazy all through his boyhood. His father worked very hard. He'd start Brad on a task and then leave him to finish it alone. If Brad stalled or played around, his father would accuse him of laziness, when it was really that Brad just wanted companionship." So when Terry was working and Brad was at leisure, the memories of his father's accusing voice were revived. In both of these young people, a critical father with high expectations had laid down a deep imprint that would influence their lives. But even recognizing his discomfort when she worked, Brad encouraged Terry to go ahead with her application. He understood her wish for a professional career.

Yet, in spite of Terry and Brad's awareness of each other's needs, their relationship soon reached a state of crisis. Terry felt such an urgent wish for a profession—for accomplishment and recognition—that if she were not accepted in graduate school, she intended to go back to Seattle. Perhaps her marriage didn't have the priority she had believed, she told me.

There was no immediate precipitant to this crisis in the marriage. Rather, it seemed that the strains of moving had been eroding it silently but seriously. Having lost her familiar pathways to achievement, her familiar sources of approval and encouragement— employers, colleagues, relatives, and friends—disappointed that she was not yet pregnant, frustrated because she hadn't yet found career opportunities that seemed challenging, and taxed by a second move within Northland, Terry was sad, lonely, anxious, and homesick. She could not, as she wanted, take care of the marriage. Nor could the marriage take care of her. Brad was having troubles of his own.

"Communication between Brad and me has been very poor. He's been working 10 hours a day, and he's feeling very dissatisfied with his teaching. He has a large class, and the students aren't very interested in the course and they complain a lot. A few days ago I came home from a lecture I'd gone to and I started to tell him an anecdote about it. He said he didn't have time to hear it, and that made me withdraw. I really wonder about the future of our relationship."

The pendulum was to swing back and forth between disappointment and fulfillment. Yet Terry's dispersion—the sense of being pulled towards different aims—was a safeguard. When Jane's marriage was in crisis, the central focus of her life was lost. In contrast, Terry's other aims could sustain her.

Terry was accepted in her program, and two years after her move she was deeply immersed. There was a troubling recognition of how important grades were to her and of her intensely competitive feelings against other students. She had recognized her competitiveness before, but it was always paralleled by her concern for others. "In engineering school, if someone came in at night to discuss problems, I wouldn't want to be unkind, so I'd listen even if I had to stay up all night to finish my work." Her ideal self included Terry the achiever and Terry the nurturer, and the power to be both in a perfect way—a heavy burden of aspirations.

Brad was not responding to Terry's immersion with the complaints that she'd expected. Instead, he had become a "workaholic" who enjoyed working on weekends when she had to study. But she noticed that she was always the first one home.

"Brad would time it intentionally so he would get home after I did. I resented always being the one to get home to a cold, dark house, and I told him so. Then we began taking turns." The need of both partners for nurturance was being expressed—nurturance symbolized by a warm, lighted house with a welcoming presence.

A few months before, Terry had felt wounded when Brad was too busy to listen to her anecdote. But now the reverse prevailed. "There've been times when he's been under pressure—for example when his teaching hasn't been going well—and I've been too busy or too burdened to listen to him. But he's usually very supportive of me." This was an ironic turnabout, since Terry's immersion had been partially motivated by Brad's unavailability.

At that earlier time, Terry had considered moving back to Seattle, giving priority to a profession over a seemingly empty marriage. But now that priority felt alien. Terry was offered an excellent summer placement in another city. She accepted it jubilantly. "But right afterwards I felt physically ill, as though a force was pressing me down into my chair. I realized the job would entail seeing Brad only on weekends, and that might happen again next year. Then it might be every other weekend and we'd drift apart. I realized I really did want to be his wife, and I didn't want to go. It was very embarrassing, but I called back and declined."

To protect her marriage, Terry accepted a less prestigious summer job. But there was a skew in priorities between husband and wife. Terry gave up a job because of Brad, but Brad was clear that he would not be willing to leave Northland because of her profession. "He's been dedicated to his field since he was five. He really loves it. He feels that my interest is recent and not consolidated. Why should he give up his goals? That could change, though, if I really became committed to my field."

As clearly as any couple, Terry and Brad played out the complex scenario of finding an equilibrium between two major realms of need: the need for expression and recognition of abilities that a professional career can fulfill in women as well as men, and the need both have for nurturance at home—nurturance represented by light, warmth, and a welcoming, listening, responding presence. These realms are perhaps the adult counterparts of childhood needs for what has traditionally been linked to the mother—warmth, comfort, and unconditional love, and also for what has been the role of traditional father—he who encourages and praises accomplishment, responding less to the child's being, as does the ideal mother, than to the child's doing.

Contemporary couples such as Terry and Brad turn to the "paternal" outside world for recognition of their doing and the "maternal" inside for nourishment of their being. They do so with greater than usual intensity when moving has deprived them of both nurturance and recognition from family, intimate friends, and associates in the marketplace. Then each must serve the other as the "maternal" inside source, and support the other in finding the "paternal" outside source that they need. That is a heavy burden on each partner, and on the relationship as well.

Stressed Husbands

Brad, Bjorn, and Derek were not only immersed in their new work, but clearly worried about their performance as well. Most of the women movers noticed signs of unhappiness and anxiety in their lovers or husbands—restless and interrupted sleep, stares of worried preoccupation, irritable responses, and gloomy expressions. It was obvious that many men, as well as women, were severely stressed by their moves.

Most, if not all, felt at least transient anxiety about whether they would be successful in their new jobs or their studies, or in finding meaningful occupations after retirement. And there were disappointments in the workplace, sometimes serious ones. In the light of our cultural assumption that moving is a significant pathway towards career success, the numbers were surprising. Among the 30 men who moved to advance their careers, 14 experienced intense disappointment within two years (according to their wives), 5 others felt uncertain whether the outcome would eventually be good, and only 11 felt well satisfied. But even the 11 didn't immediately achieve success (and, I later learned informally, professional life had gone awry for several of these men also).

At least a quarter of the men expressed keen loneliness to their wives. Whether or not they needed intimate friendship comparable to what the women longed for—and most wives felt that their husbands did not—they did miss shared recreation and camaraderie with other men. They seemed to find warm companionship no easier to come by than did their wives. And several men experienced the added bleakness of having their marriages seriously threatened as a consequence of the move.

Those men whose moves seemed unsuccessful must surely have experienced some loss of self-respect. And in all likelihood, they experienced guilt for the hardships imposed on their families.

Wives of Disappointed Men

For the wives of disappointed men, the pain of loss and the stress of transition was compounded by a bitter awareness that the disruptive move might have been made in vain.

Genuine sympathy for their husbands was mixed with apprehension. Since the family's future was again uncertain, the wives felt some futility about investing time and energy in making connections in Northland. It also occurred to several women that their highly mobile husbands might have personality problems interfering with their capacity ever to achieve satisfaction in their careers. They were worried, and the worry was paralleled by mounting resentment and anger towards their husbands, and towards the people or circumstances responsible for the husband's defeat. In two ways, the threat to the husband's career served as a serious narcissistic threat for the wife.

An intense frustration was confronted by those women who relied on their husband's public identity to fuel their own self-esteem; those women on whom the title Mrs. Doctor, Mrs. Director,

Mrs. Professor conferred pride and a feeling of special importance. They had endured the losses and disruptions of moving, but then were denied their special status when their husbands were unable to achieve success in the new workplace. Thus their husbands failed to provide narcissistic rewards needed by the wives.

The disappointed wives of disappointed men also had to confront the limitations of their own power of provision. For example, Rina, whose move was altogether in the service of her husband's aims, felt painful doubts when she realized that his aims would not be fulfilled in Northland. Reluctant as she had felt about moving, she had been among the many movers who expressed the conviction, "It's up to me to make it work," charging themselves with responsibility for the accomplishments of husband and children as well as their own. Unable to "make it work," she felt a frightening loss of confidence in herself as well as her husband.

"I can't let on how scared I really feel because then he wouldn't feel supported," she said. "But I wonder if the outcome could have been different for him if I'd been more involved, done more entertaining, or gotten to know some of the people he's had trouble with." Rina invoked the image of her ideal self, the powerful, nurturant self that could and should have provided a "fix." Recognizing her failure to fulfill that ideal, she felt helpless, guilty, and ashamed.

Rina's plight clearly showed the vulnerability of those women whose sense of empowerment is directed towards unfulfillable aims. Many influences other than a wife's will shape her husband's destiny. Rina's disappointment also showed the vulnerability of those women who seek fulfillment primarily through the achievements of loved ones. Women able to accept the realistic limits of their power to empower others, as well as their right to direct, personal fulfillment are more resilient. Caroline was such a woman.

Caroline's response to her husband's problems revealed aggression constructively used to maintain boundaries between his needs and hers, and to safeguard her own. Caroline, the frequent mover who had told me that "every move has resulted in a year of fighting," had insisted that her husband openly accept responsibility for the move to Northland. When he suggested that the move would benefit the whole family, she challenged that. She made it clear that it was he, not she nor the children, who wanted to move. She insisted that John tell the children they were moving because of him, and that he recognize that she was doing it for him. He accepted that responsibility.

But within three months, John's firm encountered financial problems and threatened to break his contract.

"John was very upset and anxious. He said, 'maybe we should never have moved here.' I just didn't want to hear that." Caroline felt overwhelmed. "I just went horizontal."

Soon afterward, John resigned from the firm that had not stood by their agreement and joined another, based in another state. He wanted to move back to the area they had left. But this time Caroline and the children confronted him with their incapacity to absorb more disruption and losses. So John accepted a compromise—a heavy schedule of business travelling.

Within 16 months after their move, John was convinced that "coming here was a terrible mistake." He felt friendless and lacking connection to the community in spite of all the efforts of his resourceful, friendly, energetic wife to build a network of connection for him as well as herself. The end of the story is not known. But because they could confront their rights and responsibilities together, I would expect that this couple would forge their future together, neither serving as sacrificial lamb for the other, each feeling clearer about individual needs and ways to find fulfillment.

Communication Barriers

Unfortunately, in the period of heightened need around moving, many couples were unable to open themselves to each other—to share their private, inner worlds and to be receptive to those of their partners. The holding back could occur on the woman's side or on the man's. Inner conflict about expressing anger and a perception of the partner as fragile played significant roles.

The belief that anger is at variance with femininity is deeply embedded in Western cultures. Early Christian teachings, for example, defined the ideal Christian wife as self-effacing and "free from anger" (Anderson & Zinsser, 1988, p. 81). This precept has persisted. The mentally healthy and feminine woman has continued to be defined as one who is devoid of anger, especially towards men—an ideal reinforced by the perception of the angry woman as "ferocious, envious, vengeful, or castrating" (Bernardez-Bonesatti, 1978, p. 216).

Women have been and are the primary caregivers to both children and men. An image of an angry woman is dissonant with the image of woman as "caring, tending, and nurturing" (Miller, 1983, p. 4). Furthermore, since caregiving is a role with great intrinsic power, the possibility that such power should be exercised under the influence of anger is a dangerous prospect. The cultural interdiction against female anger may derive from this dissonance and this threat.

To remain alive over time, a taboo must resonate between the system of meanings that is culture and the intrapsychic life of individuals. Not only men, but many women as well, dread female anger. They both "hold unconscious beliefs in women's omnipotence and potentially destructive power" (Bernardez-Bonesatti, 1978, p. 215), deriving from their experience as infants vis-à-vis the mother.

In the girl, fury generated by the inevitable frustrations imposed by the maternal caregiver and by the infant's ambivalent struggle to individuate from her, it becomes projected onto the mother and then internalized. As the girl's identification with the mother proceeds, this image of the powerful, angry, destructive mother becomes an element in her representation of self. In fact, "women's self-experience of being weak . . . is often a defensive retreat from a more frightening self-experience—that of an omnipotently destructive, castrating individual. . ." (Lerner, 1980, p. 139).

The anxiety generated by this self-representation can be reinforced by separation anxiety. That is, anger, a divisive emotion, can arouse a sense of separateness from the object of the anger, even an experience of momentary aloneness (Bernardez-Bonesatti, 1978). Such a feeling of separatedness may be tolerated less by women than men because the girl's early differentiation from the mother, who is also the object of continuing identification, is likely to be more complex and less complete than for the boy (Lerner, 1980). The subjective state of autonomy may feel less comfortable for women than for men.

Most movers disclosed and freely discussed their anger with me. Their forthright disclosures would seem to negate these beliefs that anger in women is not tolerated by either men or women. Yet that would be an inaccurate conclusion. In a few movers, anger had been unconscious earlier, and contributed to a clinical depression; it had become consciously recognized only in the process of psychotherapy. In a few movers, anger was partially expressed through symptoms such as sexual dysfunction, alcoholism, or exacerbation of a chronic illness. And among many movers, although anger was verbalized to me, a woman and a psychotherapist, it was not directly expressed to the husband. In fact, when group discussions of moving took place, both during and after the study, women asked for tapes or written material that could be played or shown to their husbands. Thus they conveyed the wish that I could tell the husbands what they felt unable to say. When their anger did break through directly, it caused intense distress.

"I was very depressed. I cried a lot," a young mover remembered. "I was angry at my husband and I told him so, and that made him feel very guilty. He's my closest friend and a wonderful man. But by the end of the day, when he came home, I'd be all pent up." She experienced a melange of feelings—the anger that erupted, concern about the guilt it caused in her husband, and regret to feel angry towards a wonderful man who was her closest friend. Most of the movers felt deep affection and concern for their mates. They felt tormented by the tension of coexisting love, resentment, anger, and envy—a tension related to the possibility that the husband or the relationship might be harmed.

Bernardez-Bonesatti (1978, p. 216) observes that there is "an unconscious belief in the excessive vulnerability of the male to critical, disapproving, rejecting, or directly attacking behavior from females . . ." Among the movers, such a belief was far from unconscious. "I don't want to burden him" was a sentiment I heard often, even from some of those women who characterized their husbands as their "best friends." The holding back seemed strangely at variance with the very qualities that had been characterized as central between female "best friends"—honest communication of deeply personal experiences and feelings, mutuality, and reciprocity. Towards their husbands, these women felt protective and concerned that the men shouldn't experience an emotional overload while they were dealing with their own transitional challenges. It was not only anger that was withheld. The women expressed doubt that their mates would have the emotional resilience to absorb troubled feelings of any sort. In this respect, the men were perceived as fragile.

Terry, for example, protected Brad from emotional distress in a variety of ways. She had taken on herself the painful task of sorting and packing when they moved because Brad seemed immobilized by the feelings that were aroused, and her protection continued long after the move.

"It makes him feel bad if he knows I'm feeling sad or homesick, so I try not to let on. I've heard so many women say how much they resent their husbands for bringing them here. Some of them seem to hate everything about life here. Why don't they leave? How can their husbands bear it?"

"I can't let the floodgates open on Gerald," Cecile told me, referring to the intense grief she was feeling and partially concealing from her husband. "It would burden him too much. He really doesn't want to know how I feel. He gets angry." Gerald warded off her feelings, she suspected, because of the threat that they would arouse his own. "He hasn't ever been able to express his own feelings. He sees emotional distress as a weakness. He's afraid that if he gives in to it, he'll really plunge."

Concern about the husband's vulnerability was a prominent motive in the attempts many women made to conceal their troubled feelings, although it was surprising that these perceptive women failed to recognize how much of their emotional state would be communicated without words—through facial expression, tone of voice, and body movement. But there was another strong motive at work, although less clearly recognized by the women themselves. Like Terry, many of the movers experienced themselves as powerful nurturers. Their ideal was to provide care and comfort to husbands as much as to children. When that ideal was unfulfilled because of their own distress, these women felt a loss of self-respect and shame.

"Women are less satisfied with the level of expressive interaction and companionship in marriage than men" writes Voydanoff (1988,

p. 272). Men's constriction in self-expression is often targeted as the source of their wives' disappointment. Yet women contribute as well. Among the movers, the woman's image of herself as powerful and of her husband as fragile inhibited expressive interaction between them. Yet, ironically, the holding back of troubled feelings could only deprive the women of the sharing and comfort their mates might have offered. It could only worsen the woman's loneliness, sadness, resentment, and in turn, intensify her shame.

"I cry a lot at night," a young wife told me.

But private tears were not only shed by the wives. One night, many months after their move, Donna realized her husband was quietly crying. For the first time, Donald admitted how unhappy he had felt in Northland. But, aware of his wife's sorrow, he hadn't wanted to burden her with his pain as well.

Many men, it seemed, played out their own lonely scenarios of stoicism, perhaps fearful of a regressive slide into childlike need, perhaps entrapped by the gender armor that our culture imposes on men—the armor that molds them to believe that emotion is weakness, weakness is womanly, and to be womanly means no longer to be a man. Whatever their motive, such withholding contributed to the loneliness and intensified the anxiety and sadness they felt about their move. They, too, were deprived of the comfort of sharing.

RESOLVING THE STRAINS

One coupled mover gave priority to her professional career above her marriage. All others were as committed to the work of affiliation as to the work of the marketplace, or more so. Their role as caregiver to the husband and caretaker of the marriage was central in their sense of self. It may have been because of that high level of commitment to marriage that only two couples separated during the two year time span of the study, in spite of the severe stresses upon their relationships.

Yet only one-third of the women formed new, intimate friendships within two years, only one-half felt at home in

Northland within that time, and only one-third of the men were satisfied in their new workplace. So many of the marriages were still burdened by heightened needs, disappointments, frustrations, and the powerful emotions associated with loss. Those relationships were at risk, and the risk would be further intensified for those couples who were to move again.

Yet among some couples, there were signs of positive change and growth, and three factors seemed crucial in fostering that: the woman's capacity to recognize, accept, and lay claim on behalf of legitimate needs of her own; the man's capacity to be responsive to those needs; and a shift in the balance of gaining and losing.

Whereas at the beginning of their lives after moving, many of the men seemed to be enjoying gain while the women were suffering loss, the woman's increasing fulfillment in her own spheres (when that did occur) allowed her to share more readily in the pleasure of her mate's fulfillment in his professional realm. It allowed her to feel more compassion as his losses became apparent. This could set into motion an upward spiral of reciprocal concern and care.

For example, Barbara's resentment and envy of Martin's excitement and sense of accomplishment in his work diminished when she began finding collegial encouragement and public recognition of her own talents as a photographer. Supported by this recognition, and by the growing friendships she was so keenly aware she needed, she felt genuine concern as Martin became anxious about his own work, and began to experience loneliness himself. Lovingly, not grudgingly, she found herself wanting to encourage him and provide social contacts for him through her own network. There seemed a growing reciprocity in their expressions of care, an acknowledged interdependence that was expressed clearly when they faced another move and actively factored into their decision the needs and preferences of both.

For many women, accomplishment in the marketplace was pivotal in reducing marital tensions after the move. Energy and interest so invested were not drawn away from the work of affiliation. To the contrary, the enhancement of the woman's self-confidence, and the validation of her worth, heightened her energy and interest at home.

Barbara had worked diligently to develop the friendships and the professional recognition she needed, and Martin had not had a major role in that (although he seemed to have fully accepted her right to fulfillment of her needs as an artist and a woman, distinct from her needs as his wife). In other instances, not only sympathetic understanding such as Martin's, but also active support and a willingness to change himself was needed from the man. Some of the men did show a capacity to respond when the problems were brought into focus. This was usually at the woman's initiative, perhaps because the woman was more attuned to the nuances of relationship, perhaps because she had greater ease in openly expressing her feelings. But an essential factor in the movement towards change was the woman's own capacity to be responsive towards her own needs, to take care not only of her husband but of herself as well.

Women like Rose could do that. "I've been very worried about Herbert," she told me half a year after her move, a retirement move that she had at first felt to be joyous. "I see him just sitting, staring off into space, not doing anything much. He tries to be helpful to me, he offers to wash the dishes or do the laundry. But I don't really want him to. I resent it when he tells me we're low on eggs. It's sweet of him to notice, but it feels like interfering. That's my domain. And when he goes to the supermarket with me, I find myself shrinking away, not wanting to be seen shopping together because that evokes an image of uselessness. He's around all the time and I feel sort of trapped. I don't feel free to go out on my own because I'm concerned about leaving him alone."

Rose's sentiments were echoed by other women who had moved later in life, and whose husbands had difficulty finding new roles and relationships to replace the ones that had been lost. These retired or retiring husbands, in fact, experienced stresses similar to those endured by the women movers of all ages.

But then the lines that Herbert had cast out caught hold; he found a challenging position in the field from which he had "retired" and, exhilarated, he became immersed.

"I was in the doldrums," Rose confided. "He began working long hours, six days a week. I felt resentful and angry. We had planned to develop new facets of our lives together after we retired, and he's breached the contract." Fortunately, Rose was able to express those feelings to Herbert, and he was responsive. He modified his schedule to make space in his life for a changing and perhaps deepening conjugal companionship.

Between Rose and Herbert, like Barbara and Martin, there already was a foundation of mutual respect, acceptance, and care. This had not been true among all the couples, especially those in which the woman had repeatedly abdicated rights and responsibilities in making choices about moving, and the man had willingly accepted the prerogative of choice as his own. Among them, there was a complementarity of roles, but not a mutuality of concern. Change within those couples involved a deeper turbulence.

For example, the psychotherapy she sought for depression not only freed Andrea to develop new friendships (Chapter 4), but profoundly affected her marriage as well. Recognition and gradual acceptance of her anger towards her husband, acceptance of her right to enjoy sustained connections of her own, and a rising self-esteem as her guilt and shame about failing as a "superwife" were reduced, allowed her at last to begin making claims on behalf of her own needs. The energy of her anger began to be used constructively.

For the first time, she participated in a decision about moving. For the first time, she destroyed the cartons afterwards declaring, "This is the last move!" And, through often-stormy arguments with her husband, she began to make requests for his increased presence, domestic responsibility, and involvement with their children. Kenneth began responding to her claims for mutuality.

This renegotiation was as troubling for Andrea as for Kenneth, or perhaps more so. It required that she challenge his expectations and her own that she be a superwife and supermom. It required that she endure the residual guilt and shame that welled up when she failed to fulfill that ideal of the powerful, all-giving self. But as her self-esteem became more resilient, she was able to do that without plunging into depression. In this couple's relationship, as well as the relationships of other movers, growth was an outcome of recognition by both partners that the woman as well as the man had both needs and limitations.

RÉSUMÉ

The intense emotional states aroused by moving resonated powerfully through the movers' marital relationships, especially in the absence of other confidantes.

Even the most loving wives struggled with envy of husbands who seemed fulfilled just when the women were feeling invisible. They struggled with resentment of husbands who were less available than usual just when the women felt a heightened need for comfort and recognition. They struggled with anger towards husbands whose needs had been the cause of the move.

Husbands were stressed as well, giving signs of loneliness and fear of failure. In fact, 14 of the 30 men who moved for career advancement experienced keen disappointment in their new workplaces. Their lack of success stirred apprehension and resentment in their wives, depriving them of vicarious recognition through their husband's accomplishments as well as the satisfaction of "making the move work."

During the stressful transition, there were barriers against effective communication between the partners. Wives were constrained by a wish to avoid burdening men whom they perceived as psychologically fragile with their own sadness, loneliness, anxiety, and depression. And they were constrained by their dread of experiencing and expressing hostile feelings towards their men. Husbands were constrained (in the view of their wives) by their greater difficulty articulating emotional states.

Many marriages seemed at risk during the two years of the study. Effective, growth-enhancing resolution to the strains seemed to depend on the woman's capacity to recognize and act responsively towards her own needs as well as her partner's, and the man's capacity to be responsive towards those needs. Both partners needed affirmation from outside the home to set in motion an upward spiral of reciprocal concern and care.

SEVEN

Concluding

In the United States, moving is a significant aspect of the lives of contemporary women. In order to learn how moving can shape women's lives, and how women's psychology can influence their moves, the subjective experience of 42 movers was explored in depth over a time span of two years. The inquiry was carried out in unstructured interviews which allowed the most compelling issues spontaneously to emerge. The insights gained were further enriched by the accounts of 100 other movers in group discussions.

CHOICE AND THE FEMALE PSYCHE

Ambiguous Choices

Moving begins with choice. Exploration of the way the movers had gone about making this choice, one that would deeply affect their lives, revealed significant aspects of these women's sense of self.

Coupled women and women moving independently dealt with their choices quite differently. Whether the move was imbued with anxiety and sadness, or with optimism and joy, the independent movers had made decisions about moving that gave recognition to their own needs—especially their needs for work in the marketplace and for sustaining relationships with relatives or friends. They felt a clarity about their needs, and took responsibility for trying to fulfill them.

Without doubt, there are also coupled women who make such authentic choices for themselves, in partnership with husbands or lovers, male or female. There were a few such women among the core population.

But, in contrast, most coupled women had great difficulty making a choice about moving that was as responsive to their own needs as to the needs of their partners—this after two decades of dialogue energized by the Women's Movement; after two decades of rethinking the roles, rights, and relationships of men and women! These women were widely varied in age and included professionals as well as homemakers. Some felt they had no right to choose. Some evaded the discomfort of choice. Some believed they had actively chosen or even had the primary influence on the decision. But when the grounds for their decisions were explored, it became clear that many of these choices were illusory. That is, consciously or unconsciously, in ways either subtle or blatant, most of these women had discounted themselves. Choices were focused predominantly on the man's needs rather than the needs of the woman.

These coupled women had difficulty distinguishing their needs from their men's needs, as though they felt undifferentiated from their men. They had difficulty recognizing what was important in their own lives as distinct from their men's lives. They had difficulty accepting the legitimacy of wishes that were identified, and difficulty taking responsibility for their fulfillment. Again and again, irrespective of whether the woman's work was primarily a professional career or the work of affiliation, I was told of decisions to move that were made with disregard for some important aspect of the woman's being—disregard that would influence her life adversely for months or even years.

The moves of these couples were not mandated by institutional requirements; they were voluntarily made. With only a few exceptions, the man had not seized the choice. Rather, the woman had given it over to the man or merged her choice with his. She had avoided asking him to take as much responsibility for her well-being as she took for his.

Helplessness and Power

Such expressions of self-disregard would seem to support the widespread belief that women have low self-esteem, generally lower than men's. Yet something different was disclosed. As the movers talked about choice, they communicated not pervasive inferiority but paradoxical self representations. They clearly experienced themselves as *both* inferior and superior, *both* unworthy and heroic, *both* helpless and powerful—sometimes simultaneously, sometimes in alternation. Such contradictions were prevalent, and in many instances quite extreme. Precariously balanced, the self-esteem of these women could see-saw up and down.

With two probable exceptions, these movers did not show the hallmarks of the borderline or narcissistic personality disorders currently receiving much attention from mental health professionals. However, if the term *narcissistic* is understood to denote mental functions that maintain the cohesiveness, continuity, and the positive emotional coloring of the sense of self (Stolorow, 1975), these women did show vulnerability in their narcissistic equilibrium. It was revealed with particular clarity in the coupled women's discussion of choice. Perhaps such vulnerability becomes heightened in an intimate relationship between woman and man. Yet it may have been just as prevalent, but less clearly expressed, among the single women as well. Such vulnerability may, in fact, be widely prevalent among women, reflecting characteristics of our culture that will be discussed in Chapter 8.

Women more comfortably disclosed their feelings of inferiority and helplessness—as though it is acceptable for a woman to have such feelings—than their sense of superiority and power. But heroism and power were revealed in their fantasies, and in the expectations they held out for themselves. Some had achieved excellence in professional work, yet the sense of empowerment was most clearly expressed in relation to the family. It was psychological power these women spoke of, power in the realm of personal relationships. It was power to shape their families' destinies, an expansive vision of the woman enabling husband and children to find happiness and achieve success in their new milieu, exemplified by the commonly spoken phrase, "It's up to me to make it work." The movers believed themselves to have greater capacities to absorb emotional distress than their men who, in this respect at least, they perceived as more fragile, more brittle. They believed themselves to be empowered to endure serious losses and myriad disruptions, not only their own but their families' as well.

Their "paradoxical selves" did not serve women well in considering their moves. Experiencing themselves as helpless and unworthy, they felt little possibility or right to make claims for their own needs. Experiencing themselves as powerful and heroic, they disregarded difficulties and overestimated their capabilities. And the vulnerability arising from these contradictions was intensified by the woman's tendency to experience herself as partially merged with her loved ones. There was a fluidity of boundaries succinctly described by one mover's words: "When things don't go right for my husband and sons, their pain is my pain."

These women failed in significant ways to clarify the elements that made their own lives meaningful, that fostered their work of affiliation as well as their work in the marketplace. They failed in significant ways to explore whether a move would allow those elements to be recaptured. These movers, it seemed, took better care of others than of themselves. Rather heedlessly, they subjected themselves to a highly stressful life experience.

Many paid a high toll in suffering. They experienced grief, depression, and anxiety related to myriad object losses as well as losses of aspects of self. Furthermore, they felt shame and guilt about those unexpected reactions—reactions which reverberated strongly in their love relationships. And even while those states were being endured and mastered, women were challenged by the three other major realms of moving: recreating home, developing new friendships, and reengaging in work.

RE-CREATING HOME: OVERVIEW AND OUTCOMES

Meanings of Home

Home, for these movers, had layers of meaning. It meant a milieu that was safe, above all, but also strong, warm, enfolding, and reliable. In a woman's absence, home would remain there dependably unchanged, awaiting her return. In these respects, home seemed an embodiment of a benign maternal presence—a "holding environment" (Winnicott, 1965). Home was a place of belonging, a milieu in which the qualities of self (taste, values, abilities, emotions) could be freely expressed and appreciated by others. In these respects it seemed an embodiment of identity. Home was a milieu in which personal and family history were recorded, and in this respect it seemed an embodiment of continuity. The loss of home could mean experiencing a profound loss of safety, and perhaps a rekindling of the deep anxiety once aroused by separation from mother; it could mean experiencing the anxiety aroused by loss of identity and loss of the secure feeling of continuing-to-be.

For a minority of the movers, the loss of the actual dwelling designated "home" had been a major source of pain. As an expression of self in its design and decoration, as a representation of self to others, as a milieu within which significant relationships developed and within which a woman experienced her nurturant power, and as a repository of personal and family history—in such ways their dwellings had been deeply imbued with special meanings.

But whether or not there had been deep attachment to the dwelling, it had been a realm of mastery that was lost. Moving meant enduring disorientation, confusion, disorganization—a loss of control, a temporary loss of the sense of competence that is a foundation of self-esteem. A few movers tried to circumvent those troubling states by settling in swiftly, with intense effort. Most movers had neither the concentrated time nor the energy available to accomplish that. The interval of feeling out of control, disorganized, or incompetent lasted weeks or even months and was rekindled among the half who moved again within Northland. It caused these women to feel irritable, anxious, and depressed.

The majority found it tolerable to leave the physical structure of their home, but the artifacts and furnishings inside the dwelling were the carriers of special meaning. With a move in the offing, choices had to be made, choices that impelled the mover (usually the woman rather than her partner) to re-experience the memories and meanings associated with those artifacts and furnishings. Usually, for practical reasons, some of those objects had to be left behind. In that divestment, relief and pain were mingled but usually askew—relief at the casting away of burdensome clutter was overshadowed by pain, sometimes exquisite pain, at the loss of a segment of personal history, a segment of the self.

Reconnecting to Home

As they felt able, movers went through rituals of possession. Some needed to "exorcise" those other presences, the previous occupants, by vigorously cleaning out their vestiges, their dust, crumbs, and stains. As they felt able, movers completed the ritual of possession by imprinting their dwellings with the stamp of new presences, themselves and their loved ones.

A third of the movers were able to recreate the sense of their home in their Northland dwellings within the two-year time span. These were the fortunates who had the opportunity and the financial means to find and buy dwellings that appealed to their taste in attractive locations. Owning their homes and having the resources, these newcomers could express themselves freely through their decorations, and could also reestablish their sense of continuity through the furnishings and artifacts they moved with them, linking past with present. The lives of almost all of these women were centered in domesticity, so they also were able to invest time and energy in homemaking. And they expected their stay in Northland to be extended, perhaps permanent, so the investment seemed worthwhile. (Yet, I later learned, some had moved again within five years because of their husbands' disappointments or difficulties.)

The majority were less favored. In some, the drive to decorate their new habitats was seriously dampened by the anxiety and depression generated by their move. Depleted of confidence and energy, they were drawn into a downward spiral. Their difficulty mastering the physical move caused further plunges in their self-esteem, which further reduced their competence and zest, and thus further delayed the satisfaction of recreating a home.

There were realistic obstacles as well as emotional ones. Many women were disappointed in the dwellings they could afford, many had to rent because buying was too costly in locations close to the workplace or in the desired school district. Many had their impulse to decorate stifled by limitations in the rental agreement, or they felt restrained by their sense of transience, knowing they would soon have to move on. The majority were forced to compromise, and giving up their daydreams about their new homes was yet another loss.

Yet some of the movers who were disappointed in their dwellings through the two year time span had come to feel "at home" in Northland. Conversely, some newcomers who were delighted with their new habitats at the end of two years still felt unconnected to Northland in significant ways. Feeling at home in the dwelling was insufficient. The psychological state of "feeling at home" included but extended beyond the dwelling into the surround.

Other Linkages

Feeling at home could creep in, unbidden, at random times and places. A scent—the pungency of a Gauloise cigarette, the tantalizing piquancy of garlic, oregano, or pepperoni near a pizzeria, the evocative sweetness of lilacs after a spring rain—might kindle memories of special times and places and (especially) relationships from the past, and the emotions imbuing those memories would well up and flow into the present. Contented feelings or joyous feelings would begin to pervade the new milieu. There would be linkage of past with present, present with past, a validation of the continuity of existence and of relatedness. Such experiences were quite common. Far less common was a linkage to the immediate environs, the neighborhood. To be sure, people seek connection in various ways. In settled life, many value privacy above proximity. For the newcomer, confronted with unfamiliarity and potential danger, there is a sense of safety and comfort in feeling connected to neighbors. Yet only six of the 42 movers felt positively connected to their neighborhoods at the end of two years.

"Community" is an abstract idea representing various units or organizations of people. Only one of the movers who was a newcomer to Northland developed a sense of connection to her particular town within two years; through her activism, she appreciated it as a political entity.

The predominant channel of connection between movers and "community" was through particular affinity groups. These were groups in which members shared common values and interests, and worked towards common goals. They were associations of people, formal or informal, in which the mover recognized others (thus experiencing a sense of mastery); gave expression to her capabilities (thus experiencing a sense of effectiveness); and was given recognition by others (thus experiencing a sense of affirmation). About half of the movers did experience such a feeling of connection.

Among the other half, a few had been so absorbed in intensive professional development or in love relationships that there was scarcely time or energy to become involved in new affinity groups. The remainder expressed disappointment at their lack of connection, or frank alienation against the mores and values that they perceived (accurately or not) in their particular Northland community. It was a question of whether the mover attributed the absence of connection to flaws in Northland or flaws in herself. In either case, it was the felt absence of having a special place in Northland that was wounding.

Overall, through one or another line of attachment, half the movers felt at home in Northland by the end of two years and half did not. For two reasons, this outcome was striking. On the one hand, the study population was composed of intelligent, educated women who had many capabilities to contribute to others, and who actively strove to make connections. On the other hand, Northland is extremely accessible. There is a low level of crime, and a high level of public friendliness and trust. Few doors are locked either literally or metaphorically—most community events and organizations are open to anyone interested, and local government is implemented through the open forums of various Town Meetings. From these perspectives, it should be easier to develop a sense of connection within Northland than throughout much of the United States.

Clearly, the state of feeling at home is composed of many elements. It includes feeling safely sheltered, it includes recapturing one's competence and expressing one's individuality within a dwelling, but it extends beyond hearth and family. Feeling at home includes a sense of familiarity and effectiveness in using the resources of the community. Of prime importance, it means developing a realm in the community in which a woman's specialness can be both expressed and given recognition. Initially experiencing the narcissistic threat of being "invisible" or "nobody," the mover needs to become a visible "somebody." A time span of two years allows all these elements to begin developing. More time may be needed to bring them to fruition.

FRIENDMAKING: OVERVIEW AND OUTCOMES

Most of the women, single and coupled, had separated from close friends when they moved. Persistent efforts were made to keep those friendships alive, either through eager visits (for those with the leisure time and financial means) or through heartfelt letters and phone conversations that were difficult to end. There was comfort from those attempts to sustain connection, to recapture an intimacy becoming elusive. But there was poignancy as well. Sending the letter or hanging up the phone made the separation feel real.

Unexpected Grief

The mover's intense focus on the new environs could mask the sense of loss. But sooner or later, almost every mover, single or coupled, began to grieve for her lost intimates—those women who were both objects of love and sources of love, those women with whom there was a deep empathic bond. Experienced in the interlude of psychological homelessness, and with myriad aspects of identity disrupted, the grief was sufficiently intense for some women to compare it to bereavement.

Grief was experienced whether the move had been wanted or unwanted, and it caught many women by surprise. The memory of painful separations in other moves had apparently dimmed. And the pain of uprooting has been a hidden story, hidden from our collective awareness. Unprepared for their powerful responses, movers expressed shame about their sadness, irritability, resentment, and loneliness, fearing that these emotions betrayed a flawed capacity to cope. They felt the coupling of grief and shame that can spiral a woman into depression.

Too, these women needed to contain their troubling emotions so that their daily functioning was not impaired. And they needed to consign them to privacy, since they were soon aware that open expression of their distress would not be well received by settled people.

Dilemmas About Initiative

Ironically, the interlude during which it was necessary to make outreaching gestures coincided with the interlude during which movers felt most saddened and depleted. In those moods, many newcomers would have enjoyed an active welcome from neighbors, colleagues, husbands' colleagues, or churches. But only a minority— about one third—were offered such a welcome. Yet neither did the movers face clear expectations that they should be the ones to exercise initiative. Instead, they faced considerable ambiguity about local customs. This ambiguity could only heighten the anxiety many expressed about taking initiative in seeking new personal contacts. It was anxiety that seemed rooted in the barely conscious but close linkage in their minds between initiative and forbidden aggression—aggression that felt taboo in themselves and might arouse retaliation from others. It was surprising to learn how many women experienced benign, friendly, and outreaching gestures towards others as dangerous. They spoke of such gestures as pushing, forcing, invading, or worming their way into others' lives, as though there was an inchoate sense that deep, powerful energies within themselves might get loose and do harm.

But the need to recapture the intimacy of lost friendship was intense. Almost all of the movers mastered their grief and their anxiety about initiative sufficiently to invest impressive amounts of time and energy in making new personal connections that might lead to deepening friendships.

The Work of Friendmaking

It became clear that friendmaking is a realm of work in its own right—an unacknowledged realm of affiliative work that women do. And, carrying the primary responsibility for the psychological complexities of moving, they did that work for their loved ones as well as themselves.

Searching for the mutuality that is the bedrock of friendship, most joined or developed networks or affinity groups. Strategically, this was relatively easy because of the open access in Northland. Emotionally, it was far less easy. The newcomer was poised at the margin. She did not share in the common experience, the collective memory of the group, and therefore experienced the painful tension of being simultaneously welcomed and yet subtlely held outside. The hurt, if not the actual memory, of childhood experiences of being "left out" was frequently reawakened.

"With new people, you're always having to prove yourself!" an anxious mover protested vehemently. This state of being at the margin was indeed a time of trial. Before it could become clear that there was common ground to be shared, newcomers needed to be discreet about what they disclosed by way of taste, preference, value, or belief. Some felt the need to conceal some significant aspect of their being—political views, passionate beliefs about population control—lest they be repudiated. The more forthright, who favored candor over discretion, were forced to absorb some bruising of self-esteem when those being approached expressed aversion or—often worse—indifference. Women with labile self-esteem, and there were many, suffered most during this time of trial. There were few who felt so confident of their value and goodness as to say, "Here I am. Take me or leave me."

Yet in spite of the risks, searching out and then being among others with whom there was a sense of mutuality was sustaining. It afforded a partial sense of feeling at home. It imbued the mover's activities with purpose and meaning. But it was not enough. Affinity groups did not substitute for close friendships. The warmth of mutuality was only a foundation on which future intimacy might grow.

The quest for intimacy mingled risk and benefit. With the tapestry of her previous connections now unraveled, the mover could be spurred to interact with people with new perspectives who could expand her awareness and enrich her experience. She could be spurred to develop greater clarity about her own needs, values, and interests, as well as more thoughtful choices about how and where to invest her time and energy. Yet the search involved pain—repeated experiences of hope and disappointment, of attachment and loss. Potential friends would move away. Budding friendships would lose momentum when there was recognition that an apparent mutuality was only an illusion. The giving up of each anticipated friendship was another loss; the promised phone call that never came, signaling that she was unwanted, was another wound to the mover's self-esteem.

Among the core population, *approximately one third made new, close friends within two years.* These were primarily full-time homemakers whose friendships were developed within their network of "colleagues in parenting." Making friends was a crucial realm within their work of affiliation. Most women who combined homemaking with professional careers, no less needful of close friends, lacked the sustained time and energy for this additional, purposeful realm of work.

Among half of those who formed close friendships, separation again occurred, or was going to occur; either the newcomer was intending to leave or the friend had already left. *Within two years, therefore, only a sixth of the movers were able to develop deep friendships expected to endure.* Only a sixth had securely recaptured the intimacy they had lost.

Among the rest, hope was faltering. There was a mingling of resignation, disappointment, sadness, depression, and loneliness ranging from moderate to intense. These women had lost relationships that fulfilled deep needs both to be understood and to be understanding, to be responded to and to be responsive—needs for mutuality and reciprocity that heterosexual love relationships did not fully meet. They had lost relationships that express core aspects of a woman's self, and enhance her self-esteem (Surrey, 1985). Two years was too short a time for new bonds to deepen, if that deepening was, in fact, to happen again.

The intensity of the movers' continued longing varied, of course, with the structure of each woman's personality, as well as the characteristics of her marriage or other love relationship. It varied significantly with the outcome of other aspects of moving, especially the development of new realms of work.

WORK: OVERVIEW AND OUTCOMES

Work and Choice

Although most of the independent movers made thoughtful choices related to their work in moving to Northland, this was true of few among the coupled movers. Even those who believed the decision to move was fully shared had weighed factors primarily concerned with their husbands' work and only minimally with their own. Women engaged in professional careers had been laconic in exploring prospective career opportunities for themselves. Women engaged in the work of affiliation had subscribed to the "Myth of the Transportable Homemaker," disregarding the myriad connections and supports that secure the capacity to be an effective homemaker and nurturer.

There were contradictions in women's views of their work. Homemakers valued their nurturant power, and recognized its crucial influence in the family. At the same time, they devalued it. That is, even while feeling responsible for the happiness and success of their families, they hesitated to claim openly that their emotional provision had a value as serious as the man's financial provision. Some conceded the right of choice about moving to their men on the grounds that the men's work was paid. Yet this was an avoidance. In reality, a move to Northland to maintain continuity of the man's income was necessary for only two families. For the rest, it was unnecessary for the man to move specifically to Northland, or it was unnecessary for the man to move at all to continue providing financial support. That was a matter of choice. There seemed a readiness, even a wish, among the women to assign the man that right of choice, justified by his salary. Overtly or covertly, they abdicated the right to make choices about moves that would significantly affect their own realms of work.

This was not only true of homemakers. With a few exceptions, those who had developed professional careers also minimized the significance of their work and their right to lay claims on behalf of it. Men were more committed and more focused, they explained.

The Sense of Dispersion

It was in exploring the realm of work that I learned how commonly women experienced a sense of dispersion—an awareness of energy flowing in and flowing out in myriad directions, seeming to flow through permeable walls in their being. This quality, too, was seen in contradictory terms. It was valued as expressing flexibility and a capacity to respond to diverse claims. It was devalued in contrast to the sharply focused commitments perceived in men.

Yet this focus was not a quality that women sought for themselves. In spite of widening access to traditionally male domains of work and male patterns of work, and even when husbands would have encouraged their wives to pursue such careers, the professional women were reaching for a different ideal. Only one aspired to emulate the male model of a hierarchical organization of priorities and a single-minded, primary commitment to professional work. Most sought to combine the work of affiliation and the work of the marketplace in a relationship of parity—a relationship in which one realm would enhance the other, and in which both realms would have parallel value.

Among virtually all the movers, the sense of self was multi-faceted, organized around various lines of connection to others and various realms of work. This dispersion made women more vulnerable than men to the disruptive potential of moving. Having had more significant lines of connection, they had more significant losses to mourn. And moving ruptured the integration they had achieved, the interweaving of the many elements of self and of outward identity. This unraveling caused anxiety that was sometimes profound.

Before a mover's work identities could be restructured, she needed to reexamine and realign her goals. Inner conflicts between affiliative work and work in the marketplace and between achievement and nurturance became unexpectedly intense. Three aspects of the special situation of being a mover contributed to this intensity: the woman's loss of accustomed roles; her feeling of invisibility or insignificance in her new community; and her husband's or lover's preoccupation with his own new work.

* * *

Over half of the coupled movers endeavored to reorganize their identities around the parallel cores of affiliative work and professional careers. Since only two had secured professional opportunities before moving, there were many who were disappointed in their search. Unable to progress towards achieving their occupational goals, they experienced interludes of depression before they were able to redirect their energies towards new aims. It seemed likely that such setbacks could have been avoided. Had these women allowed themselves to recognize the importance and the legitimacy of their needs for professional work when they were considering the move, they might have investigated prospective opportunities more thoroughly. If the outlook was bleak, they might have chosen not to move or to move to another area. Or they might have come to terms with their disappointment while they still had available their networks of support and affirmation. These movers had not taken good care of themselves.

Yet, even as they struggled through frustration and disappointment, there was no doubt that some women experienced growth.

As they developed new realms of work, new capabilities were recognized, and both self-confidence and self-respect were heightened. A few such women had needed psychotherapeutic help to make these gains; the several others enjoyed support from husbands who were unthreatened by their accomplishments.

* * *

Just under half the movers were centered in homemaking by the end of the two years. Their experience attested that the common view of homemaking as a readily transportable role ("I can do it anywhere") is indeed a myth. The efforts of young mothers to develop supportive parenting networks had been intense and not consistently successful. And most homemakers were also committed to developing some realm of activity outside of their nurturant roles, a realm that would allow expression of their talents, earn recognition of their specialness, and perhaps create the potential for future financial gain. Within two years, and with persistent effort, the majority had succeeded. Even for the many women who had not yet developed new close friendships, such outside recognition was sustaining.

The development of a realm of work—paid or not—commanding recognition outside the home was a central factor in the degree to which newcomers felt positively connected to Northland within two years. It was made clear that women, as much as men, have needs not only for nurturance (which they seek from lovers, husbands, intimate friends, or vicariously through identification with the children they nurture), but also for expression and recognition of their capabilities outside of their homes.

Developing an equilibrium between various realms of work is a lifelong challenge for women. It can be seriously impeded by moving. A new equilibrium can also be an exciting outgrowth of moving. But when that is achieved, a span of years is needed for the new and precious integration to become secure. It should not, must not, be heedlessly disrupted.

OTHER STUDIES

"You must have had an unusual group of women in your study."
"You must have had a troubled group of women." "Perhaps a
different group of women would have been more adequate." I was
to hear such assumptions repeatedly. They were voiced by settled
Northlanders who felt discomfited by what they had heard of the
study, or by what they imagined about it. They were voiced even
before my conclusions were known, as though to repudiate the
work in advance.

To avoid being influenced by other findings, I had decided not
to read published studies of migration or relocation until my own
work was complete. But then it was time to respond to those
critics who needed to disqualify whatever I might learn. It was
time to consider my own conclusions in relation to the conclusions
of others.

To survey the migration/relocation literature is to confront the
metaphorical basket of apples, pears, peaches, plums, and kiwi fruit
as well, so strikingly diverse are the goals and structures of published
work: clinical/anecdotal accounts, qualitative research, quantitative
research based on various hypotheses, on various instruments of
inquiry, on various respondent populations, focused on single or
multiple variables, carried out at different points in time in relation
to a move. There have been tides of bias, a wave of studies attesting
that moving is deleterious followed by a wave arguing its
beneficence. Sandcastles of belief have been constructed, data from
earlier studies being cited selectively (or with unconscious
distortion) and incorporated over time into new conclusions.
Research in the social sciences is imperfect, and the theory that
is its outgrowth must be flawed as well.

Yet the careful clinician rarely accepts theory as truth. Rather,
she or he maintains a dialectic between theory and clinical
exploration, between knowing and wondering. Theory suggests
fruitful pathways to explore with the client/patient; in turn,
understanding the individuality of the client/patient leads to
refinement of theory. In that spirit of continuous inquiry, I turn
to the literature.

Mobility and Well-being

Paykel, Myers, Dienelt, Klerman, Lindenthal, and Pepper (1969), comparing 185 depressed psychiatric patients to a matched sample in New Haven, found that job changes (prior to their illness) comprised the realm in which the depressed patients had been the most significantly affected compared to the controls. My own study had brought into focus that starting new work is central in the experience of moving. Although it is assumed that this is primarily the burden of the male who moves, especially if he is the chief wage-earner in a family, the male may actually experience more occupational continuity than his wife, and he may enjoy more support in the workplace. Among the Northland movers, single women and coupled women who came to further their husbands' careers were faced with a high level of work change. They were challenged to redefine their work priorities, to resolve anew their conflicts between affiliation and the marketplace, and then to seek out the opportunities and supports they needed in both spheres. They experienced loss of work-related identity and feelings of competence. They had ample cause for both anxiety and depression.

In the New Haven study, it was also found that life events associated with separation and loss had occurred with significantly greater frequency among the depressed patients than among the control group. The experience of the Northland movers was permeated with separation and loss (Chapter 2). There was a loss of identity expressed in myriad roles. There was a loss of home that was sheltering, that allowed expression of personal history and taste, that confirmed continuity of self, that was an arena in which competence was experienced. There was loss of intimates who were nurturing and could be nurtured, and who offered recognition of the woman's specialness. Significant objects as well as aspects of self were lost. Among couples there was at least temporary loss of some of the support and availability of the partner.

Weissman and Paykel (1972), studying a group of depressed women, noticed that the onset of symptoms had often been preceded by a move. The patients tended not to attribute their illnesses to moving but to other elements in their lives, such as financial problems, increased loneliness, increased marital friction, problems with children, career frustrations, or identity confusion. These were, in fact, among the very conditions generated by their moves for the Northland newcomers. Almost all of them experienced one or several of those stresses. Weissman and Paykel suggested that the depressed patients had not associated their symptoms with their moves because moving was so taken for granted in the United States that its significance was disregarded. A comparable disregard for the complexity and stresses of moving had been dramatic in Northland until my population of movers were invited to tell their stories.

I saw little relationship between the wish to move and the grief that Northland movers experienced (in fact, those who had wanted to move were surprised and dismayed by their sadness). Weissman and Paykel also found that depression occurred even when moves were voluntary and seemingly desirable.

Butler, McAllister, and Kaiser (1973), based on a national survey of residential mobility patterns, concluded that:

recent residential mobility experiences affect the mental health of females more than that of males. In fact, the only relatively large differences found in this research exist between residentially mobile males and females and symptoms of suspected mental disorder suggesting a greater effect of moves upon the mental stability of females than males. (p. 226)

They observe that females are more affected than males whether the move was voluntary or involuntary.

Deep and very prolonged sadness and depression were found by Fried (1963) among 566 Boston slumdwellers involuntarily moved (to housing that appeared much more desirable) in an urban renewal project. They intensely mourned their lost neighborhoods, in which there had been a sense of belonging. Sadness and depression were slightly more frequent among women than men. Fried commented:

This view of an area as home and the significance of local people and local places are so profoundly at variance with typical middle-class orientations that it is difficult to appreciate the intensity of meaning, the basic sense of identity involved in living in the particular area. (p. 151)

Yet, in fact, it was loss of identity and of intimates that aggrieved this "working class" population, the very losses that aggrieved the middle- and upper-middle-class Northland movers. It was merely that the objects of their connection had been different.

Bourestom (1984), reviewing studies of relocation among elderly populations, concluded that moving can have seriously adverse effects, including death. He isolated as one significant variable the voluntary or involuntary dimension of moving. Since choice was revealed to be highly complex by my own study, this dimension of moving will be considered separately.

Grinberg and Grinberg (1984), apparently drawing on clinical observation, write of the "persecutory, confusional, and depressive anxieties" that all international migrants experience in varying degrees. Writing of the process of mourning for "lost aspects of self," an experience that was central for Northland movers, they use words that almost echo the phrases of the Northland women: "In the new country, no one will know me; no one will know my family; I'll be a nobody," one of the migrants declared. Jan in Northland had voiced a typical lament, "I feel as though I'm floating. It's as though nobody knows who I really am."

Seidenberg (1973), drawing on clinical experience and observation of women in corporate sub-culture, published a clarion call.

> In contrast to her husband, whose credentials are easily transferable, her identity as a person, apart from being a wife or a mother, is rarely transferable. In a new community, she finds that she must create one all over again. It is starting from the bottom once more for most mobile wives . . . for some again and again. Often they become defeated people, casualties of "success." They are seen clinically during their third and fourth decades of life chronically depressed, lacking in hope or desire, frequently addicted to alcohol, tranquilizers, and barbiturates. (pp. 1-2)

Seidenberg wrote dramatically, apparently to highlight a compelling societal problem. Although none of the Northland movers were corporate wives, several of the highly mobile "no-choice" wives were or had been afflicted with clinical depression and/or alcoholism. Most movers were not severely or chronically impaired, and a close reading of Seidenberg suggests that he found this also. In fact, he concedes that some corporate wives develop a satisfying attachment to the paternalistic firm, and are able to reconnect with the corporate subculture wherever they move. However, the emphasis he gave to loss of identity is altogether germane to my findings, as is his conclusion that:

> When husband and wife adhere to their traditional roles, the conventional expectations arising from their roles demand exorbitant renunciation from the women. . . . These renunciations—not personal immaturities or childhood excessive problems—are enough to account for the consequences that accrue. (p. 10)

Seidenberg (1973, p. 13) believed that the negative impact of uprooting is not "episodic, idiosyncratic, or singularly pathological."

Olive, Kelsey, Viser, and Daly (1976), studying a population of corporation executives and their families with questionnaires and group discussions, gave support to Seidenberg with the observations that:

> A problem expressed . . . with strong feeling was that of reestablishing an identity within the new community. While the executive has gained status within the company among familiar people and surroundings, the wife and children must start over again to establish a new status with little support. . . . the emotional reserve necessary to "build a new nest" did become exhausted. (p. 548)

Further support for the significance of loss of identity associated with moving can be inferred from the work of Sieber (1974), Thoits (1983), and Pietromonaco, Manis, and Fohardt-Lane (1986). Expressing identity in terms of social roles, they attest that the accumulation of diverse roles/identities enhances psychological well-being, whereas the loss of roles/identities produces psychological distress.

Evidence of mobility-related psychic disarray comes from other societies as well. In Australia, 27 "low socioeconomic status" housewives and 25 "high socioeconomic status" housewives were evaluated within four weeks of relocation by Viney and Bazeley (1977). Comparison groups included successful university students, recently hospitalized psychiatric patients, and post-partal women. The researchers described these expectations:

> The ability to make accurate and useful assumptions about her environment is necessary to every woman, and gives her a sense of mastery . . . if, on relocation, she has not altered some of her assumptions appropriately . . . she should experience feelings of shame and inadequacy because she can no longer successfully deal with much of what is happening to herself and those dependent on her. She also cannot predict and so control those events well, so that she should experience anxiety based on a strong emotional need for cognitive mastery of her new environment. Her giving up any cathected [emotionally charged] object is expected to lead to emotions like separation anxiety . . . or feelings of loneliness and loss. Her positive feelings should, however, increase with the inclusion of new objects within her life space. (p. 37)

These expectations were born out. Three to four weeks after moving, levels of separation anxiety and shame were as high among the movers as among the psychiatric patients. Cognitive anxiety (as well as positive emotions) were exceeded only by the childbearing women, and were higher than among the patients and students.

These findings were strikingly similar to my own. In fact, this study is unusual in recognizing shame as a prominent affect among women movers, a finding recently confirmed in a pilot study of the "trailing spouse" being carried out by Bayes (1989). Most of the Northland movers felt considerable anxiety and shame about their reactions to their dislocation and, not appreciating that their reactions were appropriate, they even felt further anxiety and shame about their anxiety and shame.

The longitudinal perspective of my study allowed me greater depth of exploration, as well as observation of the vicissitudes of the movers' experiences over time. For example, the Australian study was carried out several weeks after moving, during the period when some movers were still experiencing a honeymoon of elation, excitement, and optimism, perhaps those states ambiguously designated by the Australians as "positive emotions." It was after those early weeks had passed that many in my study experienced a limbo, with sharpening awareness of the reality of their losses, an onset of grieving among those who had postponed it, longing for intimacy with much uncertainty about how and when new bonds would be formed, and recognition that the strands of identity had been unraveled. Anxiety and depression were prevalent.

A number of studies correlate moving and increased medical complaints. For example, Willmuth, Weaver, and Donlan (1975) noted large numbers of recently transferred corporate employees seeking medical advice for headaches, gastrointestinal distress, fatigue, and nervousness. Systematically comparing recently transferred (within 12 months) to more settled employees, as well as professionals to supportive personnel, they found medical service usage to be significantly higher among recently transferred non-professional employees than the three other groups. Usage of the plant medical facility was "taken as a measure of the amount of distress, disturbance, or illness being experienced" (p. 87). Lower usage by the executive group, they speculated, might be attributable to the fact that executives have a lifestyle more geared to transience, or executives might seek private medical care outside the company. They did not point out, however, that the executives would have been preponderantly male, whereas the supportive personnel might include many women, perhaps more stressed by relocation.

This idea is indirectly supported by the findings of Stokols, Shumaker, and Martinez (1983). In a survey by questionnaire of non-faculty university employees in California, predominantly women, it was found that high mobility was directly associated with illness-related symptoms. For these researchers, this was one of "two unpredicted main effects of mobility rate on well-being" (p. 12).

Based on a five year period of clinical observation, Stein (1984) noted that recent migrants to Oklahoma sought help in the Family Medicine Clinic for a variety of problems including anxiety, depression, marital discord, and somatic complaints. These patients recurrently characterized themselves as:

misplaced persons, displaced persons, isolated, stranded, like a fish out of water, alone.

These people not only feel out of their element, but are painfully aware that something is missing. It is as though the "element" from which they are parted is felt to be a part of themselves that they no longer have or feel that it was torn from them. The environment which had completed the very boundaries of their selves is no longer present. Their sense of "alienation" follows from a nagging feeling of uncanniness, if not an overwhelming feeling of depersonalization, for they truly do not know any longer who they are. (p. 275)

In these powerful words I heard echoes of the Northland movers.

Turning again to other cultures, Hooper and Ineichen (1972) found a heightened incidence of medical problems such as headache and gastrointestinal upsets among English families who had moved within six months, and Lock (1987) noted that relocated Japanese housewives expressed their distress through somatic complaints, a culturally accepted conduit. Such women were often diagnosed as depressed.

Women must nurture and nourish the family, and guilt associated with illness is particularly acute with women. . . . However, if symptoms can be legitimized through a doctor's opinion or by appropriate labeling . . . then somatization becomes a powerful form of nonconfrontational communication. Women, themselves, therefore, tend to welcome medicalization of their problems. (p. 151)

The studies described above attest to the psychologically, socially, and physically disruptive potentials of moving. Brett's (1982) survey of corporate families has been cited both to support and refute such ideas. She was forthright about her methodological limitations, pointing out that the sample "is probably biased in the direction of respondents with positive attitudes toward moving" and that "the comparison samples were less than ideal." (p. 461) Results were mixed. Highly mobile men and their wives believed their lives were more interesting and believed themselves to be more capable than the less mobile. Yet mobile men reported more psychological symptoms and were less satisfied with their health than less mobile men.

A frequently cited finding was that highly mobile couples were more satisfied with marriage and family life than comparison couples. Yet the work of others casts doubt on this (Mincer, 1978; Pinder, 1977, for example). Weissman and Paykel, previously cited, noted that marital discord was frequently mentioned among depressed women who had recently moved. In the Northland population, satisfaction with marriage fluctuated considerably over the two year interval, most couples struggling with disappointment, envy, and resentment that the move had ignited between them.

On the other hand, some Northland movers did observe that the experience of being outsiders in a new community caused a tightening of family bonds, at least temporarily. This could feel warmly supportive. Yet it could also be burdensome, because it placed heavy responsibility on each family member to fulfill the needs of the others. I have pointed out that when, to an excessive degree, children become "selfobjects" for their parents—"objects" needed to provide gratification for parents that parents cannot provide for themselves—the child's healthy development of an authentic self is likely to be impeded.

In Brett's (1982) study it was found that:

> Mobile men and women were less satisfied with all aspects of social relationships than were men and women in the comparison samples . . . opportunities to make friends at work, friends in general, nonwork activities, neighbors, and community. (p. 457)

This finding embraces all aspects of the dimension "gemeinschaft" (togetherness or community), which Northland women felt to be highly important. The finding is supported by the report of Stokols et al. (1983) of their second "unpredicted main effect of mobility rate on well-being," namely that "highly mobile persons reported less sense of community" (p. 12).

Contradictory evidence with respect to making friends would seem to be provided by Jones (1973). On the basis of questionnaires mailed to wives who had moved within the preceding year, Jones observed that "There is no significant relationship between the total number of times moved and agreement with the statement that the respondent is 'unable to develop intimate friendships'" (p. 213). This is an instance in which it would be illuminating to know more about the meaning of the question to the respondent. The query might be perceived as a threat to self-esteem, being understood as questioning the respondent's personality or personal capabilities rather than the circumstances of mobility. Furthermore, within the first year (Jones's time frame), Northland movers were still optimistic about the probability of developing new, close friendships.

The work of McCallister, Butler, and Kaiser (1973) might also be thought to cast doubt on the conclusions of Brett (1982) and Stokols et al. (1983), yet it does not. Questioning an assumption that mobility is related to the disruption of social relations, they carried out a nationally based survey of 500 women to determine visiting patterns before and after a change of residence took place. They concluded that the heightened social interaction reported after relocation (measured by numbers of visits) "is simply one mode of adjustment to a new community" (p. 201). Although this was apparently a new finding within sociological research, it is well supported by the Northland experience. Central in the work of moving for women is the exploration and development of new interpersonal contacts. For some, this is exhilarating, but for many it is exhausting. The quantification of social contacts tells little about their qualitative or subjectively experienced aspects, which Brett and Stokols et al. seemed to be reporting.

Jones (1973) was apparently singular in addressing the issue of perceived responsibility. Seventy-eight percent of her respondents agreed with the statement "the wife is the key person in establishing the home and making the move successful" (p. 212), a finding in strong agreement with the view of Northland women that "It's up to me to make it work."

Fischer and Stueve (1977) energetically argued against the deleterious impact of mobility. Drawing primarily on the study of men, they explored and refuted the proposition that:

> Local social relations are more likely to be communal (intimate and supportive) than are social relations with people outside the locality. . . . One derivative from this proposition is that people who cannot build strong local relations because they have recently moved are also likely to lack communal relations and, consequently, to suffer psychologically because of their isolation. (p. 165)

Unfortunately, "local" is not defined.

Although Fischer and Stueve conceded that frequent contact is needed for the *development* of intimacy, they argued that "community without propinquity" can be *maintained* through the use of modern communication and transportation systems. The experience of Northland movers does not support this. These women invested much time, energy, and money in trying to maintain closeness with friends in other locales, yet almost without exception they experienced long-distance intimacy as insufficient—and they grieved intensely for its loss. The ongoing, empathic sharing of thought, feeling, and experience were sorely missed. And propinquity was indeed needed to consolidate new friendships.

Yet Fischer and Stueve (1977) did conclude:

> One might argue that this analysis implies that no one suffers from mobility. Quite the contrary, it points to those who would be most vulnerable: those with few alternatives on when or where to move—the evicted or, often, *wives*. [emphasis added]. (p. 184)

Markham and Pleck (1986), using national survey data, examined the comparative willingness of men and women to move for occupational advancement. Finding women significantly less willing to move, they observed that "existing theory and research failed to provide completely adequate guidance about mechanisms linking sex to willingness to relocate" (p. 138). The literature yields ample evidence that moving can be deeply disruptive for both men and women, apparently more so for women. Perhaps it is less important to know which sex is more affected than to understand fully how they are each affected.

Mobility and Choice

Since attempts to establish correlations between relocation and individual or societal well-being have yielded inconsistent results, the effort has moved towards identifying the most significant intervening variables. Choice has become one such focus.

Bourestom (1984) identified as the first intervening variable "whether the move is voluntary or involuntary" (p. 61). He concluded that:

> The research is consistent in showing negative effects when individuals are forced to move. The data suggest that, for relocations within the community, forced moves impact negatively on life satisfaction and personal adjustment, whereas for those whose forced moves involve more radical environmental changes . . . the relocation may literally be lethal. (p. 67)

This conclusion, of course, strongly supports the work of Fried, cited above. The extent of the problem was attested by Rossi (1980), who estimated that one-third of residential mobility is involuntary.

Like Bourestom, Fischer and Stueve (1977) attributed high significance to choice, remarking that:

> If there is a single characteristic that distinguishes those who benefit from mobility from those who lose from it, it is the degree of choice they have. People who benefit are those who, because of their resources and knowledge, can choose whether to move or not, and where to move. (p. 182)

They concluded that married women are particularly vulnerable to adverse effects from moving because they have little choice.

Jones (1973) offered a more sanguine view, reporting that 58% of the respondent wives believed the decision to move was a joint one (the construction of the questionnaire is not known), and that "the happiness of the wife in the new community is related to the degree of her involvement in the planning stages of the move" (p. 213). Stokols et al. (1983) assessed perceived residential choice by asking respondents to rate the importance of a series of questionnaire items pertaining to reasons for moving. They concluded that "health consequences of mobility were mediated by perceptions of choice and congruence associated with one's current residence" (p. 16).

These five researchers appear to view choice as a cognitive process in which information is gathered and weighed rationally. Other studies and my own suggest that choice is far more complex.

For example, Sell (1983) recognized that "Analyzing behavior through analysis of stated reasons has several limitations. First, persons frequently either do not know their motives or may express de post facto rationalizations" (p. 300). Categorizing choice to move as "Forced Mobility," "Imposed Mobility," or "Preference-Dominated Mobility," he acknowledged some degree of ambiguity within the second and third categories. He recognized that it is "tenuous to uniformly ascribe the same moving reasons to all members of relocated households" (p. 307), noting also that one respondent member may provide reasons for the others. Nonetheless, he concluded from his national survey that the majority of moves are preference-dominated and free from excessive constraint.

Missing in these quantitative studies is access to the respondents' subjective experience. For example, among Northland movers, what of Jennifer, who voluntarily and apparently by preference moved from her family homestead into a condominium? Yet she felt internally and painfully forced, because the declining physical capabilities associated with aging made it seem impossible to maintain her beloved home. What of the many wives whose "voluntary" and "preference-dominated" moves were based on wrenching ambivalence and ultimate denial of their own needs? The complexity of migration decisions was more fully recognized by DeJong and Gardner (1981), yet even they showed a relative disregard for the powerful and often unconscious emotional elements that operate in determining choice.

Williams, Jobes, and Gilchrist (1986) observed that:

Relatively little has been written regarding the impact of gender and marital status upon migration decision . . . whether husbands, wives, or both jointly make the migration decision does not effect subsequent satisfaction and implies that other, as yet empirically unidentified, factors influence family satisfaction with the new location. (p. 641)

It is at such a juncture that qualitative research can illuminate the trends that quantitative research exposes. Among all the coupled women in my population, 60% believed that they had exercised some choice or full choice in the decision to move (a finding very similar to that of Williams and Jones). Yet in many cases that choice was illusory, based on conscious or unconscious disregard of the movers' own needs and disregard of characteristics of Northland that would prove highly significant in terms of the movers' well-being. For just this reason, satisfaction would not be expected to correlate closely with choice. Furthermore, there were so many dimensions to the psychosocial work of moving that satisfaction would have to be defined in terms of particular realms to be meaningful. Global judgments would tell little. And still further, the Northland movers made it very clear that whether a move is wanted or not, whether the long-term outcome is joyous or not, there is pain to be worked through—both the grief associated with loss, and the wounds to self-esteem associated with reconnection. Williams et al. measured "satisfaction" with the move six months after its physical occurrence, a time at which the Northland movers' pain was intense.

Yet choice does have potential as a useful intervening variable (Bourestom's 1984 review seems to demonstrate that persuasively). Clarification of choice with the prospective mover is among the realms in which mental health caregivers have a highly significant role to play.

PAIN, RECOIL, AND DENIAL

On the basis of a study of 2,000 middle- and upper-middle-class movers, *The New York Times* has reported that *Only 30% make the change without anguish. The rest suffer* (Relationships, 1983). This is not understood or accepted in the popular culture. Denial of the movers' pain was a compelling finding in my study.

Most of the Northland movers felt considerable anxiety and shame about their reactions to moving because they failed to meet their own expectations. Their distress was compounded, sometimes cruelly, because they sensed that settled Northlanders recoiled from it. "We have to wear our having-a-good-time masks," some movers said. Not sadness, not loneliness, not anger, not even spontaneity nor authenticity, but a persistently cheerful demeanor seemed the passport to acceptance.

In other studies of migration and relocation, I found more than ample corroboration for my belief that Northland movers were not "unusual" or specially "troubled" or "inadequate" in their reactions. But, I wondered, why should such corroboration be needed? Why was the community so unprepared to accept the legitimacy of the movers' experiences? Why did the community recoil from their pain?

No particular regional characteristics could be imputed to Northland, since the population is geographically diverse. It includes residents attracted from across the nation to a fine, small university, a leading medical center, sophisticated "high-tech" industries, as well as the rural calm. There was no reason to believe that the repudiation of the newcomers' distress was unique to Northland. More likely, the pain of a newcomer is an unwelcome intrusion into settled life everywhere.

It arouses helplessness and guilt in the resident who, enmeshed in her (or his) own roles and affiliations, feels a lack of time, energy, inclination, or even capability to try to assuage it. If her own being is embedded in the community, which she experiences as an extension of herself, a "selfobject," the newcomer's ache can feel like rejection of what she values and loves, and thus of herself as well. And the newcomer's suffering can threaten the equilibrium of the resident's own adjustment. It can bring latent doubts about her own life into unwelcome focus, or it can set into motion disturbing resonances in her memory. The resident will defend against the pain of the mover just as she has defended against the pain in herself, even though her compassion is thus diminished.

Perhaps it is for such reasons that:

Those who are not at the moment lonely will have little empathy for those who are, even if in the recent past they had been lonely themselves. If they had earlier been lonely, they now have no access to the self that experienced the loneliness. Furthermore, they very likely prefer that things remain that way. In consequence, they are likely to respond to those who are currently lonely with absence of understanding and perhaps irritation. . . . The frequency and intensity of loneliness are not only underestimated but the lonely themselves tend to be disparaged. (Weiss, 1973, pp. 12-13)

There are other sources of denial of the mover's distress. As feminist psychologists have been observing (Gilligan, 1982; Miller, 1976), male psychological development and male experience were long accepted as normative. Therefore, those aspects of moving which cause particular distress to women have been relatively unnoticed. For example, men appear not to form deep, emotionally intimate friendships as commonly as women. The loss of such friends has not been a wrenching experience for the male mover as it has for the female. That dimension of moving has therefore been disregarded. And that disregard is reinforced by the fact that the economic-political sphere, the "marketplace," is more highly valued in the male culture than the social sphere of interpersonal connection. The loss of a network of connection has not been accorded a significance comparable to the loss of a vocational opportunity.

Our society, shaped by a predominantly male political philosophy, has celebrated individualism. The separateness embodied in competition has been more highly valued than the connection embodied in collaboration. And sociocultural values have been embodied in precepts of mental health. Thus the significance of separation and individuation have until recently been emphasized in psychoanalytic developmental psychology (Mahler et al., 1975). Loss is viewed as a necessary stimulus for developmental progression through adulthood (Settlage, Curtis, Lozoff, Lozoff, Silberschatz, & Simburg, 1988). In such a conceptual context it would follow that the separation and loss inherent in moving would be viewed as normative and unremarkable—"no big deal" in one troubled mover's words.

Furthermore, United States society, as many societies of the world, has been traditionally virilocal. Whither he goest, she goest too, and that edict has been embodied in law. To make visible the psychological cost to women of virilocality, to encourage women to make considered choices that serve their own needs as well as their men's, and perhaps even to resist mobility is to challenge a deeply rooted tradition. Of course such a challenge arouses resistance and denial.

Also in the United States virilocality and mobility have been interwoven. Together, they have spawned and are reinforced by major industrial and commercial enterprises. Deployment of personnel in the armed forces, in corporate industry, and even in certain religious ministries has involved astonishing demands for mobility. That mobility supports, and is supported by, a complex of other enterprises, not least the real estate and transportation industries. Whenever custom becomes enmeshed in economics, opposition to change is intense.

But what is the implication of such pervasive avoidance, resistance, and denial for the troubled mover? Grinberg and Grinberg (1984) recognize that:

> In order to become integrated into the environment where he is received, the immigrant must renounce part of his individuality, at least temporarily. . . . Such renunciations or losses [of parts of the self] inevitably produce internal conflicts, since they clash with each individual's striving to assure his own distinctness from others, that is, to preserve his identity. (p. 27)

Miller (1983), discussing societal recoil from female anger, observes that:

> One of *the* most destructive psychological phenomena [is] . . . the suffering of an experience, but then not having the permission to truly suffer it—that is, not being able to go genuinely through the experience, know it, name it, and react with the emotions it evokes. . . . You suffer the experience of complex emotions and the simultaneous "disconfirmation" of them. (p. 7)

In the terms of self psychology, this disconfirmation could only be experienced as a profound deprivation, an absence of necessary validation of the authentic self. In this realm, mental health caregivers have a crucial role to play, both in validating the emotional experience of the individual mover, and in working to influence the pervasive denial of the pain of relocation.

EIGHT

Intervening

PSYCHOLOGICAL INTERVENTIONS

It will be evident to the clinician who has become attuned to the experiences of the Northland movers that there are myriad issues and conflicts around which psychological intervention could have enormous preventive and therapeutic benefit for the female mover and her family.

For months or even years after moving, she may experience a complex intermingling of pleasure and pain. Even amidst growing satisfaction with her new milieu, new acquaintances, and new work, there may be upwellings of intense longing for what has been left behind, or days that feel bleak, grey, and sad, or anger at the person or circumstances that caused the move, or anxious feelings of loss of control or incompetence. As transient states, these are expectable. Yet they may not be expected by the mover or her family, and arouse anxiety, shame, or guilt. For just that reason, support and validation from primary health care providers and the clergy can be immensely beneficial.

If the mover's grey mood becomes an enveloping mantle, if work seems futile, if life seems meaningless, if irritability is continuous, if sleep or appetite or sexual functions are consistently disturbed, if there is self-loathing and thoughts of suicide, if there is inappropriate rage and physical attack on spouse or children, and/

or there is an increase of illnesses or accidents—any such conditions signal the need for help from the clinician specially trained in psychotherapeutic intervention. Yet in addition to (and connected with) such significant disturbances of thought, mood or behavior, there are a number of complex psychological issues involved in major moves that should be the focus of intervention. Paramount among these is the issue of choice.

"Doesn't everyone have to adapt to changing circumstances?" wondered a long-settled Northland resident. Unspoken was the question I sensed: "So what?" If the millions of women who move every year are faced with unanticipated frustrations and disappointments, does it really matter?

Yes. It matters because every woman faces stressful experiences in life that are altogether beyond her control. Just for that reason, she needs to be prudent in the choices she can control. A pioneering feminist declared 200 years ago, "I do not wish [women] to have power over men, but over themselves." (Wollstonecraft, 1985, p. 57). When women abdicate their choice about moving, they relinquish power over themselves.

It matters because a woman who has abdicated her choice has abdicated some of her dignity, the dignity that is enhanced by having a clear sense of who she is and by making decisions that allow full expression of her potential.

It matters because a woman who has abdicated the responsibility of choosing for herself is prone to feel victimized. Victimization generates resentment, even rage. Resentment and rage seek a target and the most likely target is a loved one close at hand—husband, lover, or even a child. Such targets respond with guilt, anger, anxiety, and relationships are eroded.

It matters because suffering from ill-considered choices can compromise a woman's capacity for work and for love, interfering wastefully with the expression of her capabilities. Her pain will flow outward in concentric circles, affecting her intimates, her community, and her world.

For all these reasons, it is significant to explore her choice in depth with the woman mover. This exploration will lead into the central and complex realm of her sense of self.

Differentiation Between Self and Other

The momentum of our daily lives rarely allows for contemplation. Weeks, months, and years speed by and we often feel caught up by forces we hardly understand, shaped by needs we barely recognize, energized by aims that we have not consciously chosen. The opportunity to consider moving, whether accepted or not, offers a special challenge. It can spur a woman to take a fresh look, a deep look, a wide-ranging look at her life. It is as though, for an interlude, time can be frozen. It is as though the elements in her life can be crystallized and studied under a focused beam.

Many women have scarcely struggled free of the psychological cocoon of their birth family and have scarcely consolidated a distinct sense of self, when the boundaries between self and other may again feel fragile. In new love relationships—heterosexual, homosexual, maternal—women experience interludes of merging, feeling as one with the other. Such merging allows for deep intimacy, as between lovers in shared passion, as between nursing mother and suckling babe, as between close friends who seem at moments to know each other's thoughts.

But fluid boundaries can be problematical as well. It is a difficult task for many women to differentiate their thoughts and feelings, needs and goals, and fears and dreams from those of their intimates. At moments, whether single or coupled, women feel enmeshed in the assumptions and expectations of others. Yet to experience authentic interdependence, a relationship of mutual care and concern that safeguards the needs and dignity of both self and others, a woman must experience not only connection but separateness as well. Responsible choices involving major life decisions, such as moving, involve caring for self as well as for others.

As a first stage, the prospective mover needs to distinguish her own aims from those of her loved ones. Although helping them fulfill their aims may be a major goal of her own, to accept it as the entirety is precarious for her and burdensome for them. Her identity is then grounded on shifting sands. Her loved ones are cloaked with responsibility for her self-esteem. Given all the forces beyond her control, how can she possibly ensure her mate's success as a doctor, lawyer, or CEO? Or her children's success as students, hockey players, or ballet dancers? How will she feel if they fail? Who will she be if they fail?

Therefore, there is a core question the prospective mover needs to explore: "Who am I as an individual woman, deeply connected with, but also distinct from my loved ones?" It is around this complex question that the clinician can help the patient/client initiate not only a geographical move, but also a psychological journey of self-discovery. This can happen as the move is considered, when it is in progress, or when the move has taken place, because a woman's sense of self and its valuation is significantly expressed in the process of choosing to move. (In fact, such an exploration could profitably happen in any therapy, but for reasons concerned with institutional needs and the economics of mental health care, much psychotherapeutic practice has become focused on identification and amelioration of symptoms.)

The clinician, as much as the client, has internalized sociocultural assumptions. Those many assumptions which are reflected in widespread disregard or denial of the pain of relocation may be shared by the clinician—more likely, but not exclusively, if he is male. As professionals, perhaps ambitious and "upwardly mobile," clinicians are themselves likely to have moved. Their own biases need examination, especially a bias either towards or against virilocality. Neither bias is likely to serve the individual mover well, since bias may blunt sensitivity to the unique needs of that particular woman. To be sure, the concept of authentic interdependence also expresses a bias. But it is a more benign one, I believe, since it takes into account the rights and responsibilities of each partner in a coupling.

Around the issue of choosing to move, or not to move, many questions need exploration, and the shadow of the past may become apparent. For example, the sense of self as differentiated from or merged with the other is of course expressed in the here and now, but also has its antecedents in times past. Thus behind a fragile differentiation from spouse or lover may lie a precursor—the unfinished differentiation from the primary object of identification, the mother. To experience herself as separate or different may arouse anxiety or guilt in a woman. It may feel like an abandonment of mother or by mother. It may feel like a hostile or competitive repudiation of mother. Therefore, with this issue as with all others, the depth of exploration will need to be sensitively gauged and shaped by the needs of the client or patient as well as the training of the clinician.

"Who am I?" a woman should be encouraged to consider. "How would I describe my personality to a trusted friend? What do I need in my life to feel secure, effective, significant, loving, and loved?"

"How do I spend my days? What work makes me feel effective, makes me feel I have a significant role in human affairs? What or who gives recognition to my work? How would my life feel without the work, recognition, and feeling of effectiveness? Could it be developed elsewhere and fulfill those needs?

"Who are my colleagues, whether my work is nuclear physics or mothering? What role do they play in encouraging my work, affirming its importance, sharing my problems, and finding solutions? How would it feel to do my work without them? How readily could they be replaced?"

"How do I play? Is it a walk in the forest that replenishes me, or an interlude in a sidewalk cafe amidst a frenetic crowd? Do I need myriad impingements—sights, smells, movements, and sounds—to exhilarate me, or do I need tranquil times and places for dreams and meditation? Who are my playmates? How readily could they be replaced?

"What kind of milieu do I live in most contentedly? Must it have urban bustle or rural calm? Do I need exposure to the sights and sounds of neighbors to feel safely connected, or a shield of privacy to feel safely protected? Do I need a zestful melange of races and ethnic traditions, or a predictable homogeneity?"

"How much of my being is embedded in my home? Does it express my taste and values, feeling like an extension of my being? Does it embody my personal history and my family's as well? In what ways does it shape my relations to others? Does it give us the closeness we want or the distance we need? Is it the center of my life with friends? Which among those elements could be recreated in another dwelling?"

"Who are my intimate friends? What role do they play in assuaging my loneliness, comforting me in distress, rejoicing with me in gladness, clarifying my perplexities, and allowing me the warm satisfaction of doing the same for them? How would my life feel without them? How would it feel if I found nobody to take their place?"

As those complex questions are being explored, as her self-awareness is heightened, a prospective mover develops a foundation for finding out whether the move to a new community is likely to fulfill her personal needs, related to but distinct from the needs of her loved ones. This is a critical juncture, the point at which she may avoid seeking answers or begin disregarding them. This is the point at which she may abdicate her responsibility for self care.

Responsible choice about moving must be based on self-awareness as well as responsiveness to loved ones. But it must also be based on a sense of entitlement to make a choice for oneself. That is problematical for many women.

A single (uncoupled) woman is usually forced to make her own choice, and that necessity tends to relieve her guilt about being the primary object of her concern—being "selfish," as it is labeled in our culture. But a coupled woman must disentangle herself from overt and covert expectations, within as well as outside herself, that she will subjugate herself to the selfhood of her mate and children. Until she feels a clear conviction of her right to fulfillment both in the marketplace and by the hearth, and her right to the opportunities and supports she needs to attain that fulfillment, she is unlikely to make a fully responsible choice.

Feminine Paradoxes and Cultural Dualisms

A woman's conviction of her right to fulfillment is an expression of healthy self-regard, which is based on realistic appreciation of both her capabilities and her limitations. The majority of Northland movers, perhaps reflecting a much more widespread characteristic of women, gave signs of a precarious foundation for their self-regard. Their sense of self was paradoxical, including contradictory images of power and helplessness, and of heroism and unworthiness. They expected too much of themselves and too little. They mirrored the culture we live in.

Clinicians also mirror the culture in which we live. Whereas female helplessness and inferiority are readily understood (perhaps even expected), the idea of female power can be deeply threatening. The realm of women's power is one in which the perceptions and the interpretations of the clinician, female and male, may be subject to considerable bias.

In the dialogues generated by the Women's Movement, it has been the inequities in the spheres of economic and political power that have had the most prominent focus. The realm of psychological power has had little recognition. Yet those who listen closely hear women speak of their nurturant power, not only in relation to the home but in the marketplace as well. Such power is effectively exercised by the executive associate, by the woman professor who is an "academic mother" to younger teachers, and by all those women who facilitate and integrate, comfort and encourage, privately believing, "It's up to me to make it work."

Miller (1982) is among the few clinicians who have recognized authentic and benevolent power in women, and her observations correspond with what the Northland movers revealed. Defining power as "the capacity to produce a change . . . acting to create movement in an interpersonal field" (p. 2), she concludes that "women have exerted enormous powers in their traditional role of fostering the growth of others, and they have found that empowering others is a valuable and gratifying activity" (p. 1).

It is sometimes assumed that feelings of empowerment and superiority—especially among women—are spurious, serving as a defense against underlying vulnerability and inferiority. Such an assumption was prevalent among those Freudian theorists who viewed genital "inferiority" (the lack of a penis) as a central issue of female development. A feminist theorist, Friedan, has argued that *female machismo*—her term for what I would consider an exaggerated, manipulative, and hostile power in the family—is a defense. "That female machismo, passed on from mother to daughter, hides the same inadmissible self-hate, weakness, sense of powerlessness as machismo hides in men" (1981, p. 113). In turn, she views self-hate as arising from the woman's vulnerability, economic dependence, and denigration by society. Power in the family is a reaction against weakness in society.

There are indeed instances in which nurturant power is exercised in compensation for, or reaction against, restricted access to economic and political spheres. However, the opposite case can just as persuasively be argued—namely, that the restriction of women's access to the marketplace has arisen out of the urge of men (and some women as well) to contain and control the deep sexual, procreative, and nurturant powers of femaleness.

In fact, power in the marketplace, so often referred to as "real power," may be less feared and therefore more highly valued in our culture just because it can more readily be controlled. If monetary reward is provided, monetary reward can also be withdrawn. In contrast, relentless attempts to impose control on women's sexual, procreative, and nurturant capacities through demands for chastity, through regulation of conception, pregnancy, and childbirth, attest to the fears those powers arouse.

Those fears are alive in the minds of women as well as men. Therefore, whereas women do at times mobilize feelings of invincibility to defend against uncertainty, the opposite is also true. A sense of helpless inferiority can serve as a shield against deep strength derived from early identification with the powerful mother, strength that feels threatening because of its aggressive potential (Bernardez-Bonesatti, 1978; Lerner, 1980). This is the potential to "invade," to "worm my way in," to "burst through other people's boundaries," that Northland women described as their dreads.

Contradictory self-representations do serve in complex ways as defenses against opposites that feel forbidden. Yet contradictions can also coexist as authentic aspects of a woman's self which have developed, from infancy onward, through internalization of sociocultural systems of belief.

Culture is most powerfully transmitted within the family. Without doubt, the parental attributes, behaviors, and communications that shape the child's emerging self are highly variable. Every parent is an individual, interacting with an infant who is unique from the moment of birth. But every parent has been shaped by the culture and is a carrier of the culture through the model she or he presents, and through the attitudes she or he transmits.

The image, or idea, *woman*, has long been polarized in our culture (and in many others as well). *Woman* is idealized or debased, seen as pure or defiled, splendid or worthless, strong or weak. Thus the young, adult male senses himself:

> As a little boy in relation to a powerful maternal figure . . . devouring witch, feeding breast, sexual seducer, willing servant and demanding master. (Levinson, 1978, p. 107)

The contradictory views of women that pervade our culture most likely relate to man's dualistic experience of the first woman in his life, his powerful mother. He has learned to denigrate her in defense against her intrusions into his body and his psyche, in defense against his recurrent wish (often unconscious) to re-experience the early, warmly melded, suckled bliss, and in defense against the femininity he incorporated within himself through his earliest identification with her. Paradoxically, that early internalization of her ideal qualities leaves as its residue the idealization of the woman he also denigrates.

Through their own development, through the complexities of internalization and identification, through parents as intermediaries, the selfhood of women also has been imbued with those contradictions. Women, too, have become carriers of a cultural polarization of the concept *woman*.

Modifying the Paradoxes

Although Sigmund Freud's dictum that "anatomy is destiny" has outraged feminists both because of its biological determinism and its phallocentric skew, the fact that men and women alike have first developed in woman's uterus and have been nourished by her breasts has powerfully shaped the fears and longings, the denigration and idealization directed towards and against her. As men are freed to become primary caregivers, to experience their empowerment in the deepest nurturant realms, and as women are allowed more freely to carry their nurturant power into economic and political realms, society may find a new equilibrium of power between the sexes. Both sexes may become able to enjoy their personal wholeness and the unfettered fulfillment of all their potentialities. Then the debasement of woman can be expected to undergo gradual change. The polarization of the image, *woman*, can be expected to undergo gradual change.

Both men and women must become agents in that change. Just as the individual man can be helped to recognize, value, and express his own sensitivity and tenderness (the "feminine" aspects of self), the individual woman can be helped to struggle free from the polarization—the partially unconscious, contradictory representations of self. In the arena of choosing to move, she must confront some challenging questions. Do I have a right to personal fulfillment, including but extending beyond my care of others? Am I prepared to seek that fulfillment, or do I feel too helpless? Do I feel unworthy? Disturbing as they are, these recognitions of helplessness and unworthiness (traditionally linked to femininity) are easier for most women to confront than recognition of power. The more difficult question is this: Am I ignoring or minimizing obstacles because I privately imagine that I have the power to transcend them, the power to deal with anything that comes along, the power somehow to *make* things turn out for my loved ones as well as for myself?

Recognizing that exaggerated optimism, that heady vision of power or its opposite, the painful feeling of unworthiness and helplessness, means taking a significant step towards the self-awareness that helps us control our destinies. To varying degrees the introjects that have been integrated into these self-representations may need to be investigated and identified, with the aim of fostering insight and a liberating differentiation. It is as though certain introjects can be "extrajected," in a sense, leaving a woman with a clarity that "although I have internalized my father's strict standards, I am not my critical father, after all; I am Barbara, with aims of my own."

Even if the clinician does not work in sufficient depth to identify the sources of a woman's sense of self, much can be gained if a woman's contradictory self-representations can at least be drawn out of their dark mental recesses and subjected to the clear light of reality testing. Since unrealistically high expectations often lead to a sense of failure and a depressive state, a woman can fruitfully be encouraged to imagine how it would be to modify those lofty ideals just a little. Must she really stand on a shining pinnacle or else fall into a dark abyss? Are there no green pastures in between?

It is painful for a woman to question the high expectations she holds for herself, since they express both her sense of power and her ideals. "That's the way I believe all people should behave towards each other," a young therapy client told me with conviction when I pointed out her implacable need to be the healer, the fixer, to make things come out right for others. Such nurturant power should indeed be cherished. Sometimes misused, manipulative, and hostile, to be sure, it has also been a benign influence in the world, and could become much more so if it were allowed to permeate the political sphere. But it becomes a source of trouble for the individual and is wasted as a positive energy in society when the boundaries of a woman's responsibility are blurred, and when she commits herself to fixing the unfixable. So she needs to question whether her dreams are really attainable, whether and how they shape her choices, whether they set her up for inevitable disappointment, or guide her towards being and feeling effective and worthwhile.

Self-sacrificing moves can squander nurturant power, to the detriment of the individual woman, her loved ones, and society. When she undertakes a move heroically, with disregard for her needs, she allows that power to oppress her.

Loss, Grief, and Reconnection

There are no norms establishing an expectable time of onset, intensity, and duration of grief or mourning (Wortman & Silver, 1989). Yet most clinicians would agree that mourning is an essential process that allows for adaptation to loss and change, and that can have as its outcome "resolution, gain, creativity, and/or investment of psychic interest in new areas, activities, or objects" (Pollock, 1977, p. 16). The clinician can usefully foster the process of grieving (or mourning) by exploring with the mover what is being lost, what has been lost (and, for the prospective mover, what will be lost), and the meanings and emotions associated with those losses. Sorrow is likely to be accessible to conscious recognition and expression. Anger in response to those losses, and guilt in response to the anger or towards those the mover has "abandoned" may be far less accessible, but considerably more troublesome because of their role in inducing depression. Sensitive intervention will be needed to coax those powerful emotions into awareness, and to help the mover accept them with self-forgiveness.

Close friendship has not been recognized as a sociocultural institution (Rubin, 1985), perhaps because it has not been as significant for men as for women, and the male experience has in the past been accepted as normative. Therefore, close friends who are still living may not be readily recognized by the clinician or by the client as significant objects of mourning. Yet among contemporary women, intimate friendships serve crucial needs. Through her recognition, a close friend confirms a woman's identity; through her responsiveness, she replenishes a woman's self-regard; through her care and concern she nourishes a woman's own capacity for concern, love, and for work. And all those fulfillments are reciprocal. A woman's self-worth may be significantly based on her capacity to develop and sustain empathic connection. When her close friendships are disrupted by moving, not only is her self-esteem threatened, but even her core sense of self. The loss of a dear friend is thus both an object loss and a narcissistic loss— a loss disturbing the stability, continuity, and positive valuation of the self. Such meanings need recognition in therapy with troubled movers. The prospective mover should be confronted with the fact that by moving she may risk an irreplaceable loss of intimate friendship.

Many of the losses mourned by the mover are both object losses and lost aspects of self, and these continue to be experienced during the sometimes prolonged transition. The metaphor of invisibility, often used by movers, captures a spectrum of almost inevitable narcissistic losses—being unrecognized, unresponded to, excluded— that they experience as reconnection gradually takes place. Such losses arouse not only grief but depression as well, and are likely to rekindle the hurt of childhood experiences of invisibility or exclusion.

Grief in the present rekindles grief in the past, whether consciously remembered or not. The separations and losses inherent in a move cause past separations and losses to be remourned, thus contributing unexpected intensity to the mover's grief. Even in nurturing and intact families, separation anxiety reverberates across time: the babe awakens hungry and alone in the night, the five-year-old trudges with fearful excitement to the school bus, the adolescent pulls out of the family cocoon by repudiating attachments that still matter. At each of these junctures, the sadness, anger, fear, and guilt attached to prior separations may surge up afresh. By exploring the history of loss, clinician and client share the opportunity to deal anew with unfinished psychological business— perhaps uncovering and resolving a troublesome ambivalence towards an abandoning family member, perhaps uncovering and resolving the mover's own guilt for having been an abandoner.

To reexperience past wounds is to subject them to new mastery. No longer a child who is helpless in the face of adversity, the adult woman has the possibility to invoke new strengths and resources. She has the potential for insight, through which not only the realities of past events can be better understood, but also their meaning to her, the emotions they aroused, and the way they shape her present life. From her understanding, self-forgiveness and forgiveness of others can follow, as well as the changes needed to enhance her life.

Furthermore, to explore the losses connected with the recent move is not only to bring her painful emotions into awareness, but to validate their appropriateness and thus to reduce shame. It also serves to validate the significance of the lost relationship or capability. It fosters healing as well, because it confirms the mover's capacity to form deep friendship and to express her other capabilities.

Although the pain of loss can be well understood and accepted, it must nonetheless be endured. It is helpful to explore a woman's capacity for self-soothing. External separation can be endured when internal connection can be preserved. Thus Winnicott (1965) described "the capacity to be alone"—a hallmark of psychological maturity—as developing through early internalization of mental images of the mother's presence. Mahler et al. (1975) contributed the concept of "object constancy," whereby the toddler becomes able to tolerate physical separation from the mother as he or she becomes able to retain a mental image of the mother in her absence. Buie and Adler (1982) proposed the concept of *evocative memory*, the capacity to soothe and comfort oneself with images and memories derived from early interactions with the primary caregiver. Perhaps those movers who grieve most powerfully have not had reliable, consistent, empathic, and loving caregivers whose qualities and responses became a source of soothing evocative memory in times of distress. When this is the case, a prolonged psychotherapy may be needed to afford the client the opportunity for the development of new, healing relationships that can become internalized as new "structures" within the mind. A discussion of such therapy is beyond the scope of this work, but is usefully described by Adler (1985).

Yet it must also be stressed that some of those women who grieve most powerfully after a move may not have been deprived of the emotional nourishment they needed early in their lives. Rather, they may be women who form deep and precious bonds that cannot be sustained through geographic separation, or they may become overwhelmed by repeated moves and losses.

It is wise to confront prospective movers with the realization that by choosing to move they will be choosing a spectrum of losses as well as gains. The potential for loss is sometimes relieving. Certain separations are welcome, and they seem easier to effect by leaving the scene than by trying to disentangle in the same locale. Yet it can be easy to externalize an inner malaise, attributing boredom and unhappiness to outer circumstance. We imagine that by fleeing the environs and the relationships that have become dreary we will regain our zest for life. That does sometimes happen. It also happens that the bleakness we had hoped to leave behind is carried within, and it soon again pervades our lives. The clinician can usefully spur the prospective mover to examine what it is she wants to leave and whether, in fact, it really can be left behind.

The prospective mover actively needs to consider the likely balance of loss and gain. For the professional woman considering a better apartment in her own city, the transient loss of familiarity and sense of competence even such a small move entails may seem a price she would gladly pay to live in a more attractive milieu. Her identity, work, and close relationships will be undisturbed. But a move into more efficient quarters in the same town can also be castastrophic if the move symbolizes an enduring loss of competence and of personal history, as Jennifer's experience so clearly showed. Had Jennifer consulted a therapist before her move, she would have been encouraged to explore the full spectrum of alternative solutions that might have preserved her connection with the too-big but beloved home.

Work and Recognition

Women still subscribe to the pervasive belief that work is only that which is done outside the home for financial compensation. Even if they privately recognize the complexity and power of their domestic roles (as many do), women are curiously diffident about openly claiming that sphere as work. The clinician may unwittingly collude in that denial. But making a responsible decision about moving—a decision that takes into account a woman's range of needs as well as the needs of her loved ones—requires that claim. It requires that a woman scan her life and identify all the various realms of work in which she is engaged—in the home and in the marketplace, paid and voluntary, task-oriented, and interpersonal. It requires rethinking her work priorities. That self-questioning can bring into fresh focus some realms of her life that she has taken for granted. It can highlight what she stands to lose, what she wants to preserve, and what she needs to recreate if she moves.

Women tend to experience a dispersion of their energies and commitments. With several realms of work in which their sense of self is embedded, they are less likely than men to identify one sphere as the central organizer in their lives. The traditional male model of an over-riding and focused commitment to one realm of work is not a model that most women truly want to emulate (in fact, there are many men who would prefer alternative styles for themselves and, largely because of the Women's Movement, new choices are becoming available for them). Yet, in the absence of an over-riding commitment, women too easily disparage the importance of any single sphere of their work. Too readily, a coupled woman abdicates the right to make choices about moving that are based on her work, and too heedlessly she sets aside significant work in preparation for a move. However, the dispersion a woman feels can make it more difficult for her than for a man to maintain a sense of continuity through change, so preserving a satisfying realm of work is equally important for her as for him.

It is strategic for a woman mover to realize that work fulfills a dual set of needs. It allows her to experience effectiveness, the sense of fulfilling potentialities, and that idea is acceptable for most women. Work also allows her to enjoy outside appreciation of her competence and her specialness. For the mover, accepting that need to be noticed is of great significance, yet it is fraught with conflict.

There are, of course, individual men for whom visible accomplishment has deep linkages with forbidden aggression and/or sexual exhibitionism, and therefore arouses anxiety. Yet, it is a sociocultural assumption that men will and men should seek recognition. Among men, that need becomes poignantly visible at the time of retirement, when the loss of a man's public "label" is often paralleled by an anxiety-laden disturbance of the sense of self (indeed, the most distinguished labels, such as President, General, or Senator may never be set aside). At the time of retirement, men experience the same feelings that women feel at many times of their lives.

Many contradictory qualities are imputed to women. A particularly corrosive dualism, or pair of opposites, is that of altruism versus selfishness—the latter label being relentlessly applied to woman's care or concern for self. The tension between these opposites was expressed by a therapy client, a married woman with young children, as she agonized over a decision to apply to medical school. Care of her family, an altruistic responsibility, was expected of her by others and by herself. The wish for professional training was labeled by her relatives and by herself as selfish— it aroused reproach from them and guilt in her. Knowing of her fantasies of helping others through medical training, I challenged her assumptions. Why did the wish to be a physician seem to be selfish rather than being an extension of caregiving beyond her immediate family? Why would care of sick people be less altruistic than care of husband and children? Because there would be satisfactions in addition to healing, she explained. Uneasily, she confided her wish for the prestige and recognition that a medical degree would confer, as well as the power to influence health-care decisions. For a man, such wishes would be accepted as inevitable. For a woman, care of self and care of others are not yet seen as harmonious. They are held in the tension of opposition.

In the individual woman, the conflict between the drive toward achievement (with ensuing recognition) and the drive toward nurturance may be so severe that she may attempt to use a move to evade the conflict. Since avoidance does not lead to resolution, this is a motive the clinician should explore.

Overt and covert denial of women's need for recognition is expressed in a variety of ways. For example, Friedan (1981), among others, emphasizes the financial motives propeling family women into the paid workforce. To be sure, in some families the woman is the sole financial provider. In some families, a second income is essential to procure decent housing, food, clothing, medical care, and other true necessities. But many women are victimized by the relentless consumerism in our society, an ideological pressure persuading us that luxuries are necessities. Just as financial need can dictate paid work, paid work can create financial need—for more cars, clothes, and convenience foods. Ironically, the labor expended to buy labor-saving appliances stretches many employed women to their utmost, and stresses many families. In these various ways, financial need is sometimes an illusory rationale for entering the paid workforce. But perhaps we focus on it because financial need is a more acceptable motive than a woman's psychological need to leave her isolated private domain and seek public recognition—confirmation of her specialness in an impersonal society.

The issue of "specialness" is troublesome for some clinicians. Especially in the last decade, as the deep character pathologies have commanded increasing attention, I have noted among therapists for whom I provide clinical supervision a tendency to link the wish to be special, or the feeling of specialness, to the narcissistic personality disorder. Therapists belittle or deny their own wishes for specialness as though the word were a perjorative, and target such longings in patients or clients as hallmarks of pathology. Such a bias can interfere with the understanding that although fantasies of specialness can indeed be pathologically exaggerated, they are also prevalent among the myriad people on whom a technological society has imposed anonymity.

Conflicts around the mover's wish for specialness need exploration; her wish for recognition needs validation. The woman who moves directly into a new professional workplace, as men so often do, will sustain recognition. But those many women who interrupt their professional work so that their men can follow a rainbow, and those many women whose lives are centered by the hearth, will lose that sustaining recognition. Regaining it will take strategic effort, and that effort cannot fruitfully begin until the need for recognition is understood and accepted.

Reverberations in the Family

According to the Census Bureau (Current Population Reports, 1989), the highest proportion of U.S. movers are between 20-34 years of age. This, of course, is the time of life when both women and men are likely to be intensively engaged in forming love relationships and starting nuptial families, as well as building the foundations of their careers. The stresses of moving are likely to coincide with a phase of development in which young adults are already taxed to the utmost. Yet, from the Northland study as well as long experience as a clinician, I find it striking how few couples consider the effects of a major move on their relationship. Even couples whose bonds have become severely strained rarely seem to make a connection between their difficulties and an impending move, a move they are engaged in, or a recent move. Many clinicians also have participated in this pervasive denial of the significance of moving. Even when the fact of a move is recorded in the family history, the meanings of the move are often unexplored.

Just as choice about moving is an invaluable channel through which to explore a woman's sense of self, the marital or family therapist will find it a useful conduit into relational dynamics. Perceptions and fantasies about each partner will emerge, as well as the exercise of rights, responsibilities, and power. Who wished (or wishes) to move and why? Whose aims were (or are) being served? How was (or is) the decision arrived at? Has the woman participated in true partnership? Has the woman, instead, felt victimized? Who has been charged with responsibility for the success of the move? Are the fantasies of responsibility attainable? Has the couple examined the powerful emotional impact a move may have, or may have had, on their relationship?

Many psychotherapists would agree that nuclear families in the United States tend to be emotionally overburdened. Sometimes every member seems to need a "wife," if "wife" is metaphor for a soothing, loving, available presence. The mobile couple or family, separated from familiar, trustworthy, concerned, and comforting friends, relatives, colleagues, clergy, and health professionals turns in on itself and is too often unable to meet its own needs.

Dealing with anxiety, sadness, and loneliness of their own, children and father may turn to the mother for their "fix"—comfort, encouragement, reassurance, and other supplies she may be unable to provide. Deprived of all other relationships, roles, and realms of work, the woman may direct all of her emotional investment toward the family. She may feel a heightened (perhaps exaggerated) interest in their successes, which confirm her effectiveness as a nurturer and provide vicarious recognition.

Yet she may also envy and resent her family's fulfillment during that interlude when she is experiencing "invisibility" in the new community. Feeling unrecognized and grieving for close friends, she may turn to her husband with more intensity of need than the man can respond to, especially when he is anxiously preoccupied with his own new realm of work. Resentful of his unavailability and feeling sadly unvalued, she may then question whether the marriage is barren. She may turn to her offspring and create an inversion in which the child is asked to take care of her mother, and can only feel guilty when he or she cannot succeed. Or the mother's depletion may even lead to neglect or abuse of her children. Some women seek solace in alcohol, pills, desserts, shopping sprees—whatever seems momentarily to fill the empty inner spaces. And those disturbing reverberations in his wife stir guilt, anxiety, and resentment in the husband.

Couples must be helped to recognize that moving brings to the forefront in both partners their needs for nurturance and recognition. Both must untangle their view of each other and of themselves from the skew of sociocultural expectations. Whereas it has traditionally been unquestioned that a man has a need for and a right to public validation (accorded through salary, status, or reputation), this has not been accepted as a legitimate need of women. Whereas it has traditionally been unquestioned that a man has a need for and right to nurturance in the home, to be provided by his helpmate, a woman has not been accorded the same. Man has been expected to provide financially and sexually rather than emotionally. Woman is viewed, and often views herself, as the nurturer, not the nurturee, even though her need is no less than that of her mate.

Women who experience themselves as powerful caregivers may have difficulty acknowledging their own need for nurturing care, because the need threatens that image of power. But it usually does not, at least, threaten their sense of femininity. Women do seek nurturance in intimate friendships, and sometimes from their mates. But men, even though they expect and accept nurturance from wives and lovers at home, and from a variety of assistants in the workplace, have far greater difficulty admitting their need. Reflecting dependency and "weakness," it threatens their sense of masculinity.

Limitations must be appreciated as well as needs. The ideals of nurturant power and perfection that women strive to fulfill, and that men both tend to seek and to fear, need modulation. The woman's fantasy of "it's up to me to make it work," a fantasy in which her husband may collude, needs to yield to the reality that no one woman can control the destinies of others in such powerful ways. Or only very rarely so. But for a more modulated and attainable ideal self to remain energized with healthy self-love and benign aggression, a woman needs replenishment. She needs recognition of her capabilities as well as affectionate nurturance from outside the family and from within. Her husband does as well.

Both partners have to struggle through barriers within themselves in order to acknowledge those needs, which are heightened by moving since the accustomed sources of gratification have been left behind. Until the needs are examined and accepted, the couple can scarcely consider what sources of fulfillment in the new environs may be available. They can scarcely consider how they may more effectively respond to each other. Couples who move tend to erect or reinforce communication barriers. Both partners may hold back, either because of guilt or shame about their own troubled feelings, or out of a wish to protect a fragile mate against over-burdening, or both. Yet the holding back tends to intensify the anger, resentment, envy, loneliness, sadness, depression, and anxiety—states that surely are communicated without words. Understanding the psychological tasks of moving, and the powerful feelings aroused, can open the door to constructive communication. The relationship can become more empathic, more trusting, more resilient, and the resources of two minds can be pooled to solve problems.

Furthermore couples can be helped to express their mutual care by looking as seriously at the gains of not moving as of moving. They can be helped to look beyond the traditional image of betterment from external sources, especially by climbing a career ladder whose rungs are dispersed across the land. Achievement in the marketplace is exalted in our society. The clinician can serve the couple well by challenging them to consider why a new vocational opportunity should inevitably take precedence over the valued interpersonal connections that will be ruptured.

They can be helped to think creatively about ways that life can be deepened, extended, and enriched by developing potentials that lie within the personality, and within the familiar environs—new realms of learning, new roles, new relationships. Psychological moves rather than geographic moves can be chosen.

PRACTICAL STRATEGIES

Researching the Prospective Community

Four cornerstones underlying responsible choice are: self-awareness, acceptance of the right to make need-fulfilling choices, responsiveness to loved ones, and realistic information. Without that, no mover can know if a new environment has the potential to foster her security, effectiveness, significance, and capacity for work and love.

"I haven't the slightest idea how to go about finding out about a new community," a highly intelligent young woman told me as she contemplated another move, this one away from Northland. She was not unique in her perplexity, a perplexity that seems to reflect the failure of many women to clarify their needs. We cannot find answers until we understand the questions.

How might an unfamiliar community be researched? One valuable and under-recognized resource is the local librarian who can draw on expertise in the realm of information retrieval, using new computer technology at her or his command. Supplementing the library's sources of data with materials requested from the Chamber of Commerce of the new community, its Town Hall and the League of Women Voters, the initial research could yield information about climate, population characteristics, cost of living and real estate values, recreational and cultural facilities, job opportunities, political climate, level of street crime, and a great deal more.

Newspapers from the new community as well as phone books, which the librarian might help procure, could yield addresses of sources of further information: women's organizations (health, informational, legal and counseling services); childcare resources; school districts; churches; and special interest groups such as peace groups, conservation groups, political or artistic associations, and community service organizations. Some of these resources could be contacted directly, along with a women's school alumnae association and her business or professional association. Through these in turn, or through her or her husband's prospective employer, she could hope to locate an acquaintance in the community, a "friend of a friend" or someone willing to talk frankly about its characteristics.

An exploratory visit is of prime importance, but its value will be proportionate to the prospective mover's clarity of purpose and the precision of her questions: "What am I trying to find out?" she needs to ask herself in advance. "What is most important in my life?"

For example, it is helpful for the prospective mover to locate her lines of attachment to her present home as she considers leaving it. Is her sense of self strongly connected to the actual structure of her present dwelling? Is it linked to the rooms themselves, the way they have shaped activities and relationships? Is it attached to the surrounding land that has been her playground or garden? Is it connected to the views, the neighborhood? If her sense of self—history, continuity, self-esteem—seems embedded in the physical qualities of her home, the rupture will be deep. Perhaps the move should be reconsidered. Or, at the least, the mover can now identify the characteristics that a new dwelling would need for lines of positive connection to be reconstructed—a certain kind of room arrangement, a particular orientation to the sun, a special sort of view, proximity to or distance from other people. The mover's preparation for a visit might include organizing her personal "inventory" in an outline or checklist. The mover's library may also be able to supply a practical guide to househunting.

On her visit(s), the mover might accompany a realtor or rent a car and drive around different sections of the new community at different times of day. Supplied with local maps, she might observe the flow of traffic among various residential areas, schools, and her (or her husband's) prospective workplace, as well as the quality of public transportation. She might notice provisions for cyclists, joggers, and walkers. She might study the types of housing and their relationship to the land. She might notice the age range and ethnic characteristics of the dwellers in various neighborhoods, as well as their styles of outdoor interaction.

The mover could saunter around appealing neighborhoods and chat with householders about local customs and lifestyles. For every householder who might find her knock on the door intrusive, another could find it welcome, and enjoy the chance to be an "authority" about the locale. Dwellings for rent or sale could be closely investigated, with the checklist, a tapemeasure, a sketchpad, and camera to supplement the mover's memories. Not only the cost of housing, but also the typical cost of heating or cooling must be investigated.

An occasional woman dismantles her home and recreates it with unflagging confidence and cheer. For most, the transient confusion, disorganization, and helplessness are threats to self-esteem. Those with strong needs for order, predictability, and control—there are many—will feel most anxious and depressed. Such women would be wise to consider how repeated disruptions could be minimized, especially by trying to avoid short-term rentals. A woman can readily imagine, "We'll rent something for a while, and then . . ." disregarding the high cost in energy and well-being of the "and then."

Those Northland movers who most happily and smoothly recreated their homes were privileged. They had time and money to choose a truly appealing habitat. Few of us can expect to live in Camelot; compromise is an inescapable reality. But it is useful to question whether the necessary compromises will feel tolerable while it is still possible not to move. It is wise for a woman to avoid subjecting herself to the shattering of daydreams later on, at a time when she is stressed and unusually vulnerable.

The opportunity to do work commanding recognition outside the household—be it selling homemade Greek pastries, organizing fund-raising drives, or doing biochemical research—is crucial to the well-being of the woman mover. A central task for the prospective mover is to identify a sphere of satisfying and visible work that she can pursue with continuity if she moves, and to find out whether or not there will be opportunities in the new community to do that work. This task is a necessity for most single movers. It is avoided by many coupled movers, professional women as well as homemakers. Yet it should be pursued as seriously as if a woman's livelihood is at stake. That may become true in financial terms. It will almost certainly become true in psychological terms.

Opportunities can be explored through professional and business associations, journals, magazine and newspaper advertisements, and by persistent inquiries at every opportunity during an exploratory visit. If the mover's primary work is homemaking, she can easily disregard her needs, persuading herself that "I can do it anywhere." But responsible self-care requires that she ask herself what and who supports her in being effective in the domestic sphere, and who supplies her with needed recognition. She will need to search diligently for potential new colleagues, inquiring about nursery schools, play groups, parent groups, children's libraries, and recreation centers—inquiring on behalf of her own needs as well as her child's.

Women sometimes imagine that moving will provide a natural opportunity to make a work or role transition. Indeed, a work or role transition often necessitates a move. But the confluence of so much change can be overwhelming. It can be wiser to separate those transitions in time if possible, either postponing a move until after the work change is resolved, or carrying the continuity of familiar work into the new locale.

All this information, those observations, can be scanned in relation to the thoughtful appraisal the potential mover has been making of her needs. In what ways, she should ask herself, would moving to this place change my life, diminish my life, enhance my life? She may conclude that she does not want to give up the familiar elements that make her present life meaningful. She may constructively prompt her spouse or lover to think more deeply about his or her own choices.

Efforts like these take time and energy and some money as well. Most of all, they take honesty and courage. But is a woman not worthy of such an investment in her personal future? Is she not as worthy as she believes her family to be?

Research for Retirement

Although the greatest number of moves in the United States are made during the third and fourth decades of life in association with career development and marriage, many moves are occasioned by retirement. The Northland movers who were approaching or at retirement age knew with considerable clarity what elements in their lives gave it special zest or meaning, although in some cases my inquiries helped them focus their ideas (as such inquiries often do). But they had not necessarily taken into account the transformations that retirement would bring about, nor the severe stress of simultaneous retirement and moving. And that is not surprising. Thinking about retirement requires thinking about ending of one's life, and few among us do that without dismay. It is painful to consider, "The place I am now choosing to live is the place where I will die."

But just because of that implication, there are special aspects of a prospective community that the mover who has retired, or is contemplating retirement, should consider. These are based on crucial issues associated with aging. First, even beyond the losses faced by most movers, which have been discussed in detail, the older mover faces inevitable loss of physical capabilities. If possible, this should be counterbalanced by continuing growth in other spheres—new knowledge, new forms of self-expression, new contributions to society. (In this respect, the dispersion of women's roles and affiliations in their earlier years may open up more possibilities at retirement age than men experience, and a coupled woman may actively need to help her mate find new occupations and meanings in his own life, some shared with her, some separate.) Second, the older mover faces another realm of probable loss, the bleak prospect of the death of spouse and/or other loved ones. As much as possible, this needs to be offset by continuing connection to younger family members and friends. Third, the older mover (except for a privileged minority) faces a reduction of financial resources.

If these are among the major issues, what characteristics of a prospective community need to be researched, beyond those that are relevant for all movers?

Loss of physical capabilities can often be postponed if the older woman stays physically active. What facilities and programs are available for swimming, bicycling, cross-country skiing, racquet sports, low-demand dance and rhythmic movement, and at what expense? Is it safe to walk? In the north, sidewalks are icy in winter (Is there an indoor walking track?), and everywhere there are questions about street crime. Is the older walker at risk for being assaulted? Is the older walker at risk for a fractured hip?

Medical care for older women involves special issues. Will they have access to a sympathetic physician to work out the best medical regimen to prevent or reduce the scourge of osteoporosis (the thinning and increased brittleness of bones that often follows menopause and results in many a broken hip). Mammograms and pap smears are essential to detect early cancers. Are such procedures readily available and affordable? Planned Parenthood and the Visiting Nurses Association may be good sources of information about health care for the older prospective mover.

But in spite of health-sustaining efforts, loss of physical capabilities will inevitably occur. When it becomes risky to drive a car, will an efficient, safe system of public transportation be available? In the community, will there be easy physical access to shopping, recreational facilities, the library, the new workplace? Is affordable housing available with ready access (a level driveway and entry, one-story living quarters)?

Illness will inevitably occur. What general medical care will be available for the older woman, probably on a reduced income? Are there physicians with a particular interest in geriatrics (the care of aging patients)? What hospitals, nursing homes, day-care programs are available, and are there Hospice programs for the time of dying? What outreach programs are available for the homebound woman?

Since the prospect of death often gives new urgency to a religious affiliation, will a church compatible with the mover's belief system be available and accessible?

Death of loved ones, whether spouse or dear friends, is inevitable. This fact should cause the prospective mover to pause and consider deeply the wisdom of uprooting. Is the time when one faces the possible loss of one's nearest and dearest (the life expectancy of men is still shorter than women's) a wise time to sever connection with a supportive network of long-term friends and colleagues? The Northland study has shown how slowly new intimacies grow.

The mover should ask herself several questions concerning loss and replacement in relation to the prospective community. The wish of many aging women is to move closer to their offspring, or other family members. This can be an appealing prospect, but a risky one. What if that son or daughter then decides to move away? Is she or he rooted deeply enough so that moving is unlikely?

Will the mover feel more comfortable in a retirement community in which all the inhabitants share the needs and concerns of aging, or will she feel more vitalized and comforted by sustaining connection with younger people outside of her family? Where in the community could such mingling take place? A university town has a high proportion of young adults, but will the older newcomer find ways to be among them? Will there be lectures and discussion groups in which she will be a welcome participant? Might there be programs that would allow her to become a proxy grandmother to children in need of nurturance?

It has been convincingly shown that pets assuage grief and make life meaningful for the elderly, and may have direct physical benefits as well (for example, stroking a dog may reduce blood pressure). Can the mover locate safe, accessible, affordable housing that will allow pets to be in residence?

But there's much more to aging than illness and death. There is the possibility of counterbalancing loss with gain. The older mover will need to sustain her intellectual, political, and cultural interests and, hopefully, to develop new ones both with her spouse and on her own. Towards these goals, she should investigate the availability of and access to libraries, university courses, artistic and musical programs and instruction, and the possibility for active participation as a singer, painter, potter, or weaver. The mover should investigate the availability of groups dedicated to other special interests, such as conservation or nuclear disarmament. There is as much place in the Sierra Club, for example, for a woman willing to help with a mailing as a woman interested in technical rock climbing. Within such organizations, she can develop new connections with people of all ages.

The prospective mover should research opportunities for work, paid or unpaid. Easily overlooked for the older woman, sometimes still stereotyped as grandma in a rocking chair enjoying her well-earned rest, work affords her a needed sense of having a significant role in society. Some communities have organizations devoted to matching the talents of older voluntary or part-time paid workers with unmet human needs.

Finally, since the psychological work of moving tends to be done primarily by women, a coupled woman should encourage her spouse—whose life will no longer be organized around his work in the marketplace—to seek all of the same sorts of information on behalf of himself. Most of the questions raised in chapter six, questions about how moving can influence a marriage, can be just as germane for the retired couple.

Making it Work

If a truly thoughtful decision to move is made, a woman of any age is better equipped to seek out the elements to make it work for herself as well as for her loved ones.

A woman's sense of safety, competence, and continuity are both expressed in and reinforced by her home. Although her actual dwelling is rarely transportable (the mobile home being the exception), many of her possessions are. In planning the move, it is useful to consider which objects are most strongly imbued with positive memories—the battered aluminum pot, now used for spaghetti, in which the baby's bottles were once sterilized? The rocking chair in which she was soothed? The complete set of Nancy Drew mysteries? The tattered posters of Grateful Dead? It is tempting but risky to consign them to a garage sale. Are they junk or are they really treasures? It is risky to entrust them all to a van. Some need to become part of a survival kit, more important—because they are irreplaceable—than the toothbrush or can opener usually carried by hand.

What special foods express the family history? If sweet Hungarian paprika or hot green chiles season those foods, can a supply be brought along? Is there an herb tea that invokes memories of long chats with a beloved friend?

What snippets can be taken from the garden to be rooted in a mug? Can a handful of bulbs be dug? No, they won't quickly reproduce the glorious sweep of gold that was left behind. But they will foster linkages between past and present; they will help rekindle the good feelings attached to the past and allow them to imbue the present.

* * *

Among the Northland movers, there was a handful who experienced a high level of pleasure and a low level of suffering early in their transition. They were offered sponsorship. None had intimate friends already in Northland, but some had cordial acquaintances who provided a warm welcome, who served as escorts in the new community, who supplied companionship and introduced the newcomers to those with kindred backgrounds and interests, who made available information that could help the newcomer understand the customs and expectations of Northland people, as well as information about needed goods and services. "They gathered me in," said one, her phrase strikingly evocative of the formal "rituals of incorporation" practiced by traditional societies around the world, and practiced informally by tight ethnic communities in American cities as they absorb new immigrants. A few other Northland movers were similarly "gathered in" by networks of young mothers and their churches.

A sponsor—a welcoming, warming, informing, facilitating presence—was provided to only a few movers. But a potential mover able to recognize the need for such help and her right to have it, might locate a sponsor for herself through an alumnae association, professional association, women's network, Welcome Wagon, Newcomer's Club, or her church. Preferably, she should try to make such a connection even before moving for the warm reassurance of knowing a hand is being held out towards her.

The benefits of sponsorship are increasingly recognized by organizations intended to serve people with other shared needs and problems, Alcoholics Anonymous or Overeaters Anonymous, for example. Given that one out of five Americans is a mover every year, sharing a multitude of common needs and problems, the provision of easily accessible sponsorship through either private organizations or municipal government is badly overdue. This is a realm in which mental health professionals with organizational skills could serve a key role.

* * *

We rarely think of making friends as a form of work. Prospective movers may imagine that it will simply happen. But once schooldays are past, with their shared spaces, their inevitable interactions in work and play, opportunities must be intentionally sought for recurrent meetings with people who share experience, values, interest, and goals—potential friends.

In Northland, during the warm months, fruitful months, months of harvest, there is a Farmer's Market. From the verdant valleys come bearded men and sturdy women with glowing faces, plaited hair, and nursing babes. There are kids, goatlings "selling" their mothers' cheese. Trucks backed into a ring spill onto the stands their crisply frilled lettuce, their yielding red tomatoes and squash—amber, ochre, and burnt sienna, gnarled or smooth—and rough, sweet melons, pungent basil, "organic" garlic swelling plumply, fat breadloaves densely grained, clear jellies, fragrant vinegars, and still more nannygoat cheese.

Every week the professors and painters, musicians and mechanics, pathologists and plumbers of Northland gather there to choose the reddest tomato, ripest melon, and—as much—to saunter. They saunter about filling a woven basket from Kenya or Lake Titicaca, a New Guinea netbag, or a supermarket plastic sack. They saunter about, noticing. There's warm recognition of last week's faces, last month's faces, last year's—the same professor of Italian, the geologist, the tree surgeon who imposes euthanasia on ailing elms—shared memories. A small exchange each week, an unfolding of self layer by layer, and the fragmented discourses develop continuities. There's deepening recognition, dawning kinship. Let's get together. Might you become my friend?

The newcomer must seek out such gathering places, the places where recurrent encounters can take place, the places where she will begin to recognize and be recognized—the modern counterpart of the ancient agora, or the streamside washing place in a pre-technological village. Are neighborhood sidewalks or coffee houses or convenience stores the gathering places, the salad bar in the supermarket, the parks, playgrounds, tennis courts, art galleries, post offices, natural history museums? Since these informal, sometimes changing gathering places become known through word of mouth, the mover must seek them out by asking her neighbor, employer, colleague, minister, rabbi, shopkeeper, librarian, teacher, or physician.

And it is helpful for the newcomer to seek out structured affinity groups as well—political, community service, artistic, business or professional associations, parenting networks—groups whose values and interests the mover shares. Where do they meet? Where are they announced—bulletin boards, newspapers, churches, schools?

Studying troubled movers whose distress was expressed in medical disorders, Stein (1984) cautioned that it may be "anti-therapeutic" for movers to be encouraged to seek such groups. That is, by emphasizing "resocialization" (which he terms an aspect of "culturally expectable" therapy), clinician and patient may collude in avoiding the painful but necessary work of mourning those relationships which have been severed. Such a caution should be heeded, yet it may be overstated. In reality, disconnection and reconnection must proceed as parallel realms of psychological work. Until society allows a moratorium for the mover, as it does for the widow, an energetic reaching outward needs to begin during the period when the mover is depleted and in pain. It is the very time when she wants to be reached in towards, but that is unlikely to happen.

Affinity groups offer comradeship that is warming and reassuring. Affinity groups also provide the opportunity for doing work, voluntary or paid, which helps restore the mover's shaken sense of competence and gives recognition to her special capabilities.

The newcomer is most apt to be accepted if she is cautious, sensitive to the vulnerabilities of those in the group who may both welcome her potential contribution and yet also feel threatened by her talents. And she needs caution on behalf of herself, to safeguard against the chief hazards of volunteerism: ambiguity and lack of boundaries, guilt-inciting requests for just a little more effort, a little more time, a little more commitment—requests that arouse her wish to please just in the period when she is stressed and vulnerable to depletion. It can be very hard for woman—the fixer, the healer, the pleaser—to say "no."

Affinity groups offer a source of new friendships, since they include those who share a common ground. But the newcomer must be reminded that instant intimacy rarely occurs. Rather, it grows slowly and haltingly, through repeated encounters, mutual experiences, and shared memories. The warmth of comradeship can be expected to assuage but not dispel the chill of emotional loneliness, the longing for intimacy.

That interlude without intimates is painful indeed, but it is in fact needed. Loss does usually result in grief. Time is needed for the sorrow to be felt, for the memories and qualities of the lost person to be internalized, and then for the attachment to be sufficiently loosened so that love-energy is again available to flow towards new people. I do not share the belief that affinity groups impede the process of grieving. To the contrary, they may provide support that enables a woman to struggle through that necessary pain at an endurable pace.

But normal grieving can certainly be impeded and compounded by shame. When that happens, because neither the newcomer nor the new community understands and accepts the psychological complexities of moving, the newcomer suffers intensely, and reverberations will affect her loved ones. So it is essential that she be prepared for the fact that even a much wanted move will be stressful, and that it is likely to be several years before she will feel fully "at home" again.

The woman who recognizes the inevitability of some pain and decides nonetheless to move needs to ask herself, "Where can I turn for the soothing I need? What helps me feel cozy, snug, safely enfolded—a hot bath, an eiderdown quilt? Is it certain music or a well-thumbed book that helps invoke comforting images? Is it the voice of an old friend on the telephone, a cup of herb tea, a hug from my husband or lover? Might it be the deep, tension-releasing pressure of a professional massage?" Once she recognizes her sources of comfort, she needs to claim them.

And there is wisdom in the mover who sets to work when she feels at risk of drifting away in oceanic sadness. There must be a balance between allowing ourselves to experience authentic emotions, and containing them sufficiently so they don't become overwhelming. A small dose of work, whether domestic or professional, confirms that we are effective, competent women. It enhances satisfaction with ourselves, and satisfaction offsets sadness.

But grief is not just sorrow. Raging and grieving are intertwined. There is outrage kindled by the sense of lost identity, by lack of recognition in the new locale. There is outrage kindled by the loss of competence, by helplessness. These are rages that arise from wounds to self-esteem. There is anger, sometimes rage, directed towards the cause of all the pain, perhaps the spouse who wanted to move.

Anger is fueled by aggressive energy. That energy seeks release, and physical release is in harmony with deep psychophysiological urges. The mover may indeed fantasize aggressive actions against those townspeople who seem so indifferent, or flight away from the apparently alien locale. But more adaptive would be a long, rhythmical swim, a breath-pumping bike ride, walking, running, dancing, smashing a tennis ball, whacking a golf ball, hurling a snow ball—any such actions that allow the energy of anger to flow out benignly, with pleasure as a side-effect. Beset by powerful emotions, the mover also needs to counteract the anxiety and shame those emotions can generate by searching out a forum in which her sadness, anger, fear, and self-doubts can be vented, understood, and accepted. She may find an appropriate forum through the Welcome Wagon, a newcomer's club, a women's network or women's information service, or a church.

* * *

Mental health clinicians have many strategic roles to play. They can serve as conduits through whom an understanding of the mover's experience can flow to the public at large. They can interpret to institutions the mover's needs for services extending far beyond the practical help with housing, or the financial help with transporting possessions, which are sometimes provided (Gaylord, 1979). They can act as consultants fostering the development of community resources to meet both psychological and practical needs of the newcomer. They can, for example, encourage the development of a roster of sponsors for the newcomer within schools, PTOs, and churches. They can interpret the newcomer's need for a "moratorium"—an interlude during which some grief is expected, and during which the newcomer is allowed access to special interest groups without expectations of productive participation. They can become facilitators of support groups for newcomers, perhaps based in facilities such as recreational centers or libraries which do not connote maladjustment or illness (Kaplan & Glenn, 1978). And, of course, they can serve as therapists to the individuals, couples, or families of newcomers who suffer in their transitions.

REFLECTIONS

Women who have the resiliency to grieve for their losses, the capacity to endure intervals of depression and anxiety, the courage to reexamine their unraveled identities and make new choices—such women are likely to regain their sense of competence and self-respect, and energies will become available for new tasks and relationships. Clearly, moving can stimulate personal growth. It can enhance confidence to explore new realms of experience; it can contribute to a richer inner life and a clearer sense of self.

But moving can also disempower women, since it is a complex realm of work absorbing time and energy that has to be withdrawn from other goals. In a society in which there is now both a surge towards and heightened resistance against equal opportunity for women and men, powerful energies will be needed to bring about the changes in the paid workplace and in domestic arrangements that will allow true parity to develop. Moving can deplete those energies.

Moving also helps perpetuate the existing equilibrium of power between men and women. It is in their affiliative work that many women feel most empowered—empowered as the integrators of the family, empowered to influence the physical, emotional, and mental well-being of their loved ones. Tending the fire or preparing a meal can be understood as metaphors as well as actual tasks. Sharing the tasks of the hearth can be experienced as a giving over of some of this deep power. Boulding (1976, 1977) writes persuasively of the need to relieve women from the exclusive "breeder-feeder" roles that have restricted their participation in those economic and political spheres that shape human experience beyond the hearth. Pruett (1987) has argued that women, the "gatekeepers" of the realm of childcare, must allow men into that domain if men are to fulfill the potential for personal wholeness that nurturing their offspring helps them to develop. But women whose sense of competence, continuity, and significance has been threatened by the dislocations of moving, perhaps recurrently, or women whose participation in public life has been interrupted by moving, perhaps recurrently, can scarcely be expected to yield any realm in which they feel empowered.

Yet if man is needed by the cradle, so is woman needed at the podium. Hierarchies of dominance and subservience—created by men and sometimes emulated by women—have not benefited humanity. They have, in fact, brought us to the brink of annihilation. Many believe that without a genuine interdependence within societies, interdependence among nations, interdependence between humanity and the natural world, human life on our planet will not survive. In many respects, contemporary mobility obstructs the development of interdependence by women (and perhaps by men as well).

A woman's relationship to her milieu needs to be a relationship of reciprocal care. The milieu provides care insofar as it confirms a woman's safety, competence, and her identity. It supports her essential sense of going-on-being and her personal significance. In turn, care must flow from the woman towards each level of community—her dwelling, her neighborhood, her town, her state, her nation, her planet.

Among Northland movers—educated, intelligent, resourceful, and financially secure—only half regained a sense of connection to community within two years (and within five years, more than half the movers were gone again). The fact that an attachment to community did not readily develop among this privileged population, and the fact that urban gentrification is causing economically and ethnically disadvantaged women to be uprooted, coupled with the relentless mobility within the United States, has bleak implications. For prolonged interludes, many movers are psychologically homeless. Their security, dignity, and effectiveness are at risk. They feel disconnected from neighborhood and town.

One has to feel connection to feel concern. It is only when the newcomer has had time and opportunity to become psychologically rooted in her locale that its continuity becomes significant. It is only then that her interest in its past and her care for its future are likely to be aroused.

Perhaps less entangled than men in the traditions of competitive struggle and hierarchical relationships, women must use their nurturant power to move towards the ideal of interdependence. They can start by expressing that ideal in their own lives, showing clearly that a relationship of mutual concern and care—concern and care for other as much as self, self as much as other—can be truly successful between woman and man.

Moving is a major realm in which that ideal can be expressed.

References

Abelin, E.L. (1971). The role of the father. In McDevitt, J.B. & C.G. Settlage (Eds.), *The Separation-individuation process* (pp. 229-252). New York: International Universities Press.

Abraham, K. (1924). A short study of the development of the libido; viewed in the light of mental disorders. In *Selected papers on psychoanalysis* (pp. 418-501). London: Hogarth.

Adler, G. (1985). *Borderline psychopathology and its treatment*. New York: Jason Aronson.

Anderson, B.S., & Zinsser, J.P. (1988). *A history of their own: Women in Europe from prehistory to the present*. New York: Harper & Row.

Barglow, P., & Schaefer, M. (1977). A new female psychology? In H.P. Blum (Ed.), *Female psychology* (pp. 393-438). New York: International Universities Press.

Bayes, M. (1989). The effects of relocation on the trailing spouse. *Smith College Studies in Social Work, 59* (3), 280-288.

Bernard, J. (1976). Historical and structural barriers to occupational desegregation. *Signs, 1* (3, part 2), 87-117.

Bernardez-Bonesatti, T. (1978). Woman and anger: Conflicts with aggression in contemporary women. *Journal of the American Medical Woman's Association, 33* (5), 215-219.

Bernstein, D. (1983). The female superego: A different perspective. *The International Journal of Psycho-analysis, 64*, 187-201.

Boulding, E. (1976). *The underside of history: A view of women through time*. Boulder, CO: Westview Press.

Boulding, E. (1977). *Women in the twentieth century world*. New York: John Wiley.

Bourestom, N. (1984). Psychological and physiological manifestations of relocation. *Psychiatric Medicine, 2* (1), 57-90.

Brett, J.M. (1982). Job transfer and well-being. *Journal of Applied Psychology, 67* (4), 450-463.

Buie, D.H., & Adler, G. (1982). Definitive treatment of the borderline personality. *International Journal of Psychoanalytic Psychotherapy, 9*, 51-87.

293

Bureau of the Census. (1989, April). *Population profile of the United States, 1989* (pp. 18-19). Special Studies Series P-23. No. 159. United States Department of Commerce.

Butler, E.W., McAllister, R.J., & Kaiser, E.J. (1973). The effects of voluntary and involuntary residential mobility on females and males. *Journal of Marriage and the Family, 35,* 219-227.

Chodorow, N. (1978). *The reproduction of mothering.* Berkeley: University of California Press.

Davis, A.Y. (1981). *Women, race, and class.* New York: Vintage.

DeJong, G.F., & Gardner, R.W., (Eds.). (1981). *Migration decision making: Multidisciplinary approaches to microlevel studies in developed and developing countries.* New York: Pergamon.

Deutsch, H. (1944). *Psychology of women.* (Vol. 1). New York: Grune & Stratton.

Deutsch, H. (1945). *Psychology of women.* (Vol. 2, Motherhood). New York: Grune & Stratton.

Deutsch, H. (1965). Absence of grief. In *Neuroses and character types.* New York: International Universities Press.

Dinnerstein, D. (1976). *The mermaid and the minotaur.* New York: Harper & Row.

Ehrenreich, B. (1983). *The hearts of men: American dreams and the flight from commitment.* Garden City, NY: Anchor Press/Doubleday.

Erickson, E. (1985). Womanhood and the inner space. In J. Strouse (Ed.), *Women and analysis: Dialogues on psychoanalytic views of femininity.* Boston, MA: G.K. Hall.

Errington, F., & Gewertz, D. (1987). *Cultural alternatives and a feminist anthropology.* Cambridge, England: Cambridge University Press.

Fast, I. (1979). Developments in gender identity: Gender differentiation in girls. *The International Journal of Psychoanalysis, 60,* 443-453.

Fenichel, O. (1945). *The psychoanalytic theory of neurosis.* New York: Norton.

Fischer, C.S., & Stueve, C.A. (1977). "Authentic community": The role of place in modern life. In C.S. Fischer, R.M. Jackson, C.A. Stueve, K. Gerson, L.M. Jones, with M. Baldassare, *Networks and places: Social relations in the urban setting* (pp. 163-186). New York: Free Press.

Frank, A. (1983). *Ann Frank's tales from the secret annex.* New York: Pocket Books. Washington Square Press.

Freedman, B.A. (1987). *Ego identity status and the family and career priorities of college women.* Unpublished doctoral dissertation, Bryn Mawr College.

Freud, S. (1917). Mourning and melancholia. *Standard edition, 14,* 237-258.

Fried, M. (1963). Grieving for a lost home. In L.J. Duhl (Ed.). *The Urban Condition* (pp. 151-171). New York: Basic Books.

Friedan, B. (1981). *The second stage.* New York: Summit Books.

Galenson, E., & Roiphe, H. (1977). Some suggested revisions concerning early female development. In H.P. Blum (Ed.). *Female psychology* (pp. 29-58). New York: International Universities Press.

Gaylord, M. (1979). Relocation and the corporate family: Unexplored issues. *Social Work, 24,* 186-191.

Gerson, K., Stueve, C.A., & Fischer, C.S. (1977). Attachment to place. In C.S. Fischer, R.M. Jackson, C.A. Stueve, K. Gerson, L.M. Jones with M. Baldessare, *Networks and places: Social relations in the urban setting* (pp. 139-161). New York: Free Press.

Gilligan, C. (1982). *In a different voice.* Cambridge, MA: Harvard University Press.

Greenson, R. (1968). Dis-identifying from mother: Its special importance for the boy. *International Journal of Psychoanalysis, 49*, 370-374.

Grinberg, L., & Grinberg, R. (1984). A psychoanalytic study of migration: Its normal and pathological aspects. *Journal of the American Psychoanalytic Association, 32*, 13-38.

Hartmann, H. (1958). *Ego psychology and the problem of adaptation.* New York: International Universities Press.

Hooper, D., & Ineichen, B. (1972). Adjustment to moving: A follow-up study of the mental health of young families in new housing. *Social Science and Medicine, 13D*, 163-168.

Jacobson, E. (1964). *The self and the object world.* New York: International Universities Press.

Jacobson, E. (1971). *Depression: Comparative studies of normal, neurotic, and psychotic conditions.* New York: International Universities Press.

Jones, S.B. (1973). Geographic mobility as seen by the wife and mother. *Journal of Marriage and the Family, 35*, 210-218.

Jordan, J.V. (1984). Empathy and self boundaries. *Work in progress.* Wellesley, MA: Stone Center for Developmental Services and Studies, Wellesley College.

Kaplan, A.G. (1984). The "self-in-relation": Implications for depression in women. *Work in progress.* Wellesley, MA: Stone Center for Developmental Services and Studies, Wellesley College.

Kaplan, A.G., Klein, R., & Gleason, N. (1985). Women's self development in late adolescence. *Work in progress.* Wellesley, MA: Stone Center for Developmental Services and Studies, Wellesley College.

Kaplan, M.F., & Glenn, A. (1978, July). Women and the stress of moving: A self-help approach. *Social casework,* 434-436.

Kestenberg, J. (1956a). On the development of maternal feelings in early childhood. In *The psychoanalytic study of the child* (Vol. 11) (pp. 257-290). New York: International Universities Press.

Kestenberg, J.S. (1956b). Vicissitudes of female sexuality. *Journal of the American Psychoanalytic Association, 4*, 453-476.

Kleeman, J. (1977). Freud's views on early female sexuality in the light of direct observation. In *Female psychology* (pp. 3-27). New York: International Universities Press.

Kohut, H. (1971). *The analysis of the self.* New York: International Universities Press.

Kohut, H. (1977). *The restoration of the self.* New York: International Universities Press.

Kohut, H. (1980). Reflections on advances in self psychology. In A. Goldberg (Ed.). *Advances in self psychology* (pp. 473-554). New York: International Universities Press.

Kubler-Ross, E. (1969). *On death and dying.* New York: Macmillan.

Lapin, M.B. (1987, June 7). Asian refugees cleave to family. *The Boston Sunday Globe,* p. N.H. 21.

Laws, K.L. (1976). Work aspirations of women: False leads and new starts, *Signs, 1* (3 part 2), 33-49.

Lerner, H.E. (1980). Internal prohibitions against female anger. *The American Journal of Psychoanalysis, 40* (2), 137-148.

Levinson, D.J. (1978). *The seasons of a man's life.* New York: Ballantine.

Lidz, R.W., & Lidz, T. (1977). Male menstruation: A ritual alternative to the oedipal transition. *The International Journal of Psycho-analysis, 58*, 17-31.

Lidz, R.W., & Lidz, T. (1984). Oedipus in the stone age. *Journal of the American Psychoanalytic Association, 32*, 507-527.

Lock, M. (1987). Protests of a good wife and wise mother: The medicalization of distress in Japan. In E. Norbeck, & M. Lock (Eds.). *Health, illness, and medical care in Japan.* Honolulu: University of Hawaii Press.

Loewald, H. (1962). Internalization, separation, mourning, and the superego. *Psychoanalytic Quarterly, 31.*

Mahler, M.S., Pine, F., & Bergman, A. (1975). *The psychological birth of the human infant.* New York: Basic Books.

Mahler, M., & McDevitt, J.B. (1982). Thoughts on the emergence of the sense of self, with particular emphasis on the body self. *Journal of the American Psychoanalytic Association, 30*, 827-848.

Maltsberger, J.L., & Buie, D.H. (1980). The devices of suicide: Revenge, riddance and rebirth. *The International Review of Psycho-analysis, 7*, 61-72.

Markham, W.T., & Pleck, J.H. (1986). Sex and willingness to move for occupational advancement: Some national sample results. *The Sociological Quarterly, 27* (1), 121-143.

McAllister, R.L., Butler, E.W., & Kaiser, E.J. (1973). The adaptation of women to residential mobility. *Journal of Marriage and the Family, 35*, 197-204.

McCollum, A. (1981). *The chronically ill child: A guide for parents and professionals.* New Haven, CT: Yale University Press.

Meeker, M.E., Barlow, K., & Lipset, D.M. (1986). Culture, exchange, and gender: Lessons from the murik. *Cultural Anthropology, 1* (1), 6-73.

Miller, J.B. (1976). *Toward a new psychology of women.* Boston: Beacon.

Miller, J.B. (1982). Women and power. *Work in Progress.* Wellesley, MA: The Stone Center for Developmental Services and Studies, Wellesley College.

Miller, J.B. (1983). The construction of anger in women and men. *Work in Progress.* Wellesley, MA: The Stone Center for Developmental Services and Studies, Wellesley College.

Miller, J.B. (1984). The development of women's sense of self. *Work in Progress.* Wellesley, MA: The Stone Center for Developmental Services and Studies, Wellesley College.

Mincer, J. (1978). Family migration decisions. *Journal of Political Economy, 86*, 749-773.

Montrain, N. (1983). On the vicissitudes of female sexuality: The difficult path from "anatomical destiny" to psychic representation. *The International Journal of Psycho-analysis, 64*, 169-186.

Olive, L.E., Kelsey, J.E., Visser, M.S., & Daly, R.T. (1976). Moving as perceived by executives and their families. *Journal of Occupational Medicine, 18* (8), 546-550.

Ornstein, A., & Ornstein, P.H. (1985). Parenting as a function of the adult self: A psychoanalytic developmental perspective. In J. Anthony & G. Pollock (Eds.). *Parental influences in health and disease.* Boston, MA: Little, Brown.

Packard, V. (1972). *A nation of strangers.* New York: David McKay.

Paykel, E.S., Myers, J.K., Dienelt, M.N., Klerman, G.L., Lindenthal, J.J., & Pepper, M.P. (1969). Life events and depression. *Archives of General Psychiatry, 21*, 753-760.

Peck, T.A. (1986). Women's self-definition in adulthood: From a different model? *Psychology of Women Quarterly, 10*, 274-284.

Pietromonaco, P.R., Manis, J., & Frohardt-Lane, K. (1986). Psychological consequences of multiple roles. *Psychology of Women Quarterly, 10*, 373-382.

Pinder, C.C. (1977). Multiple predictors of post transfer satisfaction. *Personnel Psychology, 30*, 543-556.

Pollock, G.H. (1977). The mourning process and creative organizational change. *Journal of the American Psychoanalytic Association, 25*, 3-34.

Pruett, K. (1987). *The nurturing father.* New York: Warner Books.

Relationships. Common trauma of moving. (1983, October 17). *The New York Times* (p. A18).

Rossi, P. (1980). *Why families move.* Beverly Hills, CA: Sage.

Rubin, L.B. (1985). *Just friends: The role of friendship in our lives.* New York: Harper & Row.

Ruddick, S., & Daniels, P. (Eds.) (1977). *Working it out: Twenty-three women writers, artists, scientists, and scholars talk about their lives and work.* New York: Pantheon.

Sanford, L.T., & Donovan, M.E. (1985). *Women and self-esteem.* New York: Viking Penguin.

Schorr, P. (1975). *Planned relocation.* Lexington, MA: Lexington Books.

Seidenberg, R. (1973). *Corporate wives—corporate casualties?* Garden City, NY: Anchor Press.

Sell, R.R. (1983). Analyzing migration decisions: The first step—whose decisions? *Demography, 20* (3), 299-311.

Settlage, C.F., Curtis, J., Lozoff, M., Lozoff, M., Silberschatz, G., & Simburg, E.J. (1988). Conceptualizing adult development. *Journal of the American Psychoanalytic Association, 36*, 347-369.

Sieber, S.D. (1974). Toward a theory of role accumulation. *American Sociological Review, 39*, 567-578.

Siggins, L.S. (1966). Mourning: A critical survey of the literature. *The International Journal of Psychoanalysis, 47*, 14-25.

Smith-Rosenberg, C. (1975). The female world of love and ritual: Relations between women in nineteenth-century America. *Signs: Journal of Women in Culture and Society, 1* (1), 1-29.

Spitz, R.A. (1965). *The first year of life: A psychoanalytic study of normal and deviant development of object relations.* New York: International Universities Press.

Stein, H.F. (1984). Misplaced persons: The crisis of emotional separation in geographical mobility and uprootedness. *The Journal of Psychoanalytic Anthropology, 7* (3).

Stern, D.N. (1985). *The interpersonal world of the infant: A view from psychoanalysis and developmental psychology.* New York: Basic Books.

Stoller, R.J. (1968). *Sex and gender* (Vol. 1). New York: Science House.

Stoller, R. (1974). Symbiosis anxiety and the development of masculinity. *Archives of General Psychiatry, 30*, 164-172.

Stoller, R., & Herdt, G.H. (1982). The development of masculinity: A cross-cultural contribution. *Journal of the American Psychoanalytic Association, 30*, 25-59.

Stokols, D., Shumaker, S.A., & Martinez, J. (1983). Residential mobility and personal well-being. *Journal of Environmental Psychology, 3*, 5-19.

Stolorow, R.D. (1975). Toward a functional definition of narcissism. *The International Journal of Psycho-analysis, 56*, 179-185.

Surrey, J.L. (1985). Self-in-relation: A theory of women's development. *Work in Progress*. Wellesley, MA: Stone Center for Developmental Services and Studies, Wellesley College.

Surrey, J.L. (1987). Relationship and empowerment. *Work in Progress*. Wellesley, MA: Stone Center for Developmental Services and Studies, Wellesley College.

Thoits, P.A. (1983). Multiple identities and psychological well-being: A reformulation and test of the social isolation hypothesis. *American Sociological Review, 48*, 174-187.

Thomas, D. (1957). Do not go gentle into that good night. In *Collected poems of Dylan Thomas*. New York: New Directions.

Tyson, R.L. (1983). Some narcissistic consequences of object loss: A developmental view. *The Psychoanalytic Quarterly, LII*, 205-224.

Van Gennep, A. (1960). *The rites of passage*. Chicago: The University of Chicago Press.

Viney, L.L., & Bazeley, P. (1977). The affective reactions of housewives to community relocations. *Journal of Community Psychology, 5*, 37-45.

Voydanoff, P. (1988). Women, work, and family: Bernard's perspective on the past, present, and future. *Psychology of Women Quarterly, 12*, 269-280.

Weiss, R.S. (1973). *Loneliness: The experience of emotional and social isolation*. Cambridge: The M.I.T. Press.

Weissman, M.M., & Paykel, E.S. (1972). Moving and depression in women. *Society, 9*, 24-28.

Williams, A.S., Jobes, P.C., & Gilchrist, C.J. (1986). Gender roles, marital status, and urban-rural migration. *Sex Roles, 15* (11-12), 627-643.

Willmuth, L.R., Weaver, L., & Donlan, S. (1975). Utilization of medical services by transferred employees. *Archives of General Psychiatry, 32*, 85-88.

Winnicott, D.W. (1965). *The maturational process and the facilitating environment*. New York: International Universities Press.

Wolfman, B.R. (1984). Women and their many roles. *Work in Progress*. Wellesley, MA: Stone Center for Developmental Services and Studies, Wellesley College.

Wollstonecraft, M. (1985). *A vindication of the rights of women*. M.B. Cramnick (Ed.). London: Penguin (originally published in 1792).

Wortman, C.B., & Silver, R.C. (1989). The myths of coping with loss. *Journal of Consulting and Clinical Psychology, 57* (3), 349-357.

Zetzel, E. (1970). *The capacity for emotional growth*. New York: International Universities Press.

Author Index

Adler, G., 93, 269

Bazely, P., 20, 243
Bergman, A., 51, 93, 131, 253, 269
Bernardez-Bonesatti, T., 214, 215, 263
Bernstein, D., 132, 142, 165
Boulding, E., 17, 290-291
Bourestom, N., 241, 249
Brett, J. M., 245, 246, 247
Buie, D. H., 61n.1, 62n.4, 93, 269
Butler, E. W., 240, 247

Deutsch, H., 48, 90, 133, 142

Fenichel, O., 65, 87
Fischer, C. S., 247-248, 249
Freud, S., 65, 264
Fried, M., 20, 240, 249
Friedan, B., 262, 272
Frohardt-Lane, K., 168, 242

Gilligan, C. 57, 253
Grinberg, R., 16, 241, 254
Grinberg, L., 16, 241, 254

Jacobson, E., 51, 64, 65, 93
Jordan, J. V., 52, 134

Kaiser, E. J., 240, 247
Kaplan, A. G., 52, 134, 178, 290
Kestenberg, J. S., 133, 165
Kohut, H., 52, 62n.2, 93

Laws, K. L., 62n.3, 164, 171
Lerner, H. E., 214, 263
Levinson, D. J., 16, 130, 264
Lock, M., 16, 245

Mahler, M. S., 51, 52, 93, 131, 253, 269
Maltzberger, J. L., 61n.1, 62n.4
Manis, J., 168, 242
Markham, W. T., 164, 248
Martinez, J., 244, 247, 249
McAllister, R. L., 240, 247
Miller, J. B., 52, 134, 214, 253, 262

Paykel, E. S., 16, 239, 246
Peck, T. A., 19, 159, 201
Pietromonaco, P. R., 168, 242

Pine, F., 51, 93, 131, 253, 269
Pollock, G. H., 90, 266

Rossi, P., 147, 249
Rubin, L. B., 130, 134, 267

Shumaker, S. A., 244, 247, 249
Sieber, S. D., 168, 242
Siggins, L. S., 65, 88, 90
Silver, R. C., 90, 266
Stein, H. F., 244, 287
Stern, D. N., 52, 131
Stokols, D., 244, 246, 247, 249
Stolorow, R. D., 62n.2, 78, 224

Stueve, C. A., 247-248, 249
Surrey, J. L., 52, 134, 234

Thoits, P. A., 168, 242

Viney, L. L., 20, 243
Voydanoff, P., 175, 216

Weiss, R. S., 154, 253
Weissman, M. M., 16, 239, 246
Winnicott, D. W., 52, 93, 96, 102, 226, 268
Wortman, C. B., 90, 266

Subject Index

Adolescence, triangular relationships and, 133

Affiliative work, 23, 41, 47-50, 62n.3, 111, 177-182
continuity and, 190-194
daily life and, 67
devalued, 234
friendmaking and, 232-233
inner conflicts and, 236
power and, 290
sociocultural values and, 167
transportability and, 49, 173
valued, 174
See also Domesticity; Mothers/motherhood

Affinity groups, 147, 229, 232-233, 287-288

Aggression:
constructive, 212-213
depression and, 65
new friends and, 141-143
taboos against, 142

Aggressive cathexis, 65

Aging, fears of, 86

Alcoholism, 241-242

Alone, moving, 28-37

Altruism, 57, 271-272

Anger, 48
femininity and, 213-215

grief and, 65
losses and, 267
marriage and, 197-198
mourning and, 90
recoil from female's, 254-255

Anxiety, 64, 90, 252
about competence, 185
family members and, 274
loss of home and, 226
loss of self and, 225
new friends and, 141, 143
recreating home and, 103

Architecture, 43

Avoidance, 47, 84

Bereavement, 87

Betterment, 21, 63

Biological determinism, 164

Body self, dispersion and, 165-166

Bonding, 131

Boredom, 29, 31

Career, 62n.3
advancement in, 31
boredom with, 29
change in, 40
commitment to, 164

Career, *continued*
    continuity in, 48, 186-190
    family life versus, 46
    financial motives and, 272
    fulfillment and, 189
    growth and, 40, 58
    identity and, 35, 77-79
    inner conflicts and, 236
    marital conflicts with, 206
    nurturance versus, 187
    personal needs and, 43
    transition from studenthood to, 183-
        186
    See also Work
Career opportunities, 38, 39, 40-42
Challenges, 107, 113
Childcare:
    facilities for, 40
    unmet adult needs and, 193-194
Childhood:
    mementos from, 109
    rejection and, 143-144
Childhood experience, 47, 58
    fulfillment of innate capabilities and,
        181
    mother's anger and, 214
    sense of self and, 51-55
    unfulfilled needs and, 193
Children:
    at home with, 193-194
    friends through, 149
    independence of, 176
    individuation and, 131-132
    neighborhood connections and, 118
Choices, 27-61, 196, 249-251, 256
    ambiguous, 222-224
    female psyche and, 222-225
    illusion of, 56
    lack of, 44-50, 199, 241, 249
    loss and, 108
    merged, 39
    occupation and, 41-43
    responsible, 277
    work and, 234-235
Church affiliation, 135, 147, 282
Cleaning, ritual of, 99-100, 113
Clinical social work, 21
Clothing, physical identity and, 74-75
Cold weather, 39, 45, 72, 106

Collegial connections, 146-147, 186
Communication barriers, 23
Community:
    connection with, 229
    researching, 277-280
    welcoming gestures and, 135
Community affairs, 147
Competence, 41, 93, 270
    anxiety about, 185
    child's feelings of, 52
    glow of, 80
    home and, 204, 284
    living in disarray and, 101-103
    work and, 169, 185, 239, 288-289
    temporary homes and, 114
Competitiveness:
    ideal self and, 208-209
    husband and, 181-182
Concern, capacity for, 24
Conformity, clothing and, 74
Conscience, 57, 167
Consumerism, 272
Continuity, 22, 122
    friends and, 126
    having children and, 206
    home and, 109-110, 226, 284
    occupational, 239
    welcoming gestures and, 135
    work of affiliation and, 190-194
Cost of living, 38, 39
Creativity, 24, 33-34, 42-43, 188-189,
        194, 207
Criticism, by father, 189
Cultural dualisms, 261-266
Cultural facilities, 40

Daughterhood, transition into wife-
        hood, 177-182
Daughter-mother attachment, 132-133
Death, fears of, 86
Decoration, 104, 105, 107-109, 227-228
Defense mechanisms, loss and, 83-84
Denial, 47, 64, 84, 251-255
Dependence, 48, 49, 55, 81, 263
Depression, 16, 239-242, 268
    aggressive conflict and, 65
    anger and, 215
    anger at husband and, 199

dependence and, 48
friendmaking and, 159, 234
illness and, 90, 239
incapacity to mourn and, 90
internalized voices and, 55
loss of meaning and, 80
loss of self and, 225
re-creating home and, 103
retirement and, 80
Differentation, seeking, 31
Diffusion, child development and, 165-166
Disarray, living with, 100-103
Dispersion, 163-164, 270-271
body self and, 165-166
husband's career and, 170
interpersonal self and, 166-168
multiple roles and, 184
sexual development and, 166
work and, 168, 235-236
Divorcées, 33-34, 35
Domesticity, 69, 114, 190-194
Domestic work. *See* Housework
Dreams, 86-87
Dwelling, separating from, 67-69

Education, advanced, 47
Ego, observing, 190
Elation, 83-34
Elitism, 74
Emotional detachment, 90
Emotional states, self-expression and, 107-109
Emotional ties, 98
Empathy, 53, 130
Entertaining, friendships and, 68
Envy, marriage and, 197-198
Ethnic minorities, 118
Expectations:
fathers and, 54, 167, 184-185, 207
inadequate housing and, 106
marriage and, 198
self-imposed, 70, 252, 266
Expressive drives, 104

Failure, depression and, 65
Familiarity, loss of, 71-72, 81-82

Family:
boundaries within, 69
culture transmission and, 263-264
interventions and, 273-276
moving and, 273-276
professional careers and, 46
responsibilities to, 57
retirement and, 281, 283
sociocultural values and, 167
See also Mothers/motherhood; Father
Father, 53
boy's indentification with, 132, 166-167
girl's relationship with, 54, 55
critical, 163, 189
expectations and, 54, 167, 184-185, 207
See also Parent
Female development, 131-134. *See also* Women
Female machismo, 262-263
Femaleness, childhood experience and, 54-55
Female psychology, 22, 131, 222-225
Feminine role, 180-181
Feminine strength, 70
Femininity, anger and, 213-215
Feminist inquiry, 21
Financial resources, 106
Flexibility, 164
Foods, comfort and, 115
Friends, 34, 38, 286-288
death of, 282
husbands as, 215
idealized, 134
left behind, 84, 88-90, 124, 129, 139
long-distance, 248
loss of, 22, 82-94, 200, 201
retirement and, 281, 283
traveling in pairs, 152-153
welcoming gestures, 135-137
See also Support network
Friendship/friendmaking, 124-162, 230-234, 246-248
entertaining and, 68
gender and, 129-131
initiative and, 140-145, 231-232
longings for, 22
meaning of, 125-134
outcomes, 159-161
psychological roots, 131-134

Friendship/friendmaking, *continued*
  rhythms and, 154-158
  self-worth and, 267
  special issues, 151-152
  strategies for, 145-153
Fuel, cost of, 106
Fulfillment, right to, 261
Furniture, 104, 227

Gathering places, 286-287
Gender roles, 24, 27
Gifts, to friends, 71
Goods and services, 114-117
Goodwife, 39, 48, 56, 76
Grief, 64, 240, 266-270
  anger and, 65
  anticipatory, 83-85
  loss of friends and, 83-90, 124, 230-
    231
  loss of self and, 225
  past, 267-268
  rage and, 289
  recoil from, 92-94
  working through, 86
Guilt, 34
  anger at husband and, 215
  illness and, 245
  loss and, 91-92
  mourning and, 90
  new friends and, 141
Gypsy, modern, 29-31

Hairdressers, 85, 140
Hairstyle, 73-74
Helplessness, 47, 224-224, 262, 265
  children and, 51, 55
  disregard for well-being and, 56
  female identity and, 81
  grief and, 64
  isolation and, 117
  possessions and, 100
  professional development and, 48
  transportable homemaker and, 49
Heroines, 50, 57
Home:
  continuity and, 109-110
  disarray in, 100-103

loss of, 67-72
  meanings of, 22, 96-98
  reconnecting to, 227-228
  recreating, 96-123, 226-230
  self-expression in, 103-109
Homelessness, 98-99, 231
Homemaker. *See* Affiliative work
Hopelessness, 64, 159
Hospitality, unreciprocated, 144
Housewarming, 109
Housework, 78
  possession rituals and, 100
  relief from, 193
  shared, 176
Housing, cost of, 106
Humiliation, fears of, 144
Husbands:
  anger with, 23-215
  as friends, 215
  childhood relationship with father
    and, 55
  choices made by, 44-46, 48
  competition with, 181-182
  concealing pain from, 55-56
  disappointed, 211
  emotional protection of, 215-217
  loneliness and, 211
  protective attitudes toward, 50
  retirement roles and, 219-220
  self-esteem of, 200
  status of, 180
  stressed, 210-211
  sympathetic, 205
  unavailable, 23, 201-210, 274-275
Husband's career, 27, 35, 36-44, 154-155,
    205
  burden of, 184-185
  continuity in, 239
  dispersion and, 170
  lack of success in, 211
  women's identity and, 211-212

Identity, 260-261
  furniture and, 104
  home and, 226
  husband's career and, 211-212, 241-242
  loss of, 22, 64, 199, 200
  men and, 29, 168

physical, 72-75
  self-expression and, 108
  social, 75-82
  work and, 77-79, 168, 236-237, 239
Illness, 244-245, 250, 256
  grief and, 90
  retirement and, 282
Income, 38, 152
Incorporation, welcoming gestures and,
  135
Independence, passage into, 33
Indifference, 138, 151, 232
Individualism, 51, 253
Individuation, gender differences in, 131-
  132
Inertia, making new friends and, 139
Infants:
  bodily sensations of, 165-166
  individuation and, 131
  integration in, 96
  mother relationship, 166
  sense of self and, 51-53
Inner voice, 62n.4, 167
Institutionalized welcomes, 135
Interdependence, 60, 91
Interpersonal self, dispersion and, 166-
  168
Interventions, 24, 256-292
  family and, 273-276
  practical strategies, 277-290
  psychological, 256-276
  retirement and, 280-284
Intimacy:
  friendships and, 82, 89
  gender differences, 130-131
  merging and, 258
Introjected object, 87-88
Introjects, 62n.4, 189
Invisibility, 199, 200, 268, 274
Irritability, continuous, 256
Isolation, 33
  helplessness and, 117
  mother-daughter relationship and,
  133
  mothering role and, 203

Libidinal cathexes, 64
Library, research and, 277

Life experience, friends and, 125-126
Loneliness, 33, 154, 243
  empathy of others and, 253
  family members and, 274
  friendmaking and, 234
  husbands and, 211
Loss, 22, 63-95, 266-270
  anger and, 65, 267
  choices and, 108
  making new friends and, 139
  of friends, 82-94, 230-231
  of home, 67-72
  of physical capabilities, 281-283
  physical identity and, 72-75
  rekindling of past, 268
  sadness and, 64
  social identity and, 75-82
  welcome, 269-270
Love relationship:
  boredom with, 29
  testing, 31
  See also Marriage

Male-dominated community, 42
Marriage, 23
  choices and, 223
  communication barriers in, 213-217
  egalitarian, 44-45
  equilibrium in, 210
  expectations about, 171-172
  moving and, 196-221, 273-276
  nurturance and, 275
  priority given to, 178-180
  resolving strains, 217-220
  responsibilities in, 259
  satisfaction with, 246
  sources of tension, 196-217
  stressed husbands and, 210-211
  transition into, 177-182
  troubled wives and, 197-201
  unavailable husbands and, 201-210
Masculinity, 166-167
Mastery, 22, 268
  familiarity with surroundings and, 117
  housework and, 91
  loss of home and, 226
  of environment, 243
  past and, 134, 229

Mastery, *continued*
  safety and, 99-103
Meaning, loss of, 80
Medical complaints, 244-245, 287. *See also*
  Illness
Me Generation, 30
Melancholia, 65
Mementos, 113
Memories, 92
  friends and, 89
  furnishings and, 227
  possessions and, 69-70, 284
  reproducing the past and, 120-122
  self-constancy and, 168
Men:
  identity and, 168
  mother relationship and, 264
  See also Father; Husbands
Men, following. *See* Husband's career
Mental health clinicians:
  moves by, 95n.1
  roles of, 289-290
  sociocultural assumptions of, 259
Merging, intimacy and, 258
Mothering networks, 193, 203
Mothers/motherhood, 23, 37, 62n.3
  adult relationship with, 178
  aggressive, 142
  boys' development and, 166-167
  childhood experience and, 51-55, 131-
    133
  effectiveness of, 150
  expectations about, 41, 49, 171-172
  home as metaphor for, 97
  identification with, 193, 214, 259-260,
    263
  isolation of, 203
  man's relationship with, 264
  new, 77-79
  power of, 51-54
  respite from, 193
  separating from, 97, 178, 214, 269
  work priorities and, 39, 45
  See also Affiliative work; Parent
Mourning, 65, 87-88, 266-267, 287
Moving:
  career success and, 211
  choices and, 27-61, 249-251
  cost of, 106-107, 198
  date of, 139
  elderly populations and, 241
  family and, 273-276
  in later life, 60
  issues in, 21-24
  marriage and, 196-221, 273-276
  other studies on, 238-251
  repeatedly, 47, 110-114

Narcissistic conflict, 30, 65
Narcissistic crisis, 78, 81
Narcissistic developement, 62n.2
Narcissistic equilibrium, 224
Narcissistic injury, 138
Narcissistic loss, 82, 199, 267-268
Narcissistic personality disorder, 272-
  273
Narcissistic risk, making friends and,
  159
Neighborhoods, 118, 278-279
Neighbors, 31, 111, 135
Nesting, 107
Networks, 232
Newcomer's Club, 148-149
Newlyweds, 76-77
Newspapers, research and, 277
Nomads, psychological, 29-31
Nurturance, 23, 50
  career versus, 187
  hair care and, 85
  marriage and, 197, 275
  power from, 41, 50, 180, 204-205, 226,
    234, 262, 290-291
  self-fulfillment through, 46
  vicarious self-care and, 40
  warm house and, 209

Object, internalized, 90
Object constancy, 269
Object image, 61n.1
Object loss, 82, 267
Object relations, 62n.2
Occupation. *See* Career; Work
Older mover, 102
Olfactory experiences, 120
Other, self and, 258-261

Packing, 70
Pain, recoil from, 251-255
Paradoxical self, 50-58, 187, 224-225
Parent:
    independence from, 66
    internalized, 54
    narcissistic equilibrium of, 193
    See also Mothers/motherhood; Father
Passivity, 55, 142
Past, reproducing, 119, 133-134
People pleasers, 46, 47
Perfectionism, 47, 54, 55, 207
Personal growth, 37-38
Personality, imprinting dwelling with, 104
Personality disorders, 224
Physical appearance, 22
Physical capabilities, loss of, 281-283
Physical disarray, 100-103
Physical identity, 72, 74-75
Possession, rituals of, 99-100, 227
Possessions:
    giving up, 69-71, 110
    memories and, 284
Power, 224-225
    affiliative work and, 290
    between men and women, 290
    children and, 51
    decision to move and, 40
    maternal, 52-54, 142
    motivated by feelings of, 57
    nurturant, 41, 50, 180, 204-205, 226, 234, 262, 290-291
    through provision, 46
    work and, 175
Powerlessness, 263
Privacy, 68, 69, 141, 144, 229
Profession. *See* Career
Psychoanalytic thought, 20-21, 51-58
Psychological growth, 33
Psychotherapy, losses and, 90

Rage, 138, 256, 289
Reciprocity, friends and, 128, 134
Recognition, 207, 270, 273
Recoil, 251-255
Reconnection, 266-270
Regression, 87

Rejection, fear of, 22, 144
Relatedness, female development and, 52
Remodeling, 104
Rented dwellings, 105
Resentment:
    marriage and, 197-198
    victimization and, 256
Resiliency, 164
Resources, researching, 277-290
Retirement, 60, 69, 79-80, 219-220, 280-284
Retirement nests, 111
Rites de passage, 86
Rural home, 67-68

Sadness, 64, 85, 234, 240, 274
Safety:
    companions and, 117
    feelings of, 96-97
    foods and, 115
    grounding and, 102
    home and, 226, 284
    mastery and, 99-103
    neighbors and, 118-119
    olfactory experiences and, 120
    welcome and, 137
Salaries, 38, 39
Self:
    authentic, 52
    being versus doing and, 49
    development of, 164
    disregard for, 47
    hate of, 256, 263
    ideal, 54, 57, 141, 209
    lost aspects of, 241, 267
    love of, 62n.2, 91
    other and, 93, 258-261
    representations of, 61n.1
    validation of, 255
Self awareness, 43, 190, 261, 265, 277
Self care, 57, 187, 277-280
Self esteem, 16, 22, 62n.2
    choices and, 48
    conflict-free, 59
    depression and, 65, 92
    friends and, 127, 143, 158, 232-233, 247, 267

Self esteem, *continued*
  helplessness and, 117
  husband's status and, 180
  indifference and, 138
  living in disarray and, 101, 103
  new friends and, 143
  nurturant role and, 41
  power and, 42
  precariously balanced, 224
  retirement and, 80
  sadness and, 64
  work groups and, 189
Self expression, 33-34, 103-109, 114
Self image, 61n.1
Selfishness, altruism versus, 271-272
Self object, 54, 252
Self paradox, 261-266
Self regard, 261-262
Self representation, 61n.1, 141-142
Sense of self, 61n.1
  body and, 165-166
  contradictions in, 56-57
  dispersion and, 236
  early development of, 51, 131
  loss of, 64, 201
  self-expression and, 108
  separateness and, 52
  working and, 163-171
Separation:
  from mother, 97, 178, 214, 269
  hair cutting and, 73
Separation anxiety, 66, 243
Sexual development, dispersion and, 166
Shame, 64, 243, 252, 288
Shelter:
  home and, 96-97
  safety and, 99
Single women, 28-37
Social identity, loss of, 75
Social roles, 18
Sociocultural beliefs, internalization of, 263-264
Sociocultural values, family and, 167
Sponsorship, 137, 285
Spontaneity, 92, 126-127
Storekeepers, 115
Studenthood, transition into profession from, 183-186
Subservience, 32

Success, work and, 175
Suicide, 256
Support network, 111-112. *See also* Friends
Surroundings, affinity with, 30, 117

Telephone contacts, friends and, 126-127
Temporty housing, 105-106, 110-114, 173, 279
Things:
  arranging, 104
  divesting from, 69-71, 102
Transitions:
  hairstyles and, 73-74
  occupational, 177-186
Trust, friends and, 127-128

Unworthiness, 56
Uselessness, 79

Values, friends and, 125
Victims, 50, 256
Virilocality, 27, 253-254
Visitors, 109, 124
Vitality, 29-31
Volunteerism, 80, 147, 283-284, 287
Vulnerability, 47, 224

Warmth, friends and, 127
Weather, 42, 72, 138-139
Welcome, 135-140
Welcome Wagon, 17, 25n.2, 135
Well-being, 249
  disregard for, 56
  ethic of self-care and, 57
  mobility and, 239-248
  mourning and, 90
Wife role. *See* Affiliative work; Marriage
Womb, home as, 96-97
Woman's career, moving to advance, 58-60
Women:
  arrangement of priorities, 164
  psychological equilibrium and, 201
  socialization of, 52
  triangular relationships and, 133

vicarious fulfillment and, 170
See also Female development
Women's Movement, 20-21, 27, 262, 270
Women's Network, 18, 148
Work, 62n.3, 163-195
  advancement, 248
  choice and, 234-235
  competence and, 288-289
  conflicts and, 171-177
  continuity in, 186-194, 239
  dispersion and, 168, 235-236
  friends and, 135, 146-147

  identity and, 168
  outcomes and, 234-237
  priorities and, 23, 45
  recognition and, 22, 270
  reducing marital tensions and, 218
  researching opportunnities in, 279-280
  sense of self and, 163-171
  transitions in, 177-186
  See also Affiliative work; Career
Worthlessness, 55

About the Author

AUDREY T. McCOLLUM received her BA in Psychology from Vassar College, and her M.S.W in Psychiatric Social Work from Simmons College School of Social Work. During her many years as a family therapist and research associate in the Child Study Center and Department of Pediatrics in the Yale University School of Medicine, she explored the psychological influences of conditions such as autism, obesity, short stature, and life-threatening illness on children and their parents. Her findings were presented in numerous journal articles and in *The Chronically Ill Child*, published in 1981. That year, a major relocation kindled her interest in the psychological impact of moving upon women. She is currently in private practice as a psychotherapist in New Hampshire.